Batsford Chess Library

Beating the Flank Openings

Vassilios Kotronias

An Owl Book
Henry Holt and Company
New York

Henry Holt and Company, Inc.
Publishers since 1866
115 West 18th Street
New York, New York 10011

Henry Holt® is a registered
trademark of Henry Holt and Company, Inc.

Published in Canada by Fitzhenry & Whiteside Ltd.,
195 Allstate Parkway, Markham, Ontario L3R 4T8.
First published in the United States in 1996 by
Henry Holt and Company, Inc.
Originally published in Great Britain in 1996 by
B. T. Batsford Ltd.

Library of Congress Catalog Card Number: 95-81566
ISBN 0-8050-4731-X (An Owl Book: pbk.)

First American Edition—1996

Printed in the United Kingdom
All first editions are printed on acid-free paper.∞

10   9   8   7   6   5   4   3   2   1

Editorial Panel: Mark Dvoretsky, Jon Speelman
General Adviser: Raymond Keene OBE
Specialist Adviser: Dr John Nunn
Commissioning Editor: Graham Burgess

Contents

Introduction

When I was asked to work on *Beating the Flank Openings*, I accepted with a certain amount of scepticism, obviously finding it hard to imagine how I could demonstrate that Black has good chances to play for a win when facing ultra-solid systems such as the English or Catalan. These openings constitute a flexible alternative to mainstream theory. White will undertake decisive action only after due preparation. The play requires great accuracy from both players and in most cases it is White who dictates the pace.

However, closer examination suggests that Black need not despair. There are also pleasant aspects in this type of game from Black's viewpoint, provided one is sufficiently prepared to make use of them. A first observation is that the black king rarely becomes White's direct target. This should be of particular value to players who dislike being attacked, or want to follow a positional path unhindered. Secondly, there are not many forcing theoretical lines, a fact that enhances one's scope for originality. Finally, the idea that White is in no danger at all when playing these openings can easily work against him when facing a thoroughly prepared opponent.

In the process of preparing the manuscript, I had an enemy, changing from time to time into a useful by-stander – infrequent occurrence of the lines in question in tournament practice. This means that I had to work hard to fill my pages, but on the other hand I certainly enjoyed improvising in unknown territory and improving my positional skills. Actually, there are many beneficial points in the analysis of flank openings and so I recommend their study, regardless of more practical considerations.

The main purpose of this book is to present interesting ways to meet the various flank openings. In a very few cases, especially in the Catalan, rather dull positions will crop up, but one should be aware that this is unavoidable when playing Black. I hope that this nuisance will be compensated by a special section, where such positions will be dealt with. If this proves inadequate, switching to a study of Karpov and Andersson games should be the last resort for those wishing to extinguish the term 'dead draw' from their repertoire.

The basic criterion for choosing Black's responses to flank openings was soundness. I rejected positions with structural weaknesses or lack of space (e.g. the Hedgehog), mainly because I couldn't see a clear path to equality. However, I think that the repertoire suggested is also not lacking in sharpness.

Beating the Flank Openings, besides offering a repertoire for Black against the English and Catalan, contains a historical review on the development of hypermodern openings.

For a deeper insight to the opening ideas, I have inserted before each group of Illustrative Games, sub-sections presenting in detail the plans and typical manoeuvres for both sides. This method, which I used, I believe, successfully in *Beating the Caro-Kann*, will help readers form an overview of Black's winning possibilities.

Symbols

+	Check	0-1	Black wins
++	Double Check	$\frac{1}{2}$-$\frac{1}{2}$	Draw
#	Mate	Ch	Championship
!	Good move	Cht	Team championship
!!	Excellent move	Echt	European team championship
?	Bad move	OL	Olympiad
??	Serious blunder	Z	Zonal
!?	Interesting move	IZ	Interzonal
?!	Dubious move	Ct	Candidates event
±	Small advantage to White	Wch	World championship
∓	Small advantage to Black	jr	Junior event
±	Big advantage to White	wom	Women's event
∓	Big advantage to Black	rpd	Rapidplay game
+−	Decisive advantage to White	mem	Memorial event
−+	Decisive advantage to Black	corr.	Postal game
=	Even position	(n)	nth match game
1-0	White wins	(D)	Diagram follows

1 The Development of Hypermodern Openings

Did you ever witness an opponent playing on his first move both 1 g3 and 1 b3? It happened to me in several off-hand games and, I can assure you, it is not easy to convince a beginner that his 'move' is illegal, especially when you have a grinning face. As far as I can imagine, a similar situation occurred at the start of the 20th century, with Dr Siegbert Tarrasch, a sworn classicist, trying to refute the ideas of Nimzowitsch and Réti, introducing at the time their revolutionary 1 g3 or 1 b3 methods into practice. After a long tussle, the so-called Hypermoderns emerged victorious in the theoretical sense, proving that the centre can be controlled by other means (e.g. fianchettoed bishops), rather than sheer occupation with pawns. However, it must be pointed out that this success was enhanced by the fact their contemporaries underestimated them, or tried to refute their theories according to the old dogmas.

The story had begun earlier, around the middle of the 19th century. At that time we have the first examples by well-known players such as Morphy and Staunton using the fianchetto. Although still in its infancy, this way of developing had already made its most advantageous feature felt: avoiding early exchanges and keeping options was particularly useful against weaker opponents, especially when giving knight odds!

Staunton – Worrall
1860

(Remove White's b1-knight) 1 b3 e5 2 ♗b2 ♘c6 3 e3 ♗c5 4 ♘e2 d6 5 ♘g3 ♗e6 6 a3 ♘ge7 7 ♗e2 0-0 8 0-0 f5? 9 d4 ♗b6 10 c4 exd4 11 exd4 ♗d7 12 b4 a5 13 b5 ♘b8 14 ♖c1 c6 15 c5 dxc5 16 dxc5 ♗c7 17 ♕d4 ♖f6 18 ♗c4+ ♘d5 (18...♔h8? 19 ♕xf6!) 19 ♖c3 ♗xg3? 20 ♖xg3 ♔h8 21 ♕h4 ♗e6 22 ♖e1 ♗f7 (22...♘d7 23 ♖xe6! +–) 23 ♗xd5 cxd5 24 ♗xf6 gxf6 25 ♕h6 1-0

The next game is one of the very first featuring a double fianchetto. It is noticeable for the way in which the English master advances his central pawns, a gift almost imperceptible to the common eye of his era.

Staunton – Horwitz
London 1851

1 c4 e6 2 ♘c3 f5 3 g3 ♘f6 4 ♗g2 c6 5 d3 ♘a6 6 a3 ♗e7 7 e3 0-0 8 ♘ge2

♘c7 9 0-0 d5 10 b3 ♕e8 11 ♗b2 ♕f7 12 ♖c1 ♗d7 13 e4!

Striking in the centre once he has completed mobilization. It is true that Black's inglorious piece configuration did nothing to discourage the pawn push, but this merely underlines Staunton's expertise in positional chess rather than the weak state of his opponent.

13...fxe4 14 dxe4 ♖ad8 15 e5 ♘fe8 16 f4

Bolstering e5 and preparing a kingside attack. Black's next move saddles White with an isolated pawn, but it is highly dubious as the critical square e4 falls in Staunton's hands.

16...dxc4? 17 bxc4 ♗c5+ 18 ♔h1 ♗e3 19 ♖b1 g6 20 ♕b3 ♗c8 21 ♘e4 ♗b6 22 ♖bd1 ♘a6 23 ♕c3!

Pinpointing Black's dark-square weaknesses. The threat is c5 followed by ♘d6, so Black hurries to exchange rooks in a vain effort to avoid total paralysis. In fact, with a knight on e4 hanging above his head like the Sword of Damocles, his fate is already sealed.

23...♖xd1 24 ♖xd1 ♘c5 25 ♘d6 ♕c7 26 ♕c2 ♘g7 (D)

27 g4! ♕e7 28 ♗d4 ♕c7 29 a4 ♘a6 30 c5 ♗a5 31 ♕b3 b6 32 ♘e4 bxc5 33 ♘f6+ ♔h8 34 ♕h3 ♘e8 35 ♗a1 ♘xf6 36 exf6 ♔g8 37 ♗e5 ♕b7 38 ♗e4 ♕f7 39 ♘g1! ♗d8 40 g5 ♗b7 41 ♘f3 ♖e8 42 ♗d6 ♗xf6 43 gxf6 ♕xf6 44 ♘g5 ♕g7 45 ♗e5 ♕e7 46 ♗xg6 1-0

The idea of an attack smoothly developing on the long diagonal must

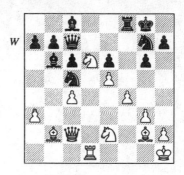

have influenced Owen, who often adopted the move 1 b3 (or 1...b6 when playing Black). However, it particularly appealed to Bird, who devised in the last decades of the 19th century a new set-up in order to prevent Black from blocking the diagonal by a timely ...e5. His system involved the moves 1 f4, 2 ♘f3, 3 e3 followed by b3 and ♗b2. The king's bishop would be developed on e2, d3, b5 or even g2, depending on the needs of the position. Bird's crude plan netted him some beautiful victories, but it was Emanuel Lasker's brilliant win over Bauer that grabbed the attention of the chess world:

Lasker – Bauer
Amsterdam 1889

1 f4 d5 2 e3 ♘f6 3 b3 e6 4 ♗b2 ♗e7 5 ♗d3 b6 6 ♘c3 ♗b7 7 ♘f3 ♘bd7 8 0-0 0-0 9 ♘e2?! c5?

9...♘c5! ∓.

10 ♘g3 ♕c7 11 ♘e5 ♘xe5 12 ♗xe5 ♕c6 13 ♕e2 a6 14 ♘h5! ♘xh5? (D)

15 ♗xh7+! ♔xh7 16 ♕xh5+ ♔g8 17 ♗xg7!! ♔xg7 18 ♕g4+ ♔h7 19

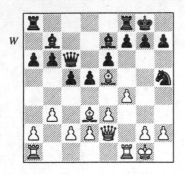

☒f3 e5 20 ☒h3+ ♕h6 21 ☒xh6+
♚xh6 22 ♕d7 and White won.

The theoretical discussion about
Bird's opening was not entirely one-
sided. The Danish player E.From
had already in 1871 invented the interesting pawn sacrifice 1...e5!?,
confronting White with difficult
problems (1 f4 e5 2 fxe5 d6 3 exd6
♗xd6 4 ♘f3 ♘f6 5 d4 ♘g4 6 ♗g5?
f6! 7 ♗h4 g5 8 h3?! ♘e3 9 ♕d3 ♗f4!
−+ was Sørensen-From, 1871, while
an encounter between the same opponents in 1874 varied with 5 g3
♘g4 6 d3 ♘xh2 7 ☒xh2 ♗xg3+ 8
☒f2 ♗xf2+ 9 ♚xf2 ♘c6 and Black
had good attacking chances despite
the material deficit). Bird himself
was in great difficulties against
Blackburne at Hastings 1895, after
the moves 1 f4 e5 2 fxe5 d6 3 exd6
♗xd6 4 g3 h5! 5 ♗g2 ♘c6 6 ♘c3 h4
7 ♘e4 hxg3 8 h3 ♘f6 9 ♘xd6+
♕xd6 10 d3 ♗e6 11 c3 0-0-0. All
this acted as a hindrance to the development of the main body of flank
openings, because ideas associated
with queenside activity or alternating positional threats all over the

board remained suppressed in the
background.

Things changed dramatically at
the start of the 20th century. This was
due to the emergence of a new gen-
eration of players, who willingly
adopted controversial ideas in an attempt to develop and systematize
theory. Aron Nimzowitsch's teach-
ings influenced many champions,
and it is not by chance that in the present era they constitute part and par-
cel of the chess player's arsenal.

Nimzowitsch's ideas had a notable impact on openings. Raging sacrificial attacks went out of fashion,
as they couldn't survive the test
against the well-founded principles
of centralization, blockade, overpro-
tection, etc. The value of a proud
pawn centre became questionable.
The new theory paved the way for a
different kind of approach, reminiscent of what has been termed by Alexander Kotov the 'Coiled Spring
Method', in his book *Train like a
Grandmaster*. As Kotov says '...some-
times grandmasters will decide to
avoid the deeply studied book lines,
by using a method that reminds one
of a coiled spring. They make just
one pawn advance to the centre, fianchetto the bishops and allow the
opponent to occupy the centre. The
calm here is only apparent since just
one incautious pawn advance by
Black will allow White's pieces to
uncoil with great force and inflict
damage on the enemy.'

These lines provide us with an excellent description of the energy

concealed in hypermodern strategy. However, we should note Kotov's remark that nowadays grandmasters attribute psychological value to their choice. In the hands of their predecessors, flank openings were just tools for theoretical applications.

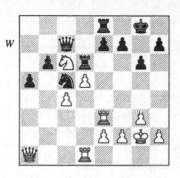

Réti – Rubinstein
Karlsbad 1923

1 ♘f3 d5 2 g3 ♘f6 3 ♗g2 g6 4 c4 d4?! 5 d3 ♗g7 6 b4 0-0 7 ♘bd2 c5 8 ♘b3!

Revealing the shortcomings of Rubinstein's early advance. Black is forced to abandon the fight for the centre after a mere eight moves.

8...cxb4 9 ♗b2 ♘c6 10 ♘bxd4 ♘xd4 11 ♗xd4 b6 12 a3! ♗b7 13 ♗b2 bxa3 14 ♖xa3 ♕c7 15 ♕a1!

A familiar manoeuvre in Réti's Opening. The queen is extremely powerful here, as it combines domination of the long diagonal with irritating queenside pressure.

15...♘e8 16 ♗xg7 ♘xg7 17 0-0 ♘e6 18 ♖b1 ♗c6 19 d4

Setting the pawn mass in motion. Rubinstein is reduced to waiting tactics, as the disappearance of the central pawns has robbed his position of its dynamism.

19...♗e4 20 ♖d1 a5

A sad necessity, but unavoidable in the long run.

21 d5 ♘c5 22 ♘d4 ♗xg2 23 ♔xg2 ♖fd8 24 ♘c6 ♖d6 25 ♖e3! ♖e8 *(D)*
26 ♕e5!

The crowning point of Réti's centralizing manoeuvres. The idea is to induce weaknesses on the kingside as well.

26...f6 27 ♕b2 e5 28 ♕b5 ♔f7 29 ♖b1 ♘d7 30 f3 ♖c8 31 ♖d3 e4?!

A desperate bid for counterplay, which fails for tactical reasons. However, Black's position was already beyond repair.

32 fxe4 ♘e5 33 ♕xb6! ♘xc6 34 c5! ♖d7 35 dxc6 ♖xd3 36 ♕xc7+ ♖xc7 37 exd3 ♖xc6 38 ♖b7+ ♔e8 39 d4 ♖a6 40 ♖b6 ♖a8 41 ♖xf6 and Black resigned on the 50th move.

Réti, who won a lot of games in the same qualitative style, was influenced to a certain extent by Nimzowitsch's opening ideas. For his game against Capablanca from New York 1924 he borrowed a move introduced in Nimzowitsch-Réti (!) at Karlsbad 1923: After the moves **1 ♘f3 ♘f6 2 c4 g6**, Nimzowitsch had unleashed the bizarre **3 b4!?** and although he couldn't eventually win, the opening was certainly a success for him: **3...a5 4 b5 ♗g7 5 ♗b2 0-0 6 e3 d6 7 d4 ♘bd7 8 ♗e2 e5 9 0-0 exd4 10 exd4 ♖e8** and now **11 ♘c3!** would have secured an edge for

White. The game Réti-Capablanca followed a different course, because Réti remained true to his style and fianchettoed both bishops: **3...♗g7 4 ♗b2 0-0 5 g3 b6 6 ♗g2 ♗b7 7 0-0 d6 8 d3 ♘bd7 9 ♘bd2 e5 10 ♕c2 ♖e8 11 ♖fd1 a5 12 a3 h6?! 13 ♘f1 c5** (13...e4!?) **14 b5 ♘f8 15 e3 ♕c7 16 d4 ♗e4 17 ♕c3 exd4 18 exd4 ♘6d7?!** (18...♘e6!) **19 ♕d2 cxd4 20 ♗xd4 ♕xc4 21 ♗xg7 ♔xg7 22 ♕b2+ ♔g8?** (22...♔h7!?) **23 ♖xd6 ♕c5 24 ♖ad1** *(D)*

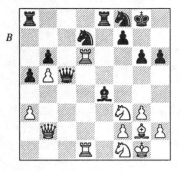

24...♖a7 25 ♘e3 ♕h5 26 ♘d4 ♗xg2 27 ♔xg2 ♕e5 28 ♘c4 ♕c5 29 ♘c6 ♖c7 30 ♘e3 ♘e5 31 ♖1d5 1-0

Following the Cuban's disaster, it became clear that Réti's Opening shouldn't be taken lightly. After all, why not play this with White if it's good enough to down the World Champion in 31 moves? At the same time Nimzowitsch was broadening the hypermodern repertoire by refining Bird's Opening and transforming it into the positional Nimzowitsch Attack, while others, like Tartakower and Alekhine were about to set foot

in uncharted fianchetto territory, later known as the Catalan. Despite Tarrasch's aphorisms, the new ideas earned a lot in respectability, and soon led to the creation of a new branch in opening theory.

However, Dr Siegbert Tarrasch was probably right in one respect: in their constant search for originality, the Hypermoderns reached in several cases the point of exaggeration. The fact that they could often escape unscathed can only be attributed to their great resourcefulness, a factor which, alas, proves inadequate if the opponent is at least as resourceful:

Réti – Em.Lasker
New York 1924

1 ♘f3 d5 2 c4 c6 3 b3 ♗f5 4 g3 ♘f6 5 ♗g2 ♘bd7 6 ♗b2 e6 7 0-0 ♗d6 8 d3 0-0 9 ♘bd2 e5 10 cxd5 cxd5 11 ♖c1?

This is too slow. White should play the energetic 11 e4! in order to take advantage of the unprotected d6-bishop. After 11...♗g4 12 exd5 ♘xd5 13 ♘c4 the position seems favourable for White. It seems, though, that Réti was keen on repeating the formation that had brought him success earlier in the tournament against Yates, with queen on a1 and doubled rooks on the c-file.

11...♕e7 12 ♖c2

White's manoeuvre is about to be completed, but Black will have few difficulties consolidating his space advantage. Lasker correctly recognizes that this advantage in itself is insufficient to break through, and initiates alternating tactics to effect weaknesses in White's game.

12...a5! 13 a4

Réti had to keep the queenside closed to prevent Black from activating his queen's rook by playing ...a4. However, the newly created weakness on b3 is more important than Black's corresponding one on b5, because it is practically impossible for White to occupy that square with a knight.

13...h6 14 ♕a1 ♖fe8 15 ♖fc1 ♗h7 (D)

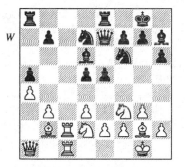

The opening struggle has ended, and both players can boast of certain achievements: White has completed his development harmoniously and controls the c-file, while Black's trumps include a strong pawn centre and wonderful centralization. On the surface chances appear even, as attack and defence seem to balance each other. Still, a closer look suffices to convince us that appearances are deceiving.

In the diagrammed position, Black enjoys a small but lasting advantage,

mainly for two reasons. The first one lies in the weakness of the b3-pawn, since the required protection would severely hamper White's strategy on the long diagonal. The second has to do with White's lack of space, an event rendering his rooks inflexible compared to Black's. It is true that they control the open c-file, but what is the point of controlling it if there are no invasion squares? Lasker's rooks, on the contrary, can be efficient in supporting a breakthrough with the central pawns after due preparation. Thus, one may dismiss Réti's manoeuvre in the present game as a mere exaggeration, based on a gross underestimation of the space element.

16 ♘f1

The prophylactic retreat of the black bishop had created a threat in ...c4-e3. Réti's move is designed to take the sting out of it since 16...e4?! would be now answered by 17 dxe4 dxe4 18 ♘d4 e3 19 ♘xe3 ♗xc2 20 ♖xc2 with tremendous compensation for the exchange. Unfortunately, the knight's withdrawal from the centre is not without drawbacks, as it allows Black to apply direct pressure on the weak spot in White's camp, namely b3.

16...♘c5 17 ♖xc5!

Displaying a willingness to cut the Gordian Knot created by his previous play. The sacrifice is objectively correct, but at the same time an admission of failure from the strategic point of view, as its character is mainly defensive.

17...♗xc5 18 ♘xe5 ♖ac8 19 ♘e3
♕e6 20 h3 ♗d6?

White has some compensation for
the exchange, but a solid move like
20...b6 would underline his lack of a
constructive plan. Lasker's move is a
serious slip, which goes unpunished
thanks to White's one track-minded
attitude in this game.

21 ♖xc8 ♖xc8 22 ♘f3?

Correct was 22 ♘5g4! ♘xg4 23
hxg4 ♗f8 24 ♗xd5 ♕d7 25 ♗f3
with a clear advantage. As it so often
happens when one is plagued by positional considerations, Réti misses
his chance and falls back on the defensive.

22...♗e7 23 ♘d4 ♕d7 24 ♔h2 h5
25 ♕h1!? h4! 26 ♘xd5 hxg3+ 27
fxg3 ♘xd5 28 ♗xd5 ♗f6! 29 ♗xb7
♖c5 30 ♗a6?

The decisive mistake. After 30
♗e4 (centralization!) 30...♗xd4 31
♗xh7+ ♔xh7 31 ♕e4+ f5 32 ♕xd4
♕xd4 33 ♗xd4 ♖c2 34 ♗b6 ♖xe2+
35 ♔g1 ♖d2 36 ♗xa5 ♖xd3 37 ♔f2
White maintains certain drawing
chances. However, it was difficult to
foresee the coming manoeuvre.

30...♗g6 31 ♕b7 ♕d8! 32 b4
♖c7 33 ♕b6 ♖d7!

Finally making use of the pin set
up by his 28th move. The exchange
of queens does not relieve White, because Black gets a dangerous passed
pawn.

34 ♕xd8+ ♖xd8 35 e3 axb4 36
♔g2 ♗xd4 37 exd4 ♗f5 38 ♗b7
♗e6 39 ♔f3 ♗b3 40 ♗c6 ♖d6 41
♗b5 ♖f6+ 42 ♔e3 ♖e6+ 43 ♔f4 ♖e2
44 ♗c1 ♖c2 45 ♗e3 ♗d5 0-1

A tremendous game by Lasker,
apart from the lapse on move 20. It
finely illustrates the dangers facing
White when his play becomes too artificial. The next example is a strictly
hypermodern affair, with Rubinstein
getting the worse of another border-
line case.

Rubinstein – Nimzowitsch
Marienbad 1925

1 d4 ♘f6 2 ♘f3 b6 3 g3 c5 4 ♗g2
♗b7 5 dxc5 bxc5 6 c4 g6 7 b3 ♗g7
8 ♗b2 0-0 9 0-0 ♘c6 10 ♘c3 a5 11
♕d2 d6

A typically hypermodern layout,
featuring a double fianchetto by both
sides. Black possesses a central pawn
majority, but it is not clear yet if this
amounts to a strength or a weakness.
White should now play 12 ♘d5 to
make the most of his bishop on b2.
Instead, he embarks on a time con-
suming manoeuvre with ill-fated
consequences.

12 ♘e1?! ♕d7 13 ♘c2 ♘b4! 14
♘e3 ♗xg2 15 ♔xg2?!

More to the point was 15 ♘xg2.
The text allows Black to grasp the
long diagonal with gain of tempo.

15...♕b7+ 16 f3? ♗h6! 17 ♘cd1

Threatening to ruin Black's pawn
formation, but Nimzowitsch strikes
first.

17...a4! 18 bxa4 (D)
18...♖fe8!

Prophylactic centralization, preparing the recovery of his pawn with
a much superior game. White's next
move looks suicidal, but Rubinstein

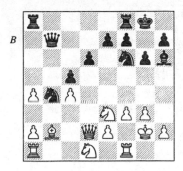

probably felt obliged to show something for his ruptured pawn structure.

19 ♗xf6? exf6 20 ♔f2 f5! 21 ♕xd6 ♗g7 22 ♖b1 ♗d4 23 ♔g2

There is no way out from the terrible pin. On 23 ♖b3 there would follow 23...♖c6 24 ♕f4 ♕e7 25 ♔g2 (what else?) 25...g5! winning a piece.

23...♗xe3 24 ♘xe3 ♖xe3 25 ♕xc5 ♖xe2+ and White resigned in a few moves.

In the 1930s the chess world witnessed a major change of scenery that has almost endured to the present day: the centre of theoretical developments was transferred to the Soviet Union and particularly Moscow, which gradually became the capital of a huge chess empire. This could be considered natural, following Alekhine's win over Capablanca in their 1927 World Championship Match, but an even more important factor was the constant danger of war in Europe, as in this respect the Soviet Republics were (or felt) less threatened than other countries, if only for geographical reasons.

Thus, a whole new galaxy of stars, soon made its appearance on the international scene. Most of these players were destined to be protagonists for many decades to come and laid the foundations of what has later been described as the Soviet Chess School. Apparently influenced by their great predecessors, they continued the research on hypermodern grounds. One of the main fields of interest in that period was the Catalan, an opening system that combines modern and classical characteristics.

The following encounter is hardly flawless, but it clearly illustrates White's aim to conduct a queenside attack with the minimum of risk.

Flohr – Szabo
Kemeri 1939

1 d4 ♘f6 2 c4 e6 3 g3 d5 4 ♗g2 ♗e7 5 ♘f3 dxc4 6 ♕a4+ ♘bd7 7 0-0 0-0 8 ♕xc4 c5 9 dxc5 ♘xc5 10 ♗e3 ♕d5 11 ♕c2 ♕e4 12 ♕c1 ♘a4 13 b3 ♘b6 14 ♘bd2 ♕h4 15 ♗d4 ♗d7 16 a3 ♕b5 17 ♖e1 ♗c6 18 ♕b2 ♘bd7 19 ♘c4 ♘c5 20 ♘cd2 ♖fd8 21 a4 ♕a6 22 ♗f1 ♘ce4 23 ♘xe4 ♗xe4 24 ♘e5 ♖ac8 25 ♖ec1 b6 26 e3 ♕b7 27 ♖xc8 ♖xc8 28 ♖c1 ♗c5 *(D)*

29 a5 ♗xd4 30 ♕xd4 ♖f8 31 a6 ♕b8 32 ♘g4 ♘xg4 33 ♕xe4 ♘f6 34 ♕b7 ♕e5 35 ♕xa7 ♘g4 36 ♕c7 ♕d5 37 ♗g2 ♕xb3 38 a7 ♕a2 39 a8♕ 1-0

The merits of the Catalan soon caught the attention of many of the newcomers to the chess world's élite. Two striking examples were

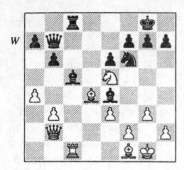

16 ♘b3 ♘c5 17 ♘xc5 ♗xc5 *(D)*

Mikhail Botvinnik and Paul Keres who both experimented with it in the early days of their career. Those days, however, were hardly inspiring for playing chess as the War was already rearing its ugly head all over Europe and the wounded chess family. The self-exiled World Champion Alexander Alekhine, one of the first to introduce the system in tournament practice, employed it in some games in his last years.

Alekhine – Junge
Prague 1942

1 d4 d5 2 c4 e6 3 ♘f3 ♘f6 4 g3 dxc4 5 ♕a4+ ♘bd7 6 ♗g2 a6 7 ♕xc4 b5 8 ♕c6 ♖b8 9 0-0 ♗b7 10 ♕c2 c5 11 a4 ♗xf3

A risky choice. More to the point is 11...♕b6 or even 11...b4!?.

12 ♗xf3 cxd4 13 axb5 axb5 14 ♖d1 ♕b6 15 ♘d2 e5

An interesting alternative is the move 15...♗c5. Worse, however, is 15...♘e5? 16 ♘b3! ♘xf3+ 17 exf3 and White has a big advantage due to Black's retarded development and the weakness at c6.

18 ♖a6!!?

A bolt from the blue. Although it is not clear whether this is winning by force, it certainly poses almost insurmountable problems for the defence in over-the-board play.

18...♕xa6 19 ♕xc5 ♕e6 20 ♗c6+ ♘d7 21 ♗xd7+ ♔xd7 22 ♕a7+ ♔c6

22...♔d6!? gives Black better defensive chances, but it was not so easy to visualize Alekhine's 24th.

23 ♗d2 ♖hc8 24 e4!! ♕b3

Editor's note: As John Nunn points out in the new edition of *Alexander Alekhine's Best Games*, there is no win for White apparent after 24...b4! 25 ♖a1 ♔b5!.

25 ♖a1 b4 26 ♖a6+ ♔b5 27 ♖a5+ ♔c6 28 ♕c5+ ♔d7 29 ♖a7+ 1-0

One of the main virtues of the Catalan is, apparently, solidity. It is not easy for Black to find or create targets, and the classical response, namely maintaining and reinforcing Black's pawns in the centre, would often succumb in the early days of acquaintance with the system to the following recipe:

1) White gets in a well-timed e4 advance.

2) The threat of advancing to e5, compels Black to take on c4, granting White a space advantage.

3) To avoid suffocation, Black reacts with ...c(7)6-c5. Then White either plays d5, obtaining a dangerous passed d-pawn and attacking chances on the kingside, or achieves a favourable liquidation, leading to a better ending, and in some cases, a complete bind on the queenside.

Black's play in the game Alekhine-Junge was an unsuccessful attempt to avoid the problems outlined above. In fact, the policy of an early capture on c4 is quite logical, as White will have to invest several tempi to recover his pawn, allowing Black to complete his development and generate freeing pawn breaks. In the next two examples Black (Keres) conforms with this strategic outline, obtaining straightforward victories against relatively inexperienced opposition.

Junge – Keres
Salzburg 1942

1 d4 ♘f6 2 c4 e6 3 g3 d5 4 ♗g2 dxc4 5 ♕a4+ ♘bd7 6 ♘d2 c6 7 ♕xc4 e5 8 dxe5 ♘xe5 9 ♕c3 ♗d6 10 ♘gf3 ♕e7 11 ♘xe5 ♗xe5 12 ♕c2 0-0 13 0-0 ♗g4 14 ♘f3 ♗c7 (D)

Black has easily equalized and now proceeds to activate his rooks on the open files. White's next is a naïve way to block the pressure on e2, as the bishop is exposed to irritating attacks from the black knight, or a potential exchange sacrifice.

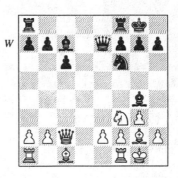

15 ♗e3?

15 b3 = was preferable.

15...♖fe8 16 ♖fe1 ♗a5! 17 ♗d2

Admitting his mistake, but at a precious cost in time. Meanwhile, the harmony in White's position has declined, as the bishop is prone to harassment on both d2 and c3.

17...♗b6 18 ♗c3 ♖ad8 19 e3 ♘e4 20 ♘d4 c5 21 ♗xe4?!

Seeking refuge in the endgame. 21 ♘b3 ♗f5 is unpleasant, but, nevertheless, a better chance than the game continuation.

21...♕xe4 22 ♕xe4 ♖xe4

Black has a clear edge in this ending, on account of his two bishops and queenside pawn majority. Keres cashed in after a further ten moves, when his opponent blundered in a hopeless position.

The second example is more instructive, since – unlike the first one – White's downfall is not caused by suspect piece manoeuvring. The main factor here is of a strategic nature and has to do with White's neglect of the centre.

Troianescu – Keres
Schawno Zdroi 1950

1 d4 ♘f6 2 c4 e6 3 ♘f3 d5 4 g3 dxc4 5 ♕a4+ ♘bd7 6 ♕xc4 a6 7 ♕c2?!

This move would have a point in preventing ...b5 if White had chosen the 3 g3 and 4 ♗g2 move-order. As it is, it commits the queen prematurely, losing the option of answering ...b5 with ♕c6.

7...b5 8 ♗g2 ♗b7 9 a4?!

Playing with fire. After 9 0-0 the position is equal.

9...c5 10 axb5?

Opening the a-file can only be good for Black, who has superior development. But White was already under pressure after his early inaccuracies.

10...axb5 11 ♖xa8 ♖xa8 12 ♘a3

Forced, in view of the devastating threat ...♗e4, winning a piece.

12...cxd4 13 0-0 ♗xa3 14 bxa3 0-0 15 ♕d3 e5 16 ♕xb5 *(D)*

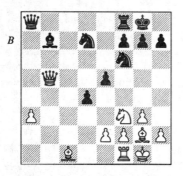

The situation has clarified. Troianescu has managed to regain his pawn and even possesses the two bishops, but in the meantime the mighty Estonian has acquired complete dominion in the centre. In fact, his central pawn duo is cramping the opponent's movements to such an extent that it would be no exaggeration to say that White's position is already lost.

16...♖b8 17 ♕c4 ♖c8 18 ♕a2 ♘e4

Heading for the square c3, a tremendous outpost. The rest of the game requires no particular comments as White's queenside soon becomes the Promised Land for the black knights.

19 ♘h4 ♘c3 20 ♗xb7 ♕xb7 21 ♕d2 ♘c5 22 ♖e1 ♘b3 23 ♕b2 g6 24 ♗h6 ♕d5 25 ♘g2 ♕c4 26 h4 ♖a8 27 h5 ♕a4 28 e3 ♕xa3 29 ♕xa3 ♖xa3 30 exd4 ♘xd4 31 ♘h4 f6 32 hxg6 hxg6 33 ♗d2 g5 34 ♔g2 gxh4 35 gxh4 ♘f5 and White resigned after the time control had been reached.

Alekhine's sudden death in 1946 ended the World Champions' arbitrary monopoly in choosing contenders for the world crown. The next World Champion (winner of a special tournament organized by FIDE during 1948) was, nevertheless, Alekhine's chosen challenger, Mikhail Botvinnik.

In the next decades, Botvinnik's personality deeply affected chess developments; even more so did his games. His universal style, disciplined and self-critical, enabled him to conduct many an arduous manoeuvring game with precision, and this helps to explain why the English (1 c4) was one of his favourite openings as White. The following example is a typical illustration of the advantages inherent in a slow build-up, by the man who brought the concept to the forefront of international competition.

Botvinnik – Szabo
Moscow 1956

1 c4 g6 2 g3 &g7 3 &g2 e5 4 ♘c3 ♘e7 5 d3 c6 6 e4

Blocking the diagonal of the fianchettoed bishop, but as Keene points out in *Flank Openings* the whole concept of erecting the structure c4-d3-e4 '... is based on one of Nimzowitsch's ideas: White holds the centre under restraint and prepares the flank advances f4 and b4'.

However, unlike positions with the queen's knight developed on c6, when the choice of White's central pawn formation would be merely a matter of taste, Botvinnik is practically forced to adopt his customary set-up here, as Black was threatening to play ...d5 under favourable conditions.

6...d6 7 ♘ge2 a6 8 a4 a5 9 &e3 &e6 10 0-0 ♕d7 11 b3 h5!? 12 h4 &h3

Szabo has played methodically enough to restrain White's ambitions on the wings and now proceeds to exchange light-squared bishops, a decision strategically justified if one

takes into account that d3-d4 always renders the position of the bishop on e6 problematic. His plan is not lacking in finesse and would have been almost perfect, were it not for the loss of time involved and the passive position of the knight on e7.

13 d4 0-0 14 ♖a2!

A fine move, highlighting Black's weaknesses along the d-file. At the same moment it reveals a fascinating aspect of flank openings, namely the ability to cause Black distress through 'indoor manoeuvring'. The psychological impact on Szabo becomes evident after a couple of moves.

14...&xg2 15 ♔xg2 (D)

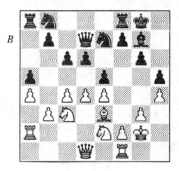

15...d5?

An unsound attempt to break free. The Hungarian had to live with the idea of defending a backward pawn and to this end the best continuation was 15...exd4 16 &xd4!? (16 ♘xd4 ♘a6 17 ♖d2 ♖ad8 looks playable for Black) 16...♘a6 17 &xg7 ♔xg7 18 ♕d4+ ♔h7 (it is important to put the king here in order to be able to repel queen invasions on f6 with ...♘g8)

19 ♖d2 ♖fd8! (19...♖ad8? 20 ♕b6) with chances to defend successfully. White can improve on this line by means of 18 ♖d2! ♖ad8 19 e5 but Black's resources are not exhausted: 19...♘f5! (not 19...d5? 20 ♕a1! with an attack) 20 ♘d4 (20 exd6?! ♘c5. 20 ♘e4!?) 20...♘c5 and it is not easy for White to win a pawn without allowing some counterplay.

16 dxe5! dxc4

16...dxe4 17 ♘xe4 is also unsatisfactory.

17 bxc4 ♗xe5 18 ♕xd7 ♘xd7 19 ♖d2

Black's pseudo-activity has backfired, but considering the undeveloped state of his queenside this was a rather inevitable conclusion. The remainder was undoubtedly sheer torture for Szabo, as he could only sit back and watch his position collapse, in order to reach a respectable number of moves.

19...♗xc3 20 ♖xd7 ♗b4 21 c5 ♖fe8 22 ♖fd1 f5 23 ♖xb7 fxe4 24 ♖d6! ♔f7 25 ♘f4 ♖eb8 26 ♖bd7 ♔e8 27 ♘e6 1-0

Botvinnik won many games with the English throughout his chess career, but in my opinion the telling factor was the strength of the player rather than the opening's objective merits. One of his rare failures with it occurred at the very beginning of his second World Championship match against Smyslov. Botvinnik employs his 'wall' again, but this time it fails to make much of an impression on Black's position.

Botvinnik – Smyslov
Moscow Wch (1) 1957

1 c4 ♘f6 2 ♘c3 g6 3 g3 ♗g7 4 ♗g2 0-0 5 e4 c5 6 ♘ge2 ♘c6 7 0-0 d6 8 a3 ♗d7 9 h3 ♘e8! *(D)*

Nowadays a standard plan. The knight is heading for c7 from where it helps to organize counterplay with ...b5. At the same time the diagonal of the g7-bishop is opened, and Black can look forward to intensifying his control over d4 with the manoeuvre ...♘c7-e6.

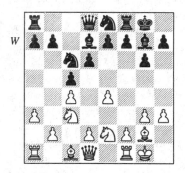

10 d3 ♘c7 11 ♖b1 ♖b8 12 ♗e3 b5 13 cxb5 ♘xb5 14 ♘xb5 ♖xb5 15 d4

Once more switching to central action, only this time Black is better poised to deal with it.

15...♕c8 16 dxc5 dxc5 17 ♔h2 ♖d8 18 ♕c1 ♘d4

Smyslov has achieved comfortable equality. The slight weakness of his queenside pawns is compensated by the strongly centralized knight and White's hole at b3.

19 ♘c3 ♖b7 20 f4 ♗c6 21 ♖f2 a5 22 ♕f1! ♘b5! 23 e5 ♘xc3 24 bxc3

♗xg2 25 ♖xg2 ♖xb1 26 ♕xb1 ♕c6 (D)

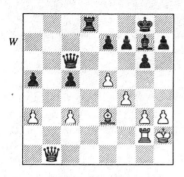

27 ♖d2?

A questionable decision. 27 c4 or even 27 ♕c2 would have yielded equal chances. Now Smyslov grasps the opportunity to fix White's queenside pawns as targets for his bishop.

27...♖xd2+ 28 ♗xd2 c4! 29 ♗e3 f6 30 ♗d4 ♔f7 31 ♕d1 a4! 32 ♕e2 ♕d5 33 ♔g1 ♗f8 34 f5

An unsuccessful try to stir up some trouble, but Botvinnik was already in great difficulties.

34...fxe5 35 fxg6+ hxg6 36 ♗xe5 e6 37 ♕f2+ ♔e8 38 ♕f6 ♗xa3 39 ♕xg6+ ♔d7 40 ♕h7+ ♗e7 41 ♗f6 and White at the same time resigned as the a-pawn is unstoppable.

Following Botvinnik's example, many top players added the English to their repertoire. These included Smyslov, Tal, Petrosian, Korchnoi, Larsen, Portisch and Uhlmann, to mention just a few. Fischer used it as a surprise weapon in several games of his 1972 match against Spassky, who would usually transpose to a Queen's Gambit, avoiding a discussion of the most straightforward replies 1...e5 or 1...c5 (which he tried only once). No doubt games like the following must have played an important role in Spassky's decision:

Botvinnik – Portisch
Monaco 1968

1 c4 e5 2 ♘c3 ♘f6 3 g3 d5

This normally leads to a type of Dragon with colours reversed. Botvinnik liked the resulting positions with either colour, the present game probably being his best performance.

4 cxd5 ♘xd5 5 ♗g2 ♗e6 6 ♘f3 ♘c6 7 0-0 ♘b6 8 d3 ♗e7 9 a3 a5 10 ♗e3 0-0 11 ♘a4 ♘xa4

Botvinnik criticized this move on the grounds that it accelerates White's mobilization. He suggested instead 11...♘d4 as a more prudent course of action.

12 ♕xa4 ♗d5 13 ♖fc1 ♖e8 14 ♖c2!

A difficult decision, but White correctly perceived that his queen's position is unassailable, e.g. 14...b5? 15 ♕xb5 ♖b8 16 ♕a4 ♗b3? 17 ♕xc6 or 14...♖b8 15 ♕b5. Thus, he achieves his aim of doubling rooks on the c-file.

14...♗f8 15 ♖ac1 ♘b8?

From the psychological point of view I would rate this as a magnificent example of history being repeated. Just as in Botvinnik-Szabo (14 ♖a2!), a cunning rook move (14 ♖c2!) initiates pressure on an open file. A couple of moves later Portisch repeats the mistake made by his compatriot: he tries to solve his problems by drastic means. Black's position cannot afford such a treatment, and he should have preferred the continuation 15...e4 16 dxe4 ♗xe4, which keeps White's edge to a minimum.

16 ♖xc7 ♗c6 *(D)*

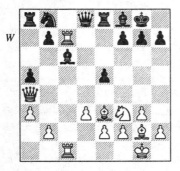

This position has been published the world over. It seems that White must lose an exchange, but in fact he is willing to give a lot more than that!

17 ♖1xc6! bxc6 18 ♖xf7!!

A brilliant shot. It suddenly turns out that Black is extremely weak on the light squares, the following line offering more than sufficient evidence: 18...♔xf7 19 ♕c4+ ♔g6 20 ♕g4+ ♔f7 21 ♘g5+ ♔f6 22 ♘xh7+ ♔f7 23 ♕f5+ ♔g8 24 ♘g5 forcing mate or win of the queen. The continuation chosen by the Hungarian grandmaster postpones the inevitable for a few moves.

18...h6 19 ♖b7 ♕c8 20 ♕c4+ ♔h8 21 ♘h4! ♕xb7 22 ♘g6+ ♔h7 23 ♗e4

Threatening 24 ♘e7+ and 25 ♕g8 mate. Black's reply is forced.

23...♗d6 24 ♘xe5+ g6 25 ♗xg6+ ♔g7 26 ♗xh6+! and Portisch resigned because 26...♔xh6 allows 27 ♕h4+ ♔g7 28 ♕h7+ ♔f6 29 ♘g4+ ♔e6 30 ♕xb7.

In the 1960s, hypermodernism had entered its second full moon. The co-existence of deep strategists and authentic researchers produced sparkling clashes, in both a theoretical and competitive sense. The theory of the King's Indian Attack was greatly enriched in that period. It is a system that can be applied almost irrespective of Black's reply. This particular feature appealed to many players, all the more so because the opening's direct object of attack is the black king.

However, despite being a regular choice in serious tournaments, the King's Indian Attack never caught on as a first-class weapon. Players such as Petrosian, Fischer and Geller used it effectively on several occasions, but only to dispose of 'ordinary' grandmaster opposition. The following games have become anthology pieces, but hardly reflect Black's chances in this opening:

Fischer – Panno
Buenos Aires 1970

1 e4 c5 2 ♘f3 e6 3 d3 ♘c6 4 g3 g6 5 ♗g2 ♗g7 6 0-0 ♘ge7

A position characteristic for the entire system, which can be reached via various move orders (French, Sicilian or 1 ♘f3). White now proceeds to establish a cramping pawn on e5, an important step towards exerting kingside pressure.

7 ♖e1 d6

For 7...0-0!? see below.

8 c3 0-0 9 d4 cxd4 10 cxd4 d5 11 e5 ♗d7 12 ♘c3 ♖c8 13 ♗f4 ♘a5 14 ♖c1 b5 15 b3 b4 16 ♘e2 ♗b5?!

Fischer is gradually massing his forces on the kingside, so 16...♖xc1! was a more appropriate continuation, deflecting them temporarily from the threatened sector.

17 ♕d2 ♘ac6?! 18 g4 a5?

The decisive error. The lesser evil was 18...♗xe2 to prevent the knight from reaching g3. Panno probably feared that White would then switch to the queenside in order to exploit his weaknesses on the light squares.

19 ♘g3

The knight finds a passage to immortality. The rest is a textbook illustration of attacking on the dark squares.

19...♕b6 20 h4 ♘b8 21 ♗h6 ♘d7 22 ♕g5! ♖xc1 23 ♖xc1 ♗xh6 24 ♕xh6 ♖c8 25 ♖xc8+ ♘xc8 26 h5 ♕d8 27 ♘g5 ♘f8 (D)

Black seems to have weathered the storm, but Fischer's next move crushes this optical illusion.

28 ♗e4!!

A move from the 21st century! Its value lies mostly in the aesthetic way the bishop joins the attack, rather than the simple variation 28...dxe4? 29 ♘3xe4, forcing immediate capitulation.

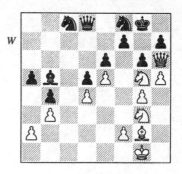

28...♕c7 29 ♘xh7!

An effective demolition of the king's fortress. The rest demonstrates Black's inability to defend in view of his uncoordinated minor pieces.

29...♘xh7 30 hxg6 hxg6 31 ♗xg6 ♘g5 32 ♘h5 ♘f3+ 33 ♔g2 ♘h4+ 34 ♔g3 ♘xg6 35 ♘f6+ ♔f7 36 ♕h7+ 1-0

Instead of 7...d6 an alternative is **7...0-0** as after **8 e5!?**, 8...b6! 9 ♘bd2 d6 does not promise White more than equality. However, the famous miniature **Petrosian-Pachman**, *Bled 1961* had long deterred Black from castling on move 7:

8...d6 9 exd6 ♕xd6 10 ♘bd2 ♕c7 11 ♘b3 ♘d4 12 ♗f4 ♕b6 13 ♘e5 ♘xb3 14 ♘c4 ♕b5 15 axb3 a5 16 ♗d6 ♗f6 17 ♕f3 ♔g7 18 ♖e4 ♖d8 (D)

19 ♕xf6+! ♔xf6 20 ♗e5+ ♔g5 21 ♗g7! 1-0

The reader may have noticed that I have refrained from criticizing Pachman's individual moves here. Actually the whole game looks like a big mistake by Black!

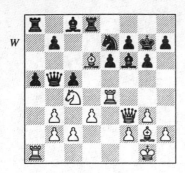

The period 1972-85 was dominated by Anatoly Karpov, a player of less romantic inclination and higher defensive skills than his predecessors. This change of guard led to a substantial strengthening of Black's chances in flank openings, as this type of game suited well the new champion's patient style and his alertness in grasping the slightest opportunity. Karpov may not be a perfectionist, but his practical attitude has usually been effective in exposing a corresponding weakness of these over-elaborate systems:

Hübner – Karpov
Tilburg 1977
English Opening

1 c4 c5 2 ♘f3 ♘f6 3 ♘c3 d5 4 cxd5 ♘xd5 5 g3 g6 6 d3 ♗g7 7 ♗d2 b6 8 ♕a4+ ♗d7 9 ♕h4 ♗c6 10 ♗g2 e6 11 ♕xd8+ ♔xd8 12 ♖c1 ♘a6 13 ♘xd5 ♗xd5 14 ♗c3 f6 15 a3 ♔e7 16 0-0 ♖hc8 17 ♘d2 ♘c7 18 b4 ♗xg2 19 ♔xg2 cxb4 20 ♗xb4+ ♔d7 21 ♗c3 ♘d5 22 ♗b2 ♗h6 23 e3 ♗xe3 24 fxe3 ♘xe3+ 25 ♔f3 ♘xf1 26 ♘xf1 ♖xc1 27 ♗xc1 ♖c8 28 ♗b2

♖c2 29 ♗xf6 ♖a2 30 ♔e3 ♖xa3 31 ♘d2 b5 32 ♘e4 b4 33 ♔d4 a5 34 ♔c4 ♖a2 35 h4 ♔c6 36 ♗d4 ♖e2 37 ♗e5 ♖e1 38 ♗f6 ♖b1 39 ♗e7 e5 40 g4 ♖c1+ 41 ♔b3 ♔d5 42 ♗g5 ♖b1+ 43 ♔c2 ♖h1 44 ♔b3 ♖h3 45 ♘f6+ ♔d4 46 ♘xh7 ♖xd3+ 47 ♔c2 a4 48 ♗e7 ♖c3+ 49 ♔b1 ♖c7 0-1

Fine endgame technique by Karpov who was, nevertheless, aided by Hübner's indecisiveness in the early stages of the struggle. An important remark here is that once Black neutralizes his opponent's main plan (which is usually stereotyped), the position rarely peters out to a forced draw. This can easily tip the scales in Black's favour, especially if White has put too much faith in his opening scheme.

Portisch – Karpov
Moscow 1977
King's Indian Attack

1 ♘f3 ♘f6 2 g3 b6 3 ♗g2 ♗b7 4 0-0 e6 5 d3 d5 6 ♘bd2 ♘bd7 7 ♖e1 ♗c5!

A strong move. By bringing pressure to bear on f2 Karpov takes the sting out of the advance e2-e4.

8 c4

On 8 e4 there follows 8...dxe4 9 ♘g5 (9 dxe4 ♘g4 and 10...♘de5) 9...e3! (the point) 10 fxe3 ♗xg2 11 ♔xg2 0-0 with a satisfactory position for Black. But now White has been lured away from well-trodden paths.

8...0-0 9 cxd5 exd5 10 ♘b3?!

A first sign of discomfort. Less artificial would have been 10 e3 but if Portisch was in dire need of moving his knight to b3 he should have prefaced it with 10 a3. Then, after 10...a5 11 ♘b3, Black can no longer play as in the game.

10...♗b4! 11 ♗d2 a5 12 ♘bd4 ♖e8 13 ♖c1 c5 14 ♘f5 ♘f8 15 d4

This allows the black knight to e4, but White had to extricate the f5-knight from potential danger. 15 a3 ♗xd2 16 ♕xd2 a4 fixing the queenside would not have appealed to Portisch either.

15...♘e4 16 dxc5? *(D)*

A bad mistake. After 16 a3 ♗xd2 17 ♘xd2 ♕f6 Black has only a slight advantage. What now follows is a debacle.

16...♘xd2 17 ♘xd2 ♕g5!

Winning material. White had probably overlooked that 18 ♘e3 loses immediately to 18...♖xe3!.

18 ♘d6?

Portisch is completely demoralized from the course of the game and fails to put up the most stubborn resistance. The best way to lose a piece

was 18 c6 ♗a6 19 ♘xg7 ♔xg7 20 e3 when the position is lost for White but he maintains a few swindling chances.

18...♗xd2 19 ♘xb7 ♗xe1 20 ♕xe1 ♖xe2! 21 ♕xe2 ♕xc1+ 22 ♕f1 ♕d2 23 cxb6 ♖c8 0-1

It is indeed rare for a player like Portisch to lose in a miniature with White. In those times his fellow grandmasters Larsen and Ljubojević were, nevertheless, getting accustomed to that, not because they had to face Karpov regularly, but rather due to their obstinacy in employing 1 b3, an opening that has its roots in the Nimzowitschian era. Their unsuccessful ride with it is one of the curiosities of the 1970s:

Larsen – Spassky
Belgrade 1970

1 b3 e5 2 ♗b2 ♘c6 3 c4 ♘f6 4 ♘f3?!

Allowing Black a free hand in the centre. 4 e3 is preferable.

4...e4 5 ♘d4 ♗c5 6 ♘xc6 dxc6 7 e3 ♗f5 8 ♕c2 ♕e7 9 ♗e2 0-0-0 10 f4?

Linked with the idea of 11 ♗xf6 ♕xf6 12 ♘c3 (Spassky), but already a decisive mistake as White's position cannot afford the luxury of another pawn move. 10 ♘c3 followed by 0-0-0 was imperative.

10...♘g4! 11 g3 h5! 12 h3

12 ♘c3 ♖xd2!! wins for Black.

12...h4! 13 hxg4

On 13 ♗xg4 Spassky offers the following winning line: 13...♗xg4

14 hxg4 hxg3 15 罝g1 罝h1! 16 罝xh1 g2 17 罝g1 豐h4+ 18 曲e2 豐xg4+ 19 曲e1 豐g3+ 20 曲e2 (20 曲d1 豐f2 21 豐xe4 豐xg1+ 22 曲c2 豐f2 −+) 20...豐f3+ 21 曲e1 魚e7 with inevitable mate.

13...hxg3 14 罝g1 *(D)*

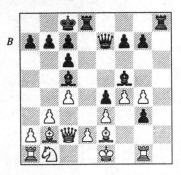

14...罝h1!!
Everything runs like clockwork! This is a brilliant example of sacrificing material in order to accelerate the attack.

15 罝xh1 g2 16 罝f1
16 罝g1 would not have altered the outcome in view of 16...豐h4+ 17 曲d1 豐h1.

16...豐h4+ 17 曲d1 gxf1豐+ 0-1

The next game is another characteristic example of what may befall White if he neglects his king's safety.

Ljubojević – Kavalek
Manila 1973

1 b3 e5 2 魚b2 d6 3 c4 ⵚf6 4 ⵚc3 g6 5 d4 exd4 6 豐xd4 ⵚc6 7 豐e3+ 魚e6 8 ⵚf3 魚g7 9 ⵚg5 0-0 10 ⵚxe6 fxe6 11 g3 d5 12 豐xe6+ 曲h8 13 ⵚxd5

ⵚxd5 14 魚xg7+ 曲xg7 15 cxd5 罝e8 16 豐g4 豐xd5 17 f3 ⵚe5 18 罝d1 ⵚxf3+ 19 曲xf2 豐xd1 20 exf3 豐d2+ 21 曲g1 罝e1 22 豐c4 罝ae8 0-1

So is 1 b3 bad after all? I wouldn't bet on this, but surely it's much more difficult to face the English or Catalan as these openings are capable of giving Black headaches right from the start. The fact that no less a player than Viktor Korchnoi has been employing them for decades is a tribute to their soundness. In reality this great fighter has contributed a lot to the middlegame theory of most hypermodern openings.

Korchnoi – Arnason
Beersheba 1987

1 c4 e5 2 ⵚc3 ⵚf6 3 ⵚf3 ⵚc6 4 g3 d5 5 cxd5 ⵚxd5 6 魚g2 ⵚb6 7 0-0 魚e7 8 b3 0-0 9 魚b2 罝e8 10 罝c1 魚g4 11 d3 魚f8 12 ⵚd2 豐d7 13 罝e1 罝ab8 14 ⵚce4 ⵚd4 15 ⵚc5 豐c8?!

Preferable was 15...魚xc5 16 罝xc5 c6 with an equal position, according to Korchnoi. Arnason is not willing to part with his bishop, even if this involves a rather odd piece configuration on the queenside.

16 ⵚf3 ⵚd7 17 ⵚxd4 魚xc5 18 ⵚf3 魚b6 *(D)*
19 罝c4!
The start of a really original manoeuvre. Arnason's last few moves have denuded his kingside from defenders, but normally there is no way to exploit that in as much as the

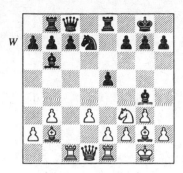

king's pawn cover has been left intact. White's intuitive rook transfer accomplishes the task of inducing weaknesses in a highly instructive manner.

19...♗e6 20 ♖h4 f6 21 d4

Korchnoi's play has been directed towards achieving this central advance. On the 19th move it would have been inappropriate as the reply 19...e4 would have then equalized.

21...g5 22 ♖h6!

Completing an incredible journey. The rook is trapped here, but its demise will add fuel to the coming attack.

22...♔g7 23 dxe5 ♔xh6 24 exf6 ♖g8

Alternatives would not have saved Black either. On 24...♔g6 Korchnoi gives the attractive line 25 ♕d2 h6 26 ♘h4+! ♔f7 27 ♕c2 ♘f8 28 ♗f3 ♕d7 (28...gxh4 29 ♗h5+ ♔g8 30 f7+ ♗xf7 31 ♕c3 +−) 29 ♖d1 ♕xd1+ 30 ♕xd1 gxh4 31 ♕d2 hxg3 32 hxg3 ♔g6 33 ♗e4+ ♗f5 34 ♗xf5+ ♔xf5 35 ♕d5+ ♔g6 36 g4 ♘e6 37 ♕h5+ ♔h7 38 ♕f7+ 39 ♕xe8+ ♖xe8 40 f7+ winning, while more prosaic methods are also available. Another

beautiful variation is 24...♘c5 25 ♕c1 ♘e4 26 ♘xg5! ♘xg5 27 h4 ♖g8 28 f7! ♗xf7 29 ♕f4, when despite White's material deficit the attack is unstoppable.

25 ♕d2 ♔h5 26 h3 ♘c5 27 g4+ ♗xg4

Or 27...♔h6 28 ♘xg5 ♖xg5 29 h4 ♕g8 30 b4! ♘a4 31 f7! ♗xf7 32 hxg5+ ♕xg5 33 ♗g7+ ♔g6 34 ♗e4+, winning the queen. The position is full of neat tactical motifs.

28 hxg4+ ♕xg4 29 ♘e5 ♕h4 30 ♕c2 ♘e4 31 ♕xe4 ♗xf2+ 32 ♔f1 ♕xe4 33 ♗xe4 ♗xe1 34 ♔xe1 and White won easily.

The last decade may well prove a turning point in the evolution of flank openings. Kasparov's successful patronage of 1 c4 has led to a resurgence of interest in many related systems, a characteristic example being the resurrection of 1 b3 in recent games by Kramnik and Adams. Kasparov's following win over Karpov was a critical encounter of great significance to the course of chess history.

Kasparov - Karpov
Seville Wch (24) 1987

1 c4 e6 2 ♘f3 ♘f6 3 g3 d5 4 b3

Karpov's win in the 23rd game had placed Kasparov in a difficult situation. He needed a win at all costs in order to even the score and save his title. The slow text move serves well the purpose of complicating the struggle as White's central pawns are kept unmoved, avoiding any chance of an early liquidation.

4...♗e7 5 ♗g2 0-0 6 0-0 b6 7 ♗b2 ♗b7 8 e3 ♘bd7 9 ♘c3 ♘e4 10 ♘e2!

The best choice, at least in a psychological sense. 10 cxd5, 10 ♕e2 and 10 ♕c2 had all been played before, but they allow simplification.

10...a5 11 d3 ♗f6 12 ♕c2 ♗xb2 13 ♕xb2

Black has achieved his aim of exchanging a pair of bishops but at the cost of allowing the white queen to b2, an excellent post from where she can observe the important squares d4 and e5. The position now resembles some of Réti's games, in which the queen also had an important task to fulfil on the long diagonal.

13...♘d6 14 cxd5 ♗xd5

14...exd5 seems more natural and would have reached a queenside structure analogous to the one from his game against Portisch. The text does not make a good impression because it accentuates White's central preponderance. It seems, however, that Karpov was solely intent on fluid piece play, a strategy which soon lands him in an inferior position.

15 d4! c5 16 ♖fd1 *(D)*

Black's pieces appear exposed along the d-file and according to Kasparov he should have now resorted to 16...c4!? 17 ♘f4 b5 18 ♘xd5 exd5 19 ♘e5 ♘f6, with an unclear game in which the queenside majority might be of some significance. Karpov's actual move shows

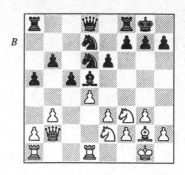

that he has reconciled himself to the idea of defending a slightly worse, yet symmetrical position after the ensuing exchange of his bishop for White's king's knight.

16...♖c8?! 17 ♘f4 ♗xf3

Forced. The variation 17...♗e4? 18 dxc5 ♘xc5 19 ♕e5 (centralization with tempo) 19...♘cb7 20 ♘h5! serves to illustrate the effectiveness of White's queen on the long diagonal.

18 ♗xf3 ♕e7 19 ♖ac1 ♖fd8 20 dxc5 ♘xc5 21 b4!

Opening a war front on the queenside. From now on White relies on alternating knight manoeuvres to take advantage of the weaknesses at b6 and c6.

21...axb4 22 ♕xb4 ♕a7 23 a3 ♘f5 24 ♖b1 ♖xd1+ 25 ♖xd1 ♕c7

25...♕a5 26 ♖c1! ±.

26 ♘d3! h6

Black has defended well in the last few moves but Kasparov opines that 26...g6 would have been more appropriate here. In any case, Karpov's real mistake comes one move later.

27 ♖c1 ♘e7?

Allowing White to strengthen his grip on the queenside by advancing the a-pawn. 27...♘d6! offered good drawing chances.

28 ♕b5 ♘f5

Hurrying back to expel the queen from her powerful station on b5. On 28...♕a7 the reply 29 ♘xc5 bxc5 20 a4 gives White a dangerous passed pawn.

29 a4 ♘d6 30 ♕b1 ♕a7 31 ♘e5!

With time pressure approaching Kasparov throws this knight into the offensive. In reality White's advantage has reached almost decisive proportions, a fact illustrated by the following long variation given by Kasparov: 31...♕xa4 32 ♕xb6 ♕a3 33 ♖d1 ♘f5 (33...♘e8 34 ♖d8 ±) 34 ♖d8+ ♖xd8 35 ♕xd8+ ♔h7 36 ♘xf7 ♕c1+ 37 ♔g2 ♕b2! 38 e4 ♘e3+ 39 ♔h3 ♕xf2 40 ♕h8+ ♔g6 41 ♘e5+ ♔f6 42 ♕f8+ ♔xe5 43 ♕xc5+ ♔f6 44 ♕f8+ ♔e5 45 ♕xg7+ ♔d6 46 e5+ ♔c5 47 ♕f8+ ♔d4 48 ♕b4+! ♘c4 (48...♔d3 49 ♕c4+! ♔d2 50 ♗g4 +−) 49 ♗g4 ♕f1+ 50 ♔h4 ♔xe5 51 ♕c5+ ♔e4 52 ♕c6+ and White should win. Since the move chosen by Karpov should have led to a picturesque loss, the sole chance of salvation lay in 31...♘f5.

31...♘xa4? 32 ♖xc8+ ♘xc8 *(D)*
33 ♕d1??

A terrible blunder that could have thrown away the fruits of his labour. Kasparov probably overlooked that Black's queen can check on a1 in many lines, for otherwise he would have opted for 33 ♕b5! (alternatively 33 ♗h5?! f6! 34 ♗f7+ ♔f8 35

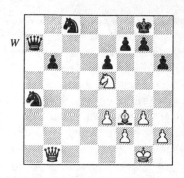

♗xe6 fxe5 36 ♕f5+ ♔c8 37 ♗xc8 ♕c7 is only a little better for White) 33...♔h7! (other moves lose easily, e.g. 33...♘d6 34 ♕c6 or 33...♔f8 34 ♘c6 ♕a8 35 ♕d3! g6 36 ♕d4!) 34 ♘c6 ♕a8 35 ♕d3+! f5 36 ♕d8 (threatening ♘e7) 36...♘c5 37 ♔g2! and Black is at a loss for a good reply, e.g. 37...♕b7 38 ♘e5 ♕b8 39 ♘f7 ♔g6 40 ♕g8 ♔f6 41 ♘h8! +− or 37...♕a2 38 ♘c5! (38 ♕xc8?? ♘d3 +) 38...♕b2 39 ♘f7 ♕f6 40 ♕h8+ ♔g6 41 ♕g8! +−. After the text the most White can hope for is a draw.

33...♘e7??

Karpov in return panics and fails to seize his chance! The simple 33...♘c5! 34 ♕d8+ ♔h7 would have left Kasparov wondering what had gone wrong, e.g. 35 ♕xc8? ♕a1+ or 35 ♗d1? f5 36 ♕xc8 ♕a1. White's best is to force a study-like draw by 35 ♔g2! f6 36 ♘c6 ♕d7 37 ♕xd7 ♘xd7 38 ♘d8! ♘c5 39 ♘xe6! ♘xe6 40 ♗g4, but in view of the circumstances, drawing would have been almost equivalent to losing.

34 ♕d7+ ♔h7 35 ♘xf7 ♘g6 36 ♕e8 ♕e7 37 ♕xa4 ♕xf7 38 ♗e4

♔g8 39 ♕b5 ♘f8 40 ♕xb6 ♕f6

The smoke has cleared, but in the meantime Black's pawn structure has been demolished. The loss of f7 has left nothing but gruesome weaknesses to defend, of which the most unpleasant is the impotent e-pawn. Black's only consolation is that all pawns lie on the same side, but this is overshadowed by the presence of queens, a factor giving White many attacking possibilities.

41 ♕b5 ♕e7 42 ♔g2 g6 43 ♕a5 ♕g7 44 ♕c5 ♕f7 45 h4 h5?! 46 ♕c6 ♕e7 47 ♗d3 ♕f7 48 ♕d6 ♔g7 49 e4 ♔g8 50 ♗c4 ♔g7 51 ♕e5+ ♔g8

Black is unable to oppose on f6: 51...♕f6 52 ♕xf6+ ♔xf6 53 f4 e5 54 ♔f3 ♘d7 55 ♔e3 ♘c5 56 ♗d5! and the march of the white king to c4 will decide the issue.

52 ♕d6 ♔g7 53 ♗b5 ♔g8 54 ♗c6 ♕a7 55 ♕b4! ♕c7 56 ♕b7! ♕d8 57 e5! +−

Kasparov must have been elated to play this move, which spreads a paralysing net over his opponent's kingside. Karpov of course now saw that he is lost − from here on he is merely dragging things out, hoping for a miracle.

57...♕a5 58 ♗e8 ♕c5 59 ♕f7+ ♔h8 60 ♗a4 ♕d5+ 61 ♔h2 ♕c5 62 ♗b3 ♕c8 63 ♗d1 ♕c5 64 ♔g2 and Black resigned, not waiting for ♗d1-f3-e4.

2 The Ideas Behind the English Opening

1) The Centre

In the theoretical section concerning the English we will encounter various types of pawn centre. It would be rather absurd to consider classifying all of them in this small survey so I will concentrate on the most important cases. These include:

A) The Nimzowitsch/Botvinnik centre (white pawns on c4 and e4)

B) The backward d-pawn centre (arising from the reversed Nimzowitsch Sicilian)

C) The amorphous centre (arising from lines with 4 d3)

D) The Scheveningen centre (with white pawns on e3 and d3)

E) Central structures arising in the 4 e3 ♗b4 variation

F) The Dragon centre

A) The Nimzowitsch/Botvinnik centre

This is a rather extreme case as White attempts to impose an early bind on d5 with pawns on c4 and e4. We have already seen in the historical introduction Botvinnik's efforts to popularize this system, but here we will deal only with the structure resulting after 1 c4 e5 2 ♘c3 ♘f6 3 e4 or 1 c4 e5 2 ♘c3 ♘f6 3 ♘f3 ♘c6 4 e4. A typical position for this opening could arise after the moves 1 c4 e5 2 ♘c3 ♘f6 3 ♘f3 ♘c6 4 e4 ♗b4 5 d3 d6 6 g3 (D):

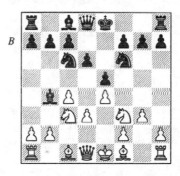

This position was reached in **Christiansen-I.Sokolov**, *Groningen 1991*, among many other games. In this type of position, Black is often tempted to retreat the bishop to c5 in an effort to increase control over d4 but I think a more thematic treatment for Black should be to undermine the white centre by ...b5 or ...f5. Let's see how Ivan Sokolov handled the problems of the position:

6...a6

Black selects the first plan.

7 ♗g2 b5 8 cxb5 axb5 9 0-0 ♗xc3 10 bxc3 ♗d7!?

Fighting chess! Sokolov is keen to prevent an early liquidation on the queenside and 10...♗d7 is directed towards achieving this objective as now 11 a4?! would be met by 11...♘e7 12 a5 ♘c6 13 a6 ♘b8 14 a7 ♘c6 and the pawn has gone straight into the wolf's mouth.

11 ♘h4

Christiansen switches his attention to the kingside. This is in fact quite natural as White enjoys enough firepower there, but an important point to be made is that his centre has lost in flexibility as a result of Sokolov's clever play. The long-term meaning of the above remark is that White may end up in a strategically lost position if he falters or vacillates in the attack.

11...0-0 12 f4 h6 13 fxe5?!

White is showing signs of impulsiveness, which usually leads to the deterioration of one's attacking chances. 13 ♘f5 or 13 ♕e1 deserved preference, keeping the position as fluid as possible for White's bishops.

13...dxe5 14 ♗e3 ♕e7 15 ♔h1?!

Pointless. As a result of his poor 13th move White will soon be experiencing pressure along the d-file, so a better move is 15 h3 to prevent bishop invasions on g4.

15...♖fd8 16 ♕c2 ♕d6 17 ♖ad1 ♗g4! 18 ♖d2 b4!

The culminating point of Black's play. White's centre has been contained and Sokolov went on to win the game with some fine technique.

Apparently Sokolov's plan is well-founded in strategic terms but I

recommend a less risky approach involving the moves ...♗xc3, ...0-0 and ...♘e8 followed by an eventual ...f5. In the resulting positions White has his chances too, but the weak central cluster (c3, c4, d3) may prove a long-term disadvantage if Black defends carefully. For a deeper insight into these ideas consult Game 2, Rohde-Wolff and the analysis contained therein.

B) The backward d-pawn centre

This central structure crops up in the reversed Nimzowitsch Sicilian (1 c4 e5 2 ♘f3!? e4 3 ♘d4 ♘c6). A typical example of this peculiar type of centre is featured in the next diagram *(D)*:

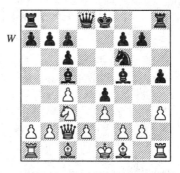

Black's pawn wedge on e4 yields him chances of expansion on the kingside by ...h4 in combination with an advance of the g-pawn. White, on the other hand, intends b3, ♗b2 and 0-0-0 followed by an eventual d3. If he can carry out this plan successfully then he gets a valuable 4-3 pawn majority on the kingside.

Which plan enjoys more realistic chances of success? Objectively speaking it should be Black's as he has more space to operate and better development. In practice, however, things are not so easy as ...h4 can be met with the interesting manoeuvre ♘e2 and g4. Then, after the *en passant* capture ...hxg3, White recaptures with the knight, initiating strong pressure against the e-pawn. For a detailed analysis of these ideas see Illustrative Game 1 (Murey-Sax).

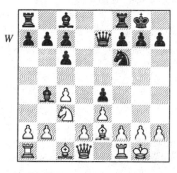

Our second example comes from the same opening variation and arose in **Sliwa-Marszalek**, *Poland 1977*. Matters are quite different here since White has castled short and should consequently get rid of the annoying pawn on e4 as quickly as possible. In my opinion the best way to do so is by playing 9 f3 but in the game White chose the prosaic 9 d3 which robs his pawn structure of its dynamism. After 9...♗xc3 10 bxc3 exd3 11 ♗xd3 ♖d8 11 ♕c2 h6 White no longer had a backward d-pawn but the newly created pawn weaknesses proved more than his queenside

could withstand. The final position provides sufficient evidence of the massacre *(D)*:

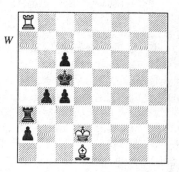

C) The amorphous (fluid) centre

This is the kind of centre that may arise when the players respect their opponent too much in the early stages of the game! What do I mean by that? The following diagram is quite enlightening *(D)*.

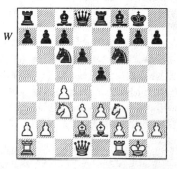

The two armies are confined to their own side of the board, and the central pawns are kept out of the reach of their opposite numbers. White is in a effect playing a Sicilian with colours reversed, while Black is about to complete his King's Indian set-up by ...g6 and ...♝g7.

This type of position arises quite often in the Four Knights Variation after 4 d3 ♝b4 5 ♝d2 and is characterized by delicate positional play.

Which policy should Black follow? It is clear that White will be playing for the b4 advance, so the black counterplay must be based on the centre as he does not have the makings of a kingside attack. There are two plausible methods of achieving this. The first one consists of luring the white rook to b1 and then exploiting its position by ...♝f5 and a timely ...e4, while in the second Black abandons for the time being the idea of kingside actions and prepares to meet his opponent's queenside demonstration by ...♞e7-g6, followed by ...c6 and ...d5. Let's watch this second plan unfold from the diagram, as exemplified by the game **Rivas-P.Nikolić**, *Manila OL 1992*:

9 a3 ♞e7!? 10 b4 ♞g6 11 ♛c2 c6 12 b5 ♝d7 13 bxc6 bxc6 14 ♖fb1 ♛c7 15 ♖b2! d5 16 cxd5 cxd5 17 d4!

The only way to maintain the equilibrium. Otherwise White would be slowly pushed off the board in view of his lack of space.

17...♖ab8!

17...e4? is a blunder because of 18 ♞xe4. However, even if the black queen were on c8 it would have been anti-positional to play this move in view of the simple 18 ♞e1 when Black is left with a weakness on d5 and no active plan.

18 dxe5 ♞xe5 19 ♞e4 ♛xc2 20 ♞xf6+ gxf6 21 ♖xc2 ♖ec8

Despite the weakening of Black's pawn structure, he maintains good play. The text embodies a plan of attack on the slightly exposed a-pawn by preparing to post the knight on c4.

22 ♖xc8 ♝xc8 23 ♞d4 ♞c4 24 ♝xc4

White is practically forced to surrender this bishop but his position is too solid for him to be in any danger of losing.

24...dxc4 25 h3 ♝d7 26 ♝c3 ♚g7 27 g4 h5! 28 f3 ♝d6 and the players struggled on for another dozen moves before finally acquiescing to the draw.

D) The Scheveningen centre

The player who follows my recommended repertoire will not face this pawn structure regularly as I have abstained from suggesting opening ideas related to a Scheveningen with colours reversed. There are, however, exceptional cases where it is worth accepting the challenge, especially if White resorts to an early ♛c2 *(D)*:

This position arose in the famous game **Ehlvest-Kasparov**, *Reykjavik 1988* (Illustrative Game 5). Foreseeing that the position of the white queen offers him enough tempi to put the so-called 'small centre' under restraint the World Champion decides to open up the game.

7...♝xc3 8 ♝xc3 d5 9 cxd5 ♞xd5 10 ♝e2 ♝f5! 11 ♖d1

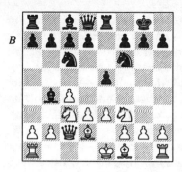

On 11 e4 Kasparov intended the interesting piece sacrifice 11...♘f4! 12 exf5 ♘d4 13 ♗xd4 exd4 14 ♘g1 ♕d5 with tremendous compensation (for more details see the Games Section). Thanks to this tactical opportunity Black gains enough time to develop his pieces in a harmonious way.

11...a5 12 0-0 ♕e7 13 a3 a4 14 ♗e1?! ♗g6

Black has obtained a solid position; for the moment there seems to be no way for White to make use of his central pawn preponderance. As I proclaimed in a friendly discussion with Grandmaster Yannis Nikolaidis, there is also no reason that White should be worse here. Just imagine a magic hand inverting the colours and then you will suddenly feel at home with Ehlvest's position. Unfortunately for the Estonian grandmaster, the game continuation didn't verify my opinion.

15 ♕c4?! ♖ed8 16 ♘d2?

Kasparov's recommendation of 16 d4 ♘b6 17 ♕c3 e4 18 ♘d2 ♕g5 19 ♘c4 ♘d5 20 ♕c1 ♖e8 should be only slightly better for Black, but it

shows the optimum way of reacting to the central advance d3-d4. The text move, on the other hand, leads to a quick disaster for tactical reasons.

16...♘d4! 17 exd4 ♘f4 and Black won in a few moves.

E) Central structures arising in the 4 e3 ♗b4 Variation

This is a variation characterized by Black's desire to establish a pawn on e4 in the spirit of Nimzowitschian strategy. White has three main methods of coping with this ambitious scheme:

a) tempting the pawn forward in the hope of winning it;

b) tempting the pawn forward in the hope of liquidating it under favourable circumstances; or

c) preventing the e pawn's advance by increasing his control over the critical square e4.

a) *White attempts to win the e-pawn*

In this case play becomes extremely sharp but practice has shown that since White's development is insufficient for his strategy to be effective, Black will usually maintain his central point even at the cost of sacrificing a wing pawn.

This position has arisen many times in international competition. Threatened with the loss of the central pawn by ♘c3 Black virtually always plays 9...b5!, a move providing the pawn with discreet protection in

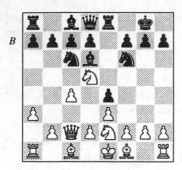

view of the tactical line 10 ♘xf6+ ♛xf6 11 cxb5 ♘e5 12 ♛xe4 ♗b7! and suddenly White comes under a strong attack. Consequently, White has usually abstained from pawn grabbing, but then Black is given time to bolster his central position and initiate pressure on the weakened light squares (for more details see Game 4).

b) *White exchanges the e-pawn for his d- or f-pawn*

This will lead to different kinds of central pawn formation according to the circumstances. Some characteristic positions are featured below *(D):*

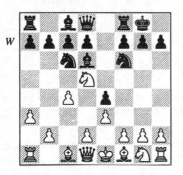

Our first example comes from **Petrosian-Timman**, *Nikšić 1983*. In the diagrammed position the ex-world champion chose the clear-cut **8 d3** which, admittedly, has a healthy appearance: White furthers his development and at the same time ensures himself a fair share of the centre. Nevertheless, Timman was able to stir up some interesting play:

8...exd3 9 ♗xd3 ♘e5 10 ♗e2 c6 11 ♘c3

11 ♘b6 is rather weak on account of 11...♗b4+! 12 axb4 ♛xb6 followed by ...d5, but 11 ♘xf6+ ♛xf6 12 ♛d4 was interesting according to Timman.

11...♗c7 12 ♘f3 d5 13 cxd5 cxd5

The central pawn structure has undergone a radical change in the last few moves. What we have now on the board is a typical isolated d-pawn position which is considered fully satisfactory for Black. Indeed, Black has good attacking chances on the kingside, while exploiting the slight exposure of the isolani is no easy job for White.

14 0-0 a6 15 ♘d4 ♛d6 16 g3 ♗h3 17 ♖e1 ♖ac8 18 ♗d2 *(D)*

18...♘c4

After this the game soon peters out to a draw. 18...h5!, with a strong attacking position, was preferable. Would it have succeeded against the magician of defence?

19 b3 ♘xd2 20 ♛xd2 ♘e4 21 ♘xe4 dxe4 22 ♗f1 and the players agreed to a draw after a few uneventful moves.

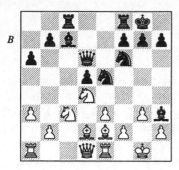

When White plays d3 without first moving or protecting his knight on c3, he risks obtaining a defective pawn structure. Then, after ...♗xc3, White enters a middlegame where his bishop pair amounts to only symbolic compensation for the doubled and isolated c-pawns.

This position arose in **Xu Jun-P.Nikolić**, *Biel IZ 1993*. Black enjoys an undisputed positional plus because the white bishops are doomed to inactivity behind his wrecked pawn structure. Let's follow the Bosnian's efforts to press home his advantage:

13 ♘b3 ♗e6 14 ♘xc5 dxc5 15 e4 f4

Also interesting was 15...fxe4 16 ♕xe4 ♕f7 but the text is the most thematic way of keeping the bishops under restraint. In addition Black creates a strong-point on e5 for his knight.

16 ♖d1 ♘e5 17 ♕b3 b6 18 a4 ♖f6! 19 a5 ♖af8

Black has massed his troops on the kingside and is now planning ...♖h6 followed by ...♕h4. With his next move the Chinese grandmaster attempts to distract Nikolić's attention from the threatened sector but the distraction, apart from being expensive, is rather short-lived.

20 ♖d5 ♗xd5 21 cxd5 c4!

Locking in the bishops for good. On other moves White obtains some counterplay by c4 and ♗b2.

22 ♕d1

The difficult part of Black's calculations was 22 ♗a3? cxb3 23 ♗xe7 bxa5 24 ♗xf6 ♖xf6 25 ♖xa5 b2 26 ♖b5 ♖b6! and wins. 22 ♕b4!? is more intriguing than the text, since the ending after 22...♕xb4?! 23 cxb4 b5 24 a6!? may offer some counterchances. Of course, Black is not forced to go for it (22...♕d7!? and 22...c5 are viable alternatives) but at least White could have given his opponent an opportunity to go wrong.

22...c5! 23 ♕a4 ♖g6 24 ♖a2 ♕h4 25 ♕d1 ♖h6 26 h3 ♖g6 27 ♔h1 b5!

White has been completely outplayed. Nikolić won on move 48 after a breakthrough with his kingside pawns.

If White is interested in obtaining a central pawn preponderance then he should strive to exchange his f-pawn for Black's pawn on e4. This idea is quite thematic but has not been played much as there is a lot of risk involved in it.

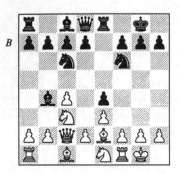

This position is from **Suba-Motwani**, *London 1989*. White is toying with the possible advances d3 or f3 so Motwani decides to clarify the situation.

8...♗xc3! 9 bxc3

9 dxc3 is clumsy, while 9 ♕xc3 runs into 9...d5! with a superb position for Black. But now White has been deprived of the possibility d3.

9...d5! 10 f3 dxc4 11 ♗xc4 ♗f5 12 a4 ♘e5

I would rather vote in favour of the immediate move 12...♕d7! with a strong initiative for Black. The text allows a pin on the b1-h7 diagonal.

13 ♗a2 ♕d7 14 ♗b1! ♖ad8 15 a5 c5! 16 c4 ♗g6 17 f4 ♘d3 18 ♘xd3 exd3 19 ♕a4 ♕g4?!

19...♕xa4! ∓.

20 h3 ♕g3 21 ♕d1 ♗e4 22 ♖f2 ♖e6 23 ♗b2

Despite the impressive appearance of Black's game, the position is now

unclear. The final outcome was a draw in 61 moves after some tragicomic twists and turns.

In conclusion, it seems that Black has excellent prospects in this variation if his pawn is allowed to reach the square e4. In practice White usually chooses the policy mentioned below.

c) *White prevents ...e4*

The only way to prevent this central advance is by playing **5 ♕c2** and after **5...0-0** either **6 ♗d3** or **6 ♘d5** (6 d3 is a likely transposition to the game Ehlvest-Kasparov). In the first of these cases it is advisable for Black to capture on c3. Then the following position may arise *(D)*:

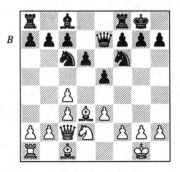

White's secret ambition is to manoeuvre his knight to d5, but he shouldn't be able to carry out this plan if Black reacts promptly. In **Korchnoi-Szabo**, *Amsterdam 1972*, Black failed to notice White's positional threat.

9...a5?!

The immediate 9...h6 (or even 9...g6) is correct, in order to answer 10 ♖e1 with a quick ...♘d7-c5. Then White would no longer have time for the above-mentioned manoeuvre.

10 ♖e1 g6 11 e4 ♘h5 12 ♘f1 ♘f4 13 ♘e3 ♕g5

Korchnoi thinks that the continuation 13...♘xd3 14 ♕xd3 f5 15 ♘d5 ♕g7 16 exf5 ♗xf5 17 ♕g3 would have been slightly better for White. This is true, but what about the more logical 16...gxf5? I believe that Black cannot be worse in the ensuing positions, e.g. 17 ♕g3 ♖f7 18 ♗h6 (18 ♗g5 f4) 18...♕xg3 19 hxg3 ♗e6 or 17 f4 ♗e6 and there seems to be no way to exploit the slight exposure of the black king. After the text Black is drifting slowly in a difficult situation.

14 f3 ♘e7 15 ♗f1

White regroups in order to attack. Black has neglected the fight for the centre and as a result will be pushed back.

15...h5 16 g3 h4 17 ♘g4! hxg3 18 hxg3 ♗xg4 19 gxf4 ♕h4 20 ♕f2 ♕xf2+ 21 ♔xf2

White has a clear advantage at this point but Black managed to draw with inventive defence.

The continuation 5 ♕c2 0-0 6 ♘d5 ♖e8 is likely to produce different types of game: a wild one, arising after 7 ♕f5!? d6 8 ♘xf6+ gxf6 9 ♕h5 d5, or a quiet one if White is content with either 7 ♗d3 or 7 ♘g5. In the former case play takes on an independent nature which is hardly

appropriate to examine in this section, so I will concentrate on the central pawn structure resulting when White adopts peaceful methods.

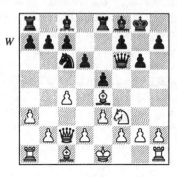

A common set-up deriving from the above-mentioned variations. The pawn structures have been left intact which is in a way reminiscent of the fluid centre discussed earlier on, but an important difference is that a pair of knights has been exchanged, a fact considerably aiding Black's plan of contesting the centre as his f-pawn is free to advance. In **Ljubojević-Karpov, *Linares 1993***, play continued:

11 b3?!

This is rather feeble. Better is 11 b4, which – in combination with d3 and ♘d2 – maintains the prospect of some pressure on the queenside. However, even then Black would maintain at least equality by following the plan Karpov adopts in the game.

11...♘d8! 12 ♗b2 ♕e7 13 ♖c1 c6!

The beginning of a methodical occupation of the centre. The obvious threat of ...f5 and ...e4 creates unpleasant congestion in the white camp.

14 ♕b1 ♗g7 15 0-0 ♗d7 16 b4 f5 17 ♗c2 ♘f7 18 ♘e1 c5!

Emphasizing the artificial placement of the white bishops. In the next few moves Black concentrates on stamping out any counterplay based on central pawn breaks.

19 ♗c3 b6 20 ♕b2 ♘g5! 21 f3

After 21 f4 exf4 22 ♗xg7 ♕xg7 23 ♕xg7+ ♔xg7 White has a sad choice between 24 ♖xf4 ♗c6 or 24 exf4 ♘e6, in both cases with the inferior endgame.

21...♗c6 22 ♗b3 ♘e6 23 ♘c2 ♕h4!

Black completes the encirclement. White has been deprived of a last faint hope to free his position by advancing d4 and can only sit back and watch his opponent's position improve.

24 ♘e1 ♖e7 25 ♕c2 ♖f8 26 ♕d3 ♖d8 27 ♕c2 ♗f6 28 ♖d1 *(D)*

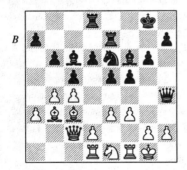

28...♘d4!

A tremendous shot, based on the lack of co-ordination among White's forces.

29 exd4 exd4 30 ♖f2

Karpov had calculated everything to a hair as the following variations show:

a) 30 ♗b2 ♗e5 (30...♖e2 31 ♘d3 ♖de8 also wins) 31 f4 ♗xf4 32 ♖xf4 ♕xf4 33 d3 ♖de8 34 ♕f2 ♕xf2+ 35 ♔xf2 ♖e2+.

b) 30 ♗a1 ♗e5 31 f4 ♗xf4 32 ♖xf4 ♕xf4 33 d3 ♖de8 34 ♕f2 ♕g4 35 ♘f3 ♖e2 36 ♕g3 ♗xf3 37 gxf3 ♖e1 and the poor bishop falls again.

30...dxc3 31 dxc3 ♗g5

Black has a strong attack without any material investments. The execution, however, was not particularly convincing.

32 g3 ♕h5 33 f4 ♖de8 34 ♘g2 ♖e2?

This looks hasty. 34...♗f6! was preferable, as 35 ♖xd6 is answered by 35...♖e1+! 36 ♘xe1 ♖xe1+ 37 ♖f1 ♖e2 −+. 34...♗xg2!? 35 ♔xg2 ♗xf4! is also interesting, with a clear advantage for Black.

35 ♖d2??

The players were probably in time trouble. Otherwise it would have been hard to explain how Ljubojević missed the simple 35 ♖xe2 ♖xe2 36 ♖d2 which allows him to stay in the game. What is really strange, however, is that Karpov in his *Informator* notes does not even mention this possibility!

35...♖e1+!

Now Black is back on the winning track. 36 ♘xe1 leads to a spectacular finish after 36...♖xe1+ 37 ♖f1 ♕f3! 38 ♖xe1 ♕h1+ 39 ♔f2 ♕g2+ 40 ♔e3 ♕f3 mate!

36 Ⅲf1 Ⅲxf1+ 37 ⬡xf1 ⬤xh2 38 Ⅲd5 ⬥xd5 39 cxd5 ⬤xg3 40 fxg3 ⬤f3+ and White resigned.

F) The Dragon centre

This a key theme for the repertoire player as the Reversed Dragon is the backbone of the suggested system of defence. Having gone through decades of games for the needs of this book I'm convinced that the whole fight revolves around the critical central squares c5 and d4.

From White's point of view c5 is very important as it constitutes the most accessible point of entrance in Black's territory. White often employs the manoeuvre ⬤a4(e4)-c5 in order to put Black's queenside under pressure or simply force an advantageous exchange of knight for bishop. There are also cases in which Black will get his pawn to c5, only to realize that it becomes the direct object of attack of White's pieces. In the following example disaster strikes from an apparently unpretentious opening *(D)*:

The Dutch grandmaster Loek van Wely chose this rather bizarre set-up with White in the game **Van Wely-Brunner**, *Biel IZ 1993*. At this point nothing indicates that we will be treated to a methodical siege of Black's c-pawn.

10...⬤d4 11 e4 f5 12 ⬡h1 c5

This natural move signals the start of Black's difficulties. 12...c6 was more prudent, with an even game.

13 ⬥c3 ⬥e6 14 ⬤g5

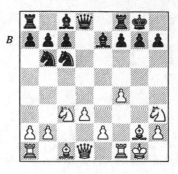

An important move. White not only obtains the advantage of the two bishops but also removes the chief defender of Black's c-pawn.

14...⬥xg5 15 fxg5 ⬤d7 16 ⬤d2 Ⅲac8 17 Ⅲf4 Ⅲf7 18 Ⅲaf1

White increases the pressure in order to force his opponent to capture on e4. With a knight on that square Black's task of defending c5 would be rendered unbearable.

18...fxe4 19 Ⅲxf7 ⬥xf7 20 ⬤xe4 ⬤e6 21 ⬤f2!

A strong move, threatening both ⬤xc5 and ⬤xf7+. White has a distinct advantage, which Van Wely converted into a win, not without mistakes, on move 30.

To avoid similar accidents one requires a detailed understanding of the position. In the above case Brunner failed to perceive that the combination of b6-knight and pawn on c5 was an unwieldy one, and this led to a critical situation for him within only nine moves. The next example is a fine piece of judgement by a devoted practitioner of the black side *(D)*:

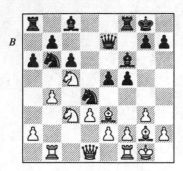

This position arose in the game **Kveinys-Smejkal**, *Lubniewice 1994*. The Czech grandmaster of course appreciated that in case of 15...♘d7 16 ♘3a4 ♘xc5 his opponent would recapture with the pawn in order to generate play along the b-file – and yet he falls in with White's plans.

15...♘d7 16 ♘3a4 ♘xc5! 17 bxc5 ♗e6 18 ♗xd4 exd4 19 ♖b2 ♖ae8 20 ♕d2 ♕f7!

There lies the point! Black intends to neutralize White's pressure on b7 by setting up a defence along his second rank.

21 ♖fb1 ♖e7 22 a3 ♖fe8?!

But this is inexact. After the immediate 22...g5! 23 ♖b4 ♕g7 24 ♕b2 ♖ff7! Black would have magnificently orchestrated his pieces for both attack and defence. Now Kveinys is given the chance to create waves with an inspired exchange sacrifice.

23 ♗f1 g5 24 ♖b4 h5 25 ♕b2 ♗a2 26 ♖xb7!? ♗xb1 27 ♖xe7 ♖xe7 28 ♕xb1 ♖b7 29 ♘b6

White has a slight initiative. The game eventually in a draw on move 49.

While a knight on c5 is quite often the head of the javelin in White's strategy, Black's plans of expansion are almost exclusively associated with ...♘d4. Playing the knight to d4 can have multiple defensive purposes, such as shielding an attack on e5 or preparing to block the action of White's king's bishop by ...c6, but its most important merits are attacking: pressure on e2 and b3, as well as provocation of a weakness along the d-file if White decides to evict the knight by playing e3. Some of these motifs are vividly illustrated in the following example *(D)*:

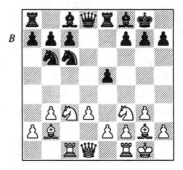

This is a typical configuration of Black's pieces, enabling the knight to play an active role in central affairs. In **Serper-A.Sokolov**, *Moscow 1990* the continuation was:

11...♘d4 12 ♘d2 c6 13 e3

White is practically forced to expel the black knight in order to prevent the unpleasant ...♗g4. But now Black has something to play for in the shape of the backward d-pawn.

13...♘e6 14 ♘f3 ♘g5! 15 ♘xg5 ♕xg5 16 ♘e4 ♕g6 17 ♘c5 ♘d7!

With every exchange the d-pawn becomes weaker. In addition Black solves once and for all his problems on the queenside.

18 ♘xd7 ♗xd7 19 ♕c2 ♖ad8 20 d4

Trying to get rid of the unhealthy job of defending this pawn, but the move creates other weaknesses.

20...e4!

Sokolov is not willing to settle for a draw by 20...♕xc2. The stabilization of the pawn structure in the centre ensures him useful transfer points at d5 and e6 for his rooks. This fact, in conjunction with the light-squared weaknesses surrounding the white king, offers Black excellent attacking chances.

21 ♗c3?

Serper's position was difficult, but with 21 f4 he could have avoided serious difficulties. Now his game collapses into pieces in less than five moves.

21...♗g4! 22 ♕d2?! ♕h5! 23 ♗b4 c5 24 ♗c3 ♖e6 25 ♕c2 ♗f3 0-1

White's resignation may appear premature but his position was already untenable, e.g. 26 dxc5 ♖h6 27 h4 ♕g4! and there is no defence to the threatened 28...♖xh4.

We have already noticed that the advance d4 is usually unsatisfactory for White if Black has the reply ...e4 in store. However, this advance can be particularly dangerous if it has been preceded by e4 and Black's control of d4 is loose at the moment of its execution *(D)*:

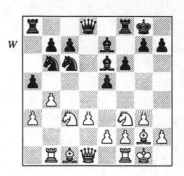

This well-known theoretical position arose in the game **Serper-Mainka**, *Vienna* 1991. With his next move (instead of the virtually universally adopted 12 b5) the resourceful player from Uzbekistan takes the game into muddy channels.

12 bxa5!? ♖xa5 13 ♘b5 ♕d7?!

A casual reply. As Korchnoi correctly points out, 13...♘a7! would have yielded equal play. Now, however, White has the chance to maintain his knight on b5 and prepare a combined advance of his central pawns.

14 ♗e3!

A strong move, luring the knight to d5 in order to play e4 with gain of tempo.

14...♘d5 15 ♗d2 ♖a6 16 ♕c2 ♘d8 17 c4 ♖c6 18 ♖d1 ♘b6 19 ♗e3 ♘f7 (D)

20 d4!

The right moment for this advance as the clumsy position of the black rook is causing a traffic jam. The game continuation saw Mainka put up stiff resistance, which, however, didn't change the assessment that White stands clearly better here.

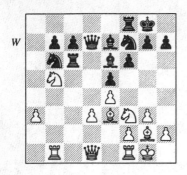

Our final example is **Ljubojević-Chernin**, *Wijk aan Zee 1986*. White applies the same idea but this time Black is better placed to meet it *(D)*.

15 b5?!

15 &c5!? is an interesting alternative. Black cannot play 15...&xc5 16 &xc5 &xf3?! 17 &xf3 &d4? as after 18 &xb7 &ab8 19 &d5 he would be a pawn down without compensation. Better is 15...b6! 16 &xe7 &xe7 17 e4 (17 &e1!? c6 =) 17...&g8! as then both 18 d4 &ad8 and 18 ₩c3 &ac8 19 d4 exd4 20 ₩xd4 (20 &xd4 c5) 20...₩xd4 21 &xd4 c5! leave Black with a satisfactory game.

15...&d8 16 &c5 &xc5 17 &xc5 c6 18 e4 &g8 19 d4

Ljubo has done all he can but in this case the central advance does not live up to White's expectations as the black pieces are ideally placed to deal with it.

19...&e6?!

Chernin could have considered playing for a win by 19...exd4, since 20 ₩xd4 ₩e7! is slightly better for Black. White may follow *Informator*'s recommendation of 20 &ac1 but after 20...cxb5 21 &c7 ₩d6 (unclear according to Stetsko) he will have to uncork miracles in order to prove sufficient compensation.

20 bxc6 bxc6 21 &h3 &fd8 22 d5 cxd5 23 &xd5 ₩e8 and the players soon agreed to a draw.

2) Neutralizing White's Queenside Pressure

In this chapter we deal only with positions where White develops his king's bishop on the long diagonal. The fianchettoed bishop, in combination with knight manoeuvring, forms the main source of trouble for Black's queenside *(D)*:

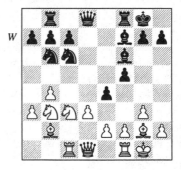

Black's game looks impressive, but on closer examination the defects of his position are manifest. He has no control over the critical square c5, while the trifling barrier to the activity of White's light-squared bishop is going to collapse with the first blow of the wind. In the game **C.Hansen-Sosonko**, *Jerusalem 1986*, White made use of his advantages in exemplary fashion:

15 ♘c5 exd3 16 ♘xb7! dxe2 17 ♕xe2 ♘d4?

The lesser evil was the continuation 17...♖xb7 18 ♗xc6 ♗c4 19 ♕c2 ♗xf1 20 ♗xb7 when White's position is slightly better in view of his superior pawn structure. The text allows Hansen to produce some interesting fireworks.

18 ♕d1 ♕c8 19 ♘d6!! ♕a6

The knight was untouchable as 19...cxd6? 20 ♘d5! leads to an immediate loss. One would now expect White to slow down a bit by 20 ♘xf7 but the Danish grandmaster continues to play energetically.

20 b5!

Guarding against checks on e2, so as to meet 20...♕a5 by 21 ♘xf7 ♖xf7 22 ♘d5! Sosonko finds the only move:

20...♘xb5! 21 ♘dxb5 ♘c4 22 ♘xc7 ♕a5 23 ♗a1 ♗xc3 24 ♗xc3 ♕xc7 25 ♕d4! *(D)*

Black has regained his piece but the outcome of the complications is clearly in White's favour in view of his razor-like bishops and excellent centralization. Hansen achieved a smooth win in 41 moves.

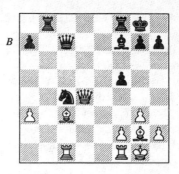

This particular example was a bit scary, but everyday life is not like this. With prudent play, Black should be able to contain or even exchange White's dangerous bishop.

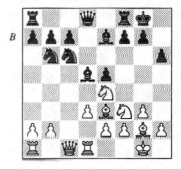

This position arose in **Lautier-Hübner**, *Baden-Baden 1992*. White's last move (12 ♖d1) has prevented any ideas associated with ...♘d4 and White now intends ♘c3 followed by an advance of his d-pawn. If this plan materializes Black will soon have problems on the long diagonal so Hübner resorts to a radical solution:

12...♗xe4!

Trading this bishop for a knight is not a common occurrence in this type of opening but the German player correctly realized that in this case the advantages by far outweigh the disadvantages: Black obtains a valuable queenside pawn majority while rendering White's kingside pawn structure inflexible. In addition, the chief pride of White's set-up is incarcerated on g2 and will have to work hard to find its way back into the game.

13 dxe4 ♕c8 14 h4 ♕e6 15 ♔h2?! ♕c4!

Simplification is highly unwelcome for White as his pawn mass on the kingside only offers attacking chances with queens on the board. For this reason it was worth considering the extravagant 15 b3 ♖fd8 16 ♖f1!? or the simpler 16 ♕b2 ♖xd1+ 17 ♖xd1 ♖d8 18 ♖c1 with unclear play.

16 ♖d2 ♕xc1 17 ♖xc1 ♖fd8 18 ♖dc2 ♗d6 19 a3 a5 20 h5 ♘d7! 21 ♘d2 a4 22 ♘c4 ♘f6 23 ♗f3 ♗e7

Black has an edge in this endgame. Lautier achieved a laborious draw on move 87.

An exchange of light-squared bishops should, in general, be thematic as a response to White turning the screws on the queenside, but Black must be careful not to relax afterwards and allow his opponent a bind on the light squares. This warning applies especially in cases where Black already has a pawn on d4.

This is a fragment from the game **Ljubojević-Hjartarson**, *Reykjavik 1991*. The Icelandic grandmaster has conducted the game excellently up

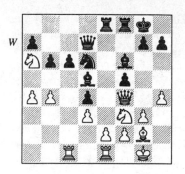

to this point, leaving White no other choice but to exchange bishops voluntarily in order to avoid even bigger problems with his displaced knight.

22 ♘d2 ♗xg2 23 ♔xg2 ♔h8?

An incomprehensible move, failing to take advantage of the imprisoned knight. After the correct move 23...♖e7! (Hjartarson) White is hard-pressed to find an adequate reply. The reason becomes apparent in a couple of moves.

24 ♘f3 ♖d8 25 e3! ♕b7 26 b5 c5

A sad necessity, but on 26...cxb5, 27 ♘c7 creates a lot of problems. By playing 23...♖e7! Black would have denied White this opportunity.

27 exd4 ♗xd4 28 ♔g1 ♗f6 29 d4!

Suddenly the knight is out for good. In addition Black has to take care of a whole complex of light-square weaknesses.

29...c4 30 ♘b4 ♕d7 31 ♘c6 ♖c8 32 ♘fe5 ♗xe5 33 dxe5 ♘e4 34 ♖xc4

White's positional advantage has been transformed into a material one but in the continuation Ljubojević failed to exploit his extra pawn, the game ending in a draw after 120 moves!

We have already witnessed several examples where the fight for c5 was of major importance for the outcome of the struggle. In these games White employed the knight manoeuvre ♘a4(e4)-c5 to occupy the square but an equally popular method lies in ♗e3-c5 with the aim of transforming that point to a permanent base for the most agile minor piece, which in our case is the knight. This idea sounds interesting but in practice White experiences difficulties in carrying it out unperturbed because Black has tactical possibilities at his disposal. The following example is simple enough, but also quite characteristic *(D)*:

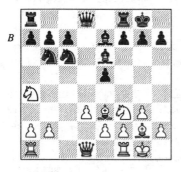

This position was reached in **Uhlmann-Romanishin**, *Dresden 1988*. White's last move (10 ♘a4) was pursuing the plan of planting a piece on c5 but Romanishin's reply nips the idea in the bud.

10...e4! 11 ♘e1 exd3 12 ♘xd3 ♗d5

Emphasizing the centralization theme. Swapping light-squared bishops relieves Black from any worries

he might have had about his queenside.

13 ♘xb6 axb6 14 ♗xd5 ♕xd5 15 ♗f4 ♗d6 16 ♗xd6 ♕xd6 17 a3 ♖fe8 18 ♘b4? ♕xd1 19 ♖fxd1 ♘xb4 20 axb4 ♖xa1 21 ♖xa1 ♔f8

The wholesale exchanges that took place do not grant Uhlmann an automatic draw in view of his inferior pawn structure. In fact, Black's compact mass of queenside pawns deprives White of the usual counterplay enjoyed in rook endings of this type.

22 ♖c1 c6 23 b5 c5! 24 b4 cxb4 25 ♖c4 ♖xe2 26 ♖xb4 ♔e7 27 ♔f1 ♖e5 28 f4 ♖d5 29 ♔e2 ♔d6 30 ♔e3 f5 and Black won easily with an extra pawn and better king.

Black has gained many points in similar fashion, as the reader can find out in the next chapter, but has more complex problems to solve if the moves a4 and ...a5 have been inserted in ♗e3 schemes. Then the move ♘a4 is no longer possible, but Black has to tolerate a knight on b5 which, in fact, looks like an excellent outpost in combination with ♖ac1. This type of position is very sharp, so the reader is advised to consult Game 10, Korchnoi-Petursson and the corresponding analysis in the next chapter for a deeper insight into Black's defensive resources.

White's queenside activity in the main line of the Reversed Dragon involves the pawn moves a3 and b4, supporting a knight journey to c5 or simply preparing b5 in order to evict the knight from c6 and clear the long diagonal. In order to neutralize the pressure Black should try to create strong-points in the threatened sector and he often accomplishes this with the thrust ...a5. Then the following situations may arise according to White's reaction.

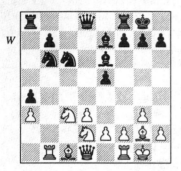

White has pressure down the b-file but it is not easy to exploit it as Black's last move (14...a4!) prevents ♘a4 and at the same time creates an important outpost at b3 for his minor pieces. In the game **Vladimirov-Savchenko**, *Helsinki 1992*, White realized that he could not make use of the backward b-pawn and changed course by playing 15 ♗xc6!? bxc6 16 ♕c2.

If White tries to prevent Black from playing ...a4 by pushing his own pawn to a4 then he concedes the outpost b4 to Black's minor pieces. A bishop anchored on that square can be particularly well placed and often exerts irritating pressure on White's position. Witness the following case *(D)*:

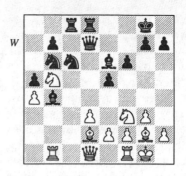

White is facing problems with the deployment of his pieces and the weakness on a4. In the game **C.Hansen-Romanishin**, *Tåstrup 1992* the exchange of dark-squared bishops led to the creation of a dangerous passed pawn:

19 ♗xb4 axb4! 20 ♘d2 ♕e7 21 ♖c1 ♘a5 22 ♖xc8 ♖xc8 23 d4!?

White has to resort to drastic measures or else he will be simply pushed to the wall.

23...♖d8

23...b3!? was interesting but there is nothing wrong with the text move. I have the feeling that Black should be winning somewhere in the continuation.

24 ♕a1 ♘bc4 25 ♘xc4 ♗xc4 26 ♖c1 ♘b3 27 ♕a2 ♕f7?

Why not 27...♕e6? Then 28 d5 does not work because of 28...♘xc1 29 ♕xc4 ♕c8! and Black saves his knight, while after 28 ♗h3 ♕f7 White loses the possibility of interference on the a2-g8 diagonal.

28 d5! ♗xd5 29 ♗xd5 ♕xd5 30 ♖b1 ♘d4 31 ♕xd5+ ♖xd5 32 e4! and at this point the players agreed to a draw.

3) Counterattacking on the Kingside – Tactical Skirmishes

Attacking on the kingside can be justified if Black has built a space advantage on that wing or when White gets carried away with his queenside aspirations, but its chances of success are dependent on the amount of central tension and the type of defensive structure he has to overcome. Realistic chances of success derive from positions that combine minimal central activity with non-g3 pawn skeletons. Such a situation arose in the game **Spraggett-Eslon**, *Seville 1993 (D)*:

This is the kind of attack that everyone likes to conduct. White has no real prospects of counterplay in the centre while his queenside advance is more of a diversion than a genuine threat. In addition, his kingside structure poses no obstacles to the avalanche of black pawns.

20...g4 21 ♖a1 ♖xa1 22 ♕xa1 f4! 23 b5 fxe3 24 fxe3 ♘d8 25 ♘b3 b6

26 ♕a8 ♘e6 27 ♕d5 ♔h7 28 ♗d2 e4!

The centralization of the queen did nothing to improve White's chances of survival. With his last move Black has created the possibility of a devastating sacrifice on f3.

29 d4 ♘g5 30 ♖f1 ♗h6 31 ♖f2 ♖g8 32 ♔h1 ♘f3!

Delivering the knock-out blow! What is particularly pleasing about this sacrifice is the aesthetic way in which it opens lines of attack for no fewer than four black pieces.

33 gxf3 exf3 34 ♗f1 ♕h4 35 ♔g1 g3 36 hxg3 ♕xg3+ 0-1

We have already witnessed several examples where a pawn on e4 offered significant attacking possibilities. In the next one Black exploits this attacking potential to win material, but this time on the queenside.

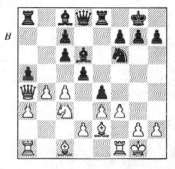

The diagrammed position was reached in the game **Larsen-C.Hansen**, *Odense 1988*. Larsen has taken his queen away from the threatened sector and he soon pays the penalty.

12...exf3 13 &xf3 ♘g4 14 &xg4 &xg4 15 c5 &e5! 16 d4 axb4 17 ♕xb4 &xh2+!

A bolt from the blue! It turns out that Black's target was the wandering white queen.

18 &xh2 ♕h4+ 19 ♔g1 ♖eb8 20 ♘xd5

This is the best practical chance for White but it turns out to be insufficient.

20...♖xb4 21 ♘xb4 &e2 22 ♖f2 &b5 23 &d2 h5 24 ♖f3 ♕e4 25 ♔f2 ♕e6 26 ♖h1? ♖xa3 27 d5 ♕e5 28 ♖h4 ♖a1 29 &e1 ♕b2+ and White resigned.

There are, of course, examples where an attack against the castled king may arise from a fluid central structure but these are very rare and almost always border on the miraculous. If a prescription for these cases exists it should lie in just one word: centralization.

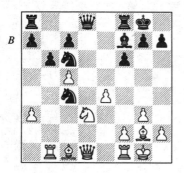

An interesting position from the game **Suba-Thorsteins**, *New York 1989*. White has the advantage of the two bishops, but his opponent enjoys good prospects in the centre. Play went on:

19...♘d4 20 a4 ♕d7 21 &f4 ♖ad8 22 cxb6 axb6 23 ♘b4 c6

Thorsteins attaches an ?! to this move in view of 24 ♘d5 cxd5 25 ♕xd4 dxe4 26 ♕xd7 ♖xd7 27 &xe4 ± but I think that after 24...♘e6! Black is winning.

24 &e3 c5 25 ♘d5 &xd5 26 exd5 ♘f5 27 &f4 ♘d4 28 h4?!

Suba has played well up to this point but his last move is rather meaningless. 28 ♖e1 or 28 ♕d3!? was much stronger.

28...♖fe8 29 ♔h2? ♖e2!

Suddenly Black is in full control. The threat is 30...♘b2 31 ♕c1 ♘d3.

30 ♕c1 ♕xa4 31 &c7 ♖de8 32 ♖a1 ♕b3 33 d6 ♘e5

Thorsteins has attained the position of his dreams. It requires, however, an utterly morbid imagination to predict the continuation.

34 ♖a3 ♕e6 35 &xb6 ♘g4+ 36 ♔g1 ♘xf2! 37 &xc5 ♖c2 38 ♕e3 ♘e2+ 39 ♔xf2 ♘f4+ 40 ♔f3 ♕d5+ 41 ♔xf4 g5+??

The simple 41...♖c4+ wins immediately. Apparently both players were in time trouble.

42 ♔g4 h5+ 43 ♔xh5 ♕f7+ 44 ♔g4 ♖xe3 45 &xe3 ♕e6+ 46 ♔h5 ♕e8+?

46...♕f7+ is a draw.

47 ♔h6! ♕f8+ 48 ♔g6 ♕f7+ 49 ♔f5 ♕d7+ 50 ♔xf6 and White finally won this game!

By studying the games section readers should be able to discover more attacking motifs, but most of them do not have a general significance. In fact the English is a positional opening and in the majority of cases tactics serve to carry out strategic ideas. A fragment from the game **Hodgson-Romanishin**, *Groningen 1993* illustrates this perfectly *(D)*:

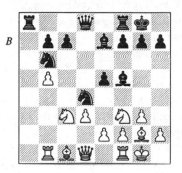

Black's b7-pawn is apparently under pressure but thanks to a small piece of tactics he blunts the attacking force of White's king's bishop:

13...♗g4! 14 ♖e1

The Englishman has to be modest. The point of Romanishin's move lay in 14 ♘xe5?? ♘a4! and White has no legal way of saving himself.

14...♘xf3+ 15 exf3 ♗f5

Black has achieved a solid position. The game ended in a draw on move 32.

A more complicated case arose in the game **Portisch-Karpov**, *Linares 1981*.

1 c4 e5 2 ♘c3 ♘f6 3 g3 d5 4 cxd5 ♘xd5 5 ♗g2 ♘b6 6 ♘f3 ♘c6 7 d3 ♗e7 8 a3 ♗e6 9 b4 a6!? 10 ♗b2 ♕d7 11 ♘e4 f6 12 ♕c2 ♗h3!

An original concept. Exchanging light-squared bishops is strategically desirable but there is a danger that White may exploit the loss of time involved with a quick reaction in the centre. Karpov, however, has calculated that he can prevent it in the nick of time.

13 0-0 ♗xg2 14 ♔xg2 g5! 15 d4?!

The critical reply, but it doesn't quite succeed. Portisch should have been content with the unclear position resulting after 15 ♘c5.

15...g4 16 ♘h4 exd4 17 ♘f5

White's position looks imposing but a couple of strong moves by Karpov sufficed to change the picture.

17...0-0-0! 18 ♖fd1 *(D)*

18...♘c4!!

A magnificent tactical retort. It suddenly turns out that 19 ♗xd4 is not possible in view of 19...♕xf5! 20 ♘d6+ ♘xd6! while on 19 ♘xd4 the simple reply 19...♘xb2 wins a piece. Portisch found nothing better than 19 ♘xe7+ ♕xe7 20 ♘c5 after which Black consolidated his extra pawn and won easily.

4) Another approach (for players who adopt the King's Indian)

During my preparation for the 1993 zonal tournament I chanced across an interesting new way of playing the King's Indian set-up against the English. My second, Albert Blees, suggested that I should refrain from the traditional 7...♘c6 in favour of a new set-up involving the moves ...h6, ...♖e8, and ...c6 followed by an eventual ...d5. The idea became more appetizing when I saw a couple of games by the originator of the system, Loek van Wely, so I tried the variation myself on several occasions, obtaining excellent positions out of the opening. Since then there has not been much going on in this line but this fact rather suits players who like to investigate untrodden opening paths.

What is the main idea behind Black's scheme? It is hard to give a concrete answer to this question as any plan depends very much on the set-up chosen by White, but a few general remarks should help in outlining the spirit of this interesting sideline. First of all, early simplification is prevented (this is where ...h6 fits in). If White could play ♗g5 and ♗xf6 followed by ♘d2 he would run no serious risks of losing, while now he has to start thinking how to meet the above-mentioned advance by ...c6 and ...d5. Secondly, Black's game gains in elasticity. The knight

can be developed on a6 or d7, according to circumstances, leaving the central pawns free to roll forward and occupy the centre. As a consequence, Black keeps open the option of playing on a wide front, which is a significant improvement compared to other lines of this variation. But the most important point which derives from an analysis of the above features is that this continuation creates obstacles to White's main strategic idea of a smooth enterprise on the queenside. In chess you don't necessarily need a plan to win. Sometimes you can achieve it by refuting your opponent's plan.

The basic position for the system arises after 7...h6 8 ♖b1 a5 9 a3 ♖e8 *(D)*.

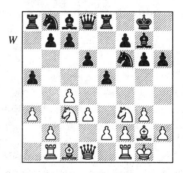

White has two plans from the diagram: he can either pursue the usual strategy of expanding on the queenside by ♘d2 and b4 or try to prevent Black's counterplay in the centre by an immediate 10 e4. The disadvantage entailed in the second continuation is that it limits the activity of the fianchettoed bishop but White gains the valuable option of trans-posing to a g3 King's Indian struc-ture by advancing the d3-pawn to d4 after due preparation.

A notable feature of the position is that the immediate 10 b4 has been rendered problematic as a result of Black's clever piece configuration. After 10...axb4 11 axb4 e4! 12 dxe4 ♘xe4 13 ♘xe4 ♖xe4 14 ♗b2 (what else?) 14...♗xb2 15 ♖xb2 (15 ♘d2 ♖e8 16 ♖xb2 ♕f6 17 ♖b1 ♗f5! 18 e4 ♗e6 ∓) 15...♕f6! Black gets ex-cellent play in view of the magnifi-cent placement of his major pieces. Thus, queenside aggression has to start with 10 ♘d2 which will, more or less, steer the game towards the following type of position *(D)*:

This is from the game **Zlotnikov-Van Wely**, *New York* 1993. Black has a space advantage, which is more relevant than White's plan of pene-trating via the a-file.

16...♘a6 17 ♘a2?

Too passive. 17 ♖a1 was prefer-able, with an unclear position.

17...♗g4 18 ♖fe1 ♕d7 19 ♘f3 ♗d6 20 ♗c3 *(D)*

This also makes an artificial im-pression. Nevertheless, White does not seem to have too much choice af-ter his 'paradoxical' 17th move.

20...♗h3 21 ♕c1 d4 22 ♗d2 ♗xg2 23 ♔xg2 ♘c5 24 ♘b4 h5! *(D)*

With his knight unchallenged on c5 Van Wely is certainly entitled to play this. In contrast, White's knight on b4 cuts an inglorious figure.

25 ♕c2 ♘g4 26 ♖a1 ♖xa1 27 ♖xa1 e4

This typical breakthrough carries the day for Black.

28 dxe4 ♘xe4 29 ♘d3 h4 30 ♘xh4 ♘exf2! 31 ♘xf4 ♘e4 32 ♘f3 g5 33 ♘h5 ♘gf2 34 ♘f6+ ♘xf6 35 ♔xf2 ♕h3 36 ♖g1 ♘e4+ 37 ♔e1 g4 and White resigned.

If White adopts the second plan Black has to be more patient, but he has a wider choice of ideas.

He may:

a) play for control of d4 by ...♗g4 and ...♘c6;

b) follow a pure King's Indian set-up by ...c6 and ...♘bd7; or

c) decide on elastic development with ...c6, ...♘a6 and ...♗d7.

All these schemes are interesting but they await serious practical tests. The reader may form an opinion on the scant tournament evidence by consulting the illustrative games in the following chapter.

3 Beating the English Opening

1) Early Deviations from the main lines

Game 1
Murey – Sax
Bagneux 1984

1 c4 e5 2 ♘f3!?

A continuation that has been unjustly underrated, mainly because of unfortunate results in tournament practice. In applying a strategy already tested with colours reversed in the Nimzowitsch Sicilian (1 e4 c5 2 ♘f3 ♘f6!?) and Alekhine's Defence, White hopes to lure forward Black's e-pawn and then use it as a target of attack. According to circumstances White may consider trading his d-pawn for the opponent's e-pawn, with the aim of accelerating his development and obtaining a central superiority (c4-pawn vs nothing).

White has several viable alternatives to 2 ♘f3 but most of them transpose to lines analysed in subsequent games. Here we will deal only with continuations that have independent significance or surprise value.

a) 2 ♕c2?! is not a good idea since Black has not yet committed himself to ...d5. Thus 2...d6! 3 ♘f3 f5 4 d4 e4 reaches a favourable version of the Old Indian in which the white queen is not doing much on c2, e.g.: 5 ♘g5 c6 6 ♘c3 ♘f6 7 d5 ♗e7 8 f3?! ♘xd5 9 ♘gxe4? (9 cxd5 ∓) 9...♘b4 10 ♕b3 d5! 11 ♘d2 dxc4 12 ♕d1 ♗c5 13 a3 ♘d5 14 ♘xd5 cxd5 –+ Schmittdiel-Psakhis, Leeuwarden 1993.

b) 2 e4 may transpose to the Nimzowitsch Variation of the English Opening, which is examined in our second illustrative game. However, the present move-order is inaccurate as Black can exploit the fact that he has not yet played ...♘f6 by advancing his f-pawn: 2...♗c5 3 ♘c3 d6!? (3...♘f6 is a direct transposition to the Nimzowitsch Variation) 4 g3 ♘c6 5 ♗g2 f5 6 d3 ♘f6 7 ♘h3?! 0-0 8 0-0 h6 9 ♕d2? fxe4 10 ♘xe4 ♘xe4 11 dxe4 ♗e6 12 ♔h1 ♕d7 13 ♘g1 ♗xc4 0-1 Colin-Gulko, Saint Martin 1992.

c) 2 a3 is not bad and should be treated carefully. 2...♘f6 3 ♘c3 (3 e3 c6 4 ♘f3 {4 d4 exd4 5 exd4 d5 =} 4...e4 5 ♘d4 ♗c5 is another move-order) 3...c6 4 ♘f3 e4 5 ♘d4 ♗c5 6 e3 (6 ♘b3 ♗e7! is unclear) 6...0-0 7 d3 d5 8 cxd5 and now *(D)*:

c1) 8...♗xd4?! 9 exd4 exd3 10 ♗xd3 ♖e8+ 11 ♗e3 ♘xd5 (Plachetka-Farago, Zemun 1980) 12 0-0! ♗e6 (12...♘xe3 13 fxe3 ♖xe3 looks

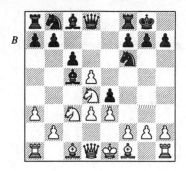

dangerous but may be possible; note that White has at least a draw by playing 14 ♗xh7+) 13 ♕h5! ♘f6 14 ♕h4 ♘bd7 15 ♖fe1 and the threat ♗g5 gives White a strong initiative.

c2) 8...cxd5! 9 ♘b3 (9 ♗e2 exd3 10 ♕xd3 ♘c6 is unclear) 9...♗d6 10 ♘b5!? (10 dxe4 dxe4 11 ♘b5 ♗e5 ∓) 10...♗e7 11 dxe4 ♘xe4 12 ♗e2 ♘c6 with a typical isolated pawn position in which Black enjoys fair chances.

The move 2 b3 transposes to lines of the Nimzowitsch-Larsen Attack.

2...e4!?

Black takes up the challenge. After the alternative 2...♘c6 White may transpose to known continuations examined later in this book.

3 ♘d4 ♘c6 4 ♘xc6?!

After this the central structure stabilizes in Black's favour. It is advisable for White to refrain from this move and follow one of the alternatives:

a) 4 e3 (this is similar to 4 ♘xc6?!, only perhaps a bit better) with a further subdivision:

a1) 4...♘xd4 (an old line that involves the sacrifice of a pawn) 5 exd4 ♕f6 6 d5 ♗c5 7 ♕e2 ♕g6 8 ♘c3 ♘f6 9 d3 0-0 10 dxe4 (10 ♘xe4 ♘xe4 11 ♕xe4 {11 dxe4 ♖e8 12 f3 f5 ∓} 11...♕f6 gives Black good compensation) 11...♘g4 12 ♘d1 ♖e8!? (after 11...d6 12 f3, 12...♘e5 was probably quite OK for Black in Murey-Udov, USSR 1966, but I regard 12...♖e8!? as a more exact way to play) 12 f3 f5! and Black has enough compensation.

a2) 4...♘f6 is a more solid choice:

a21) 5 ♘xc6 turned out badly in O'Kelly-Portisch, Palma de Mallorca 1966 after 5...dxc6 6 d4 ♗f5 7 ♘c3 ♕d7 8 h3 h5 9 ♕a4 a6 10 b3? (10 g3!?) 10...h4! (an important motif in this variation; Black grabs the opportunity to prepare a potential breakthrough by means of ...g5-g4) 11 ♗a3 ♗d6 12 ♗xd6 cxd6 13 ♗e2 ♔f8 14 c5 dxc5 15 dxc5 ♕e7 16 ♕a5 ♘d7 and Black had a clear advantage.

a22) 5 ♘c3 ♗b4 6 ♘xc6 dxc6 7 ♗e2 (or 7 d4 cxd3 8 ♗xd3 ♘g4! with initiative for Black) 7...0-0 8 0-0 ♕e7 (8...♗f5 9 ♕b3!?) 9 d3 (9 d4 exd3 10 ♕xd3 ♖d8 11 ♕c2 ♕e5! is ∓) 9...♗xc3 10 bxc3 exd3 11 ♗xd3 ♖d8 12 ♕c2 h6 13 a4 ♘g4 14 h3 ♘e5 15 ♗e2 ♗e6 16 ♕e4 ♘d7 17 ♗a3 ♕f6 and Black had good chances in the game Sliwa-Marszalek, Poland 1977.

b) 4 ♘c2! (the best move) 4...♘f6 5 ♘c3 ♗c5 6 g3 and now:

b1) 6...d6 7 ♘e3! (7 ♗g2 ♗f5! 8 ♘e3 ♗g6 9 b3 0-0 10 ♗b2 ♖e8 11 0-0 a5 12 a3 h5 was unclear in Lysenko-Itkis, Bucharest 1993) 7...0-0 8 ♗g2

♖e8 9 0-0 ±. This is a 2 ♘f3 ♘c6 3 ♗b5 Sicilian with colours reversed. White has good chances to gain the advantage, e.g. 9...♘d4?! 10 d3! or 9...h6 10 b3 and White may try slowly to improve his position while Black lacks a constructive plan.

b2) 6...♘e5! (the most exact) 7 ♗g2 (7 b4?! ♗e7 8 ♗g2 ♘xc4 9 ♘xe4 10 ♗xe4 d5 11 ♗g2 c6 12 ♖b1 a5 13 b5 c5 14 d4?! ♗f5 15 dxc5 ♗xc5 16 0-0 0-0 17 ♖b3 ♖c8 18 ♘d4 ♗e4 was clearly better for Black in Lysenko-Cebalo, Makarska 1994; White's careless advances have only created weaknesses along the c-file) 7...♘xc4 8 ♘xe4 ♘xe4 9 ♗xe4 d5 (White possesses a central pawn majority but Black has enough manoeuvring room for his pieces to neutralize this advantage) 10 ♗g2 c6 with an unclear position. A possible continuation is 11 0-0 0-0 12 d3 ♘d6 13 e4 dxe4 14 dxe4 ♗e6 15 b3 f5! and Black gets enough counterplay.

4...dxc6 5 ♘c3 ♘f6 6 ♕c2

After other moves Black also seems to enjoy a slight initiative:

a) 6 d4 exd3 7 e4 (7 ♕xd3 ♕xd3 8 exd3 ♗f5 followed by ...0-0-0 and 7 exd3 ♗c5 both look slightly better for Black; the text is extremely risky) 7...♗c5 8 h3 (8 ♗xd3? ♘g4) 8...♗e6 9 ♗xd3 ♘d7! 10 ♗e2 ♕h4 11 g3 ♕f6 12 f4 0-0-0 gave Black a strong attack in Shatskes-Seredenko, USSR 1967.

b) 6 h3 ♗b4 and now (D):

b1) 7 g4 ♕e7.

b2) 7 e3 ♕e7 8 ♕c2 ♗f5!? (or 8...♕e5) 9 a3 (9 f4? is bad because

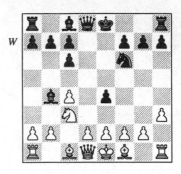

of 9...♘h5, while 9 g4 would be answered by 9...♗g6 with the idea ...♘d7-e5) 9...♗d6 10 b4 a5! yields Black excellent play as 11 c5 ♗e5 12 f4? can be met by 12...exf3! 13 ♕xf5 axb4 −+.

b3) 7 ♕c2 ♕d4 8 e3 ♕e5 9 d4 exd3 10 ♗xd3 ♗xc3+ 11 bxc3 ♗e6 12 0-0 0-0-0 13 ♗a3 ♖d7 14 ♖fb1?! ♕a5 15 ♗b4 ♕g5 led to a disaster for White in Murey-A.Ivanov, New York 1989.

6...♗f5 7 h3 ♗c5

Sax considers this to be inaccurate and proposes instead 7...♗g6 8 e3 ♗d6! 9 b3 ♗e5 10 ♗b2 ♕d6 11 0-0-0 0-0-0 12 ♘e2 ♖d7 13 ♗xe5 ♕xe5 14 ♕b2 (14 ♘f4 ♖hd8 15 ♘xg6 hxg6 16 ♔b1 ♕f5 ∓) 14...♕c5! 15 ♘f4 ♖hd8 16 ♘xg6 hxg6 with a slight advantage for Black. 7...h5!? is also interesting.

8 e3 h5 9 b3 ♕e7 10 ♗b2 0-0-0 11 0-0-0 *(D)*

11...h4?!

An attractive choice but here it doesn't quite work. Black was probably inspired by the opening of the above-mentioned game O'Kelly-Portisch. 11...♖d7 12 ♘e2 ♖hd8

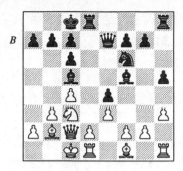

(Sax) was preferable, with roughly even chances.

12 ⌓b1

Murey should have preferred 12 ♘e2! (and not 12 d4? exd3 13 ♗xd3 ♗xe3+! −+), preparing to undermine Black's grip on the kingside by playing g4. With the text move White initiates preparations for the d4 advance, but he gets too absorbed in them, allowing the Hungarian grandmaster to carry out his plan on the kingside unhindered.

12...♕d7

12...♖d7! is better, concentrating on centralization. In that case 13 f3 is not dangerous and can be answered by 13...♗g6 14 ♘xe4 ♘xe4 15 fxe4 ♗xc4 16 d3 ♖hd8 17 ♗c2 ♗g6 18 e4 f5 ⩱ (Sax). White should prefer 13 d4! ♗h4, with an unclear position.

13 ♘e2! ♖h6 14 ♘c1?

Black's last revealed his aggressive intentions on the kingside which White ignores with the text move. With 14 g4! hxg3 15 ♘xg3 ♗e7 16 ♗g2 ♗xh3 17 ♗xh3 ♖xh3 18 ♖xh3 ♕xh3 19 ♘xe4 White would have liquidated the annoying e-pawn and obtained the better pawn structure,

although this advantage is rather symbolic after 19...♕f3.

14...g5!

Sax doesn't need to be asked twice. Now that White has deserted the kingside the advance ...g4 will be more effective at creating weaknesses in that sector of the board.

15 ♗e2 g4 16 ♗xf6?!

A questionable decision. Murey perceives that Black's knight would exert uncomfortable pressure, for instance after 16 hxg4 ♘xg4, and hurries to exchange it. However, the weaknesses created around the white king will prove fatal in the long run.

16...♖xf6 17 hxg4 ♗xg4 18 d4 exd3 19 ♘xd3 ♗f5! 20 ♖xh4 ♖d6

Sax has, naturally, changed plans and gathers his forces for an assault against the new target. The h-pawn has served as a distraction in order to achieve an awesome pin along the d-file.

21 e4 ♕e7 22 ♖h5

On 22 exf5? Black continues 22...♕xh4 23 ♘xc5 ♖xd1+ 24 ♗xd1 ♕d4! forking White's uncoordinated minor pieces.

22...♕xc4 23 f3

Thus, Sax has regained his pawn with interest. On 23 g4? the crude answer 23...♗xg4! 24 ♗xg4+ ♕xg4 25 ♖xc5 ♖xd3! 26 ♖xd3 ♖xd3 27 ♕xd3 ♕g1+ leaves White two pawns down in a queen endgame.

23...♕e6 24 g4 ♗xd3 25 ♗xd3 ♕e3 26 ♗f5+ ⌓b8 27 ♖xd6 ♗xd6 28 ♗e4 ♗a3 29 ♖h1 a5!

The exchanges that took place did not relieve White from his difficulties.

The rest of the game is a typical example of helplessness on the dark squares.

30 ♕h2 a4 31 ♕h4 ♕d4 32 ♕h2 ♕c3 33 ♕c2 ♕e3 34 bxa4 ♖d4!

A strong manoeuvre in mutual time trouble. It practically immobilizes White's forces since 35 ♕b3? would be now met by 35...♖xe4!.

35 a5 ♔a7! 36 a6 b5! 37 ♕h2 (D)

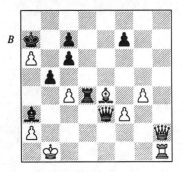

37...♔b6! 38 a7 ♖xc4! 39 a8♘+ ♔a5?!

In time pressure Black misses the immediate victory resulting after the continuation 39...♔a6! 40 ♘xc7+ ♔a5. Fortunately for him the game is still won.

40 ♕xc7+ ♔b4 41 ♕d6+

41 ♗c2 ♖xc2!.

41...c5 42 ♕d1 ♖xe4!

The final blow. The black rook has done some fine work along the fourth rank.

43 ♖f1 ♕c3 44 ♕b3+ ♕xb3+ 45 axb3 ♖e2 46 ♘c7 ♖b2+ 47 ♔a1 ♔xb3 48 f4 ♔a4 49 ♖b1 ♖f2 and White resigned because capturing on b5 with either piece is answered by 50...♗b4 with devastating effect.

2) The Nimzowitsch Variation

Game 2
Rohde – Wolff
Boston 1994

1 c4 e5 2 ♘c3 ♘f6 3 ♘f3

White may instead play 3 e4 in order to keep the f-pawn unblocked. In that case he has to reckon with the immediate 3...♗c5!, aiming at the weak point f2 and setting a trap for those who wish to transpose back to the Four Knights Variation. Indeed, after the blunder 4 ♘f3? there follows 4...♘g4 5 d4 exd4 6 ♘xd4 ♘xf2! 7 ♔xf2 ♕f6+ 8 ♔e3 ♘c6 (D) with a dismal position for White, e.g.:

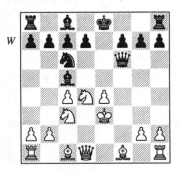

a) 9 ♘e2 0-0 10 b3 ♖e8 (alternatively 10...♕e5!?) 11 ♗b2 d5! 12 cxd5 ♗f5 and then:

a1) 13 dxc6 ♖xe4+ 14 ♔d2 (or 14 ♔f2 ♗g4+ 15 ♔g1 ♗xe2 −+) 14...♗b4+ −+.

a2) 13 ♘g3 ♕g5+ 14 ♔d3 (14 ♔f2 ♕f4+ −+) 14...♗xe4+! 15 ♘xe4 ♘b4+ −+.

b) 9 ♘b5 0-0 10 a3 a5 11 b3 ♖e8 12 ♗b2 d5! 13 cxd5 ♗f5 14 dxc6 (14 ♗d3? ♕g5+ 15 ♔f2 ♗xe4 16 ♗xe4 ♖xe4 17 dxc6 ♕e3+ 18 ♔f1 ♖f4+ –+) 14...♖xe4+ 15 ♔d2 ♗xd4 16 ♘xd4 ♖xd4+ 17 ♗xd4 ♕xd4+ 18 ♔e1 ♕h4+! 19 g3 ♕e4+ 20 ♔f2 ♕xh1 21 ♗g2 ♕xd1 ∓.

Better seems, therefore, 4 g3 d6 5 h3! (5 ♗g2?! ♘g4! 6 ♘h3 ♘c6 ∓, planning ...h5) 5...♘c6 6 ♗g2 0-0 7 d3 (if White tries to do without this move here is what may follow: 7 ♘ge2 a6!? 8 0-0 b5! 9 cxb5?! {9 d3! =} 9...axb5 10 ♘xb5? ♗a6 11 ♘bc3 ♗d3! ∓) 7...a6!? 8 ♘ge2 b5! 9 0-0 (9 cxb5?! axb5 10 ♘xb5 ♗a6 11 ♘ec3 ♕b8 12 a4 ♘b4 with initiative) 9...bxc4 10 dxc4 ♘d4 with an unclear position. Black's plan with ...a6 and ...b5 is well-founded as it takes the sting out of the advance f4, which is White's main idea in this system.

3...♘c6 *(D)*

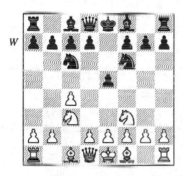

The position after 3...♘c6 is a basic position for the English Opening and characterizes the Four Knights Variation. Here we will deal with 4 e4!?, an old continuation that was a favourite of Nimzowitsch and Botvinnik.

4 e4 ♗b4!?

I have chosen this as main line because it suits well the recommended repertoire against 4 d3. Indeed, after 4...♗b4 White can switch back to our featured game by playing 5 e4!?, which would render the alternative 4...♗c5 of small practical importance. However, I disagree with the present theoretical evaluation that 4...♗c5 is inferior to 4...♗b4. After 5 ♘xe5 (the critical move) 5...♘xe5 6 d4 ♗b4 7 dxe5 ♘xe4 White has several queen moves but not one of them promises an advantage:

a) 8 ♕g4? ♘xc3 9 a3 ♗f8 10 bxc3 d6 11 ♕g3 dxe5 12 ♕xe5+ ♕e7 ∓ Taimanov.

b) 8 ♕c2 ♘xc3 9 bxc3 ♗c5 10 ♗d3 ♕h4 11 0-0 0-0 12 ♖b1 (12 ♖e1!?) 12...b6 13 ♗e4 ♖b8 14 g3 ♕h5 15 ♗f4 d6 = Taimanov-Platonov, USSR Ch 1971.

c) 8 ♕f3 f5!? (8...d5?! 9 ♗e2 with 0-0 and ♖fd1 to follow is better for White; 8...♘xc3 9 bxc3 ♗a5 was played in the game Rohde-Dlugy, New York 1990, but it also looks inferior) 9 ♗e2 (9 exf6?! 0-0!) 9...0-0 10 0-0 ♗xc3 11 bxc3 ♕e7 (Tartakower-Thomas, Ujpest 1934) 12 ♕e3 b6! (12...♕xe5? 13 f3 ♕xc3 14 fxe4 ♕xa1 15 ♗a3 +–) 13 f3 ♘c5 14 ♗a3 results in a double-edged position in which Black's chances are not inferior.

d) 8 ♕d4 (the main line) 8...♘xc3 9 bxc3 ♗e7!? (9...♗a5?! 10 ♗a3 d6

11 exd6 0-0 12 0-0-0 cxd6 13 ♕xd6
♕xd6 14 ♗xd6 ♖e8 15 ♔b2 ♗d7 16
♗d3 ♗c6 17 f3 left White better in
the game Korchnoi-Hübner, Solin-
gen (m) 1973) 10 ♕g4 ♔f8! 11 ♕g3
(11 ♗e3 d6 12 ♕h5 c6!? planning
...♕a5 with counterplay) 11...d6 12
♗e3 and now 12...♗h4!? looks like
a good improvement over Taimanov's analysis 12...dxe5?! 13 ♖d1
♕e8 14 ♕xe5 ♗d6 15 ♕h5 with a
slightly better position for White.

5 d3 0-0

Another plan is 5...d6 6 g3 (6 ♗e2
transposes to the game) 6...♗c5!? 7
♗g2 ♘d4 8 ♘xd4 ♗xd4 9 h3 (9 0-0
♗g4! followed by ...♕c8 gives counterplay) reaching a critical position
(D):

a) 9...♗e6?! is, I think, somewhat
suspicious because the bishop's position is subject to harassment after
either f4-f5 or d4:

a1) 10 f4 a6 11 ♕f3 h6 12 ♘e2
♗c5 13 ♗d2? ♕e7 14 ♗c3 ♗d7 15
b4 ♗a7 16 a4 ♘h7 17 ♔d2?! 0-0 18
g4 b5! 19 axb5 axb5 20 cxb5 ♗b6!
21 ♖hd1 ♗xb5 22 ♔e1 ♖fe8 23
♖xa8 ♖xa8 24 ♖a1 ♖d8! 25 ♔d2 c6

26 ♔c2 ♘f8! gave Black a big advantage in Gulko-Karpov, Reykjavik
1991, but Gulko's opening play could
hardly stand up to critical analysis.

a2) I think that White could get a
substantial edge by playing 10 0-0.
Then Karpov's recommendation of
10...♕c8 11 ♔h2 h5 ('with counterplay') seems rather absurd in view of
12 ♘e2! h4 (12...♗b6 can be met by
13 d4 ± or 13 b3!?) 13 g4 ♗xg4 (on
other moves White simply pursues
the plan of advancing his d- or f-
pawn; Black has no compensation
for the odd configuration of his
pieces and the time lost in ...h5-h4)
14 hxg4 ♘xg4+ 15 ♔h1 (15 ♔g1!?)
15...h3 16 ♗f3 ♘xf2+ 17 ♖xf2 ♗xf2
18 ♕f1 when despite the material
deficit White's minor pieces should
carry the day for him.

b) 9...c6!? 10 0-0 0-0 11 ♔h2!
(planning f4; on 11 ♘e2?! there follows 11...♗b6 12 ♔h2 d5! with an
unclear position) 11...♗xc3!? 12
bxc3 d5 13 cxd5 cxd5 14 exd5 ♘d5
and now instead of 15 ♕b3 ♘f6!? 16
♗a3 ♖e8 17 ♖fd1 ♗e6!? 18 ♕xb7
♗d5 with counterplay for Black, I'd
prefer 15 ♗d2!? and White is a shade
better.

6 ♗e2!?

A new idea. The traditional Nimzowitschian approach would be 6 g3
d6 7 ♗g2 (in order to intensify control of d5) when existing theory considers White's chances to be slightly
better. I think that this assumption is
far from clear as it is mainly based
on the game Cifuentes-Groszpeter,
Novi Sad OL 1990, which continued

7...♘e8 8 0-0 ♗xc3 9 bxc3 f5 10 exf5 ♗xf5 11 ♘h4 ♗e6 12 ♖b1 ♖b8 13 f4!? (13 ♗e3 ♘f6 14 ♕a4 ♗d7 was unclear in the game Zagorovsky-Krzyston, corr. 1975) 13...exf4 14 ♗xf4 ♕d7 (14...g5? 15 ♗xc6 ±; 14...♘f6?! 15 ♗g5) 15 ♕a4! ♘f6 and now *(D)*:

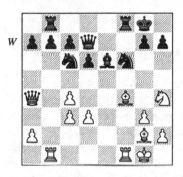

a) 16 ♗g5 (White can try to improve – see below) and now:

a1) 16...♘e5 (it seems to me that this is inexact) 17 ♕xa7 ♘xd3 18 ♗xf6 gxf6 19 ♖xb7 ♖xb7 20 ♕xb7 ♘c5 21 ♕b1 ♗xc4 22 ♖f4! and in Cifuentes-Groszpeter, Novi Sad OL 1990 White was slightly better due to his more secure king position.

a2) I suggest instead 16...♘g4!? with good play for Black:

a21) 17 ♖fe1 ♔h8 18 d4 ♕f7! (18...d5? 19 ♖xe6! +–) 19 ♖f1 (19 ♖xe6? ♕xe6 20 d5 ♕e5 –+; 19 d5? ♕f2+ 20 ♔h1 ♗d7! ∓) 19...♕h5 with counterplay.

a22) 17 ♖xf8+ ♖xf8 18 ♖xb7 ♘d4! 19 ♕d1 ♘f2! (19...♕a4 20 ♕e1 ♕a5 21 ♖b2! ±) 20 ♕e1 (20 ♕d2 ♘h3+ 21 ♗xh3 ♗xh3 22 ♖b1 ∓) and now Black has:

a221) 20...♘xd3!? 21 ♕d2 ♘c5 22 ♕xd4! (22 cxd4? ♘xb7 23 ♗xb7 ♗xc4 ∓) 22...♘xb7 23 ♗xb7 c6 24 ♗a6 c5 25 ♕e4!. This position requires further analysis but White looks better.

a222) 20...♘h3+! (leading to an unbalanced ending) 21 ♗xh3 ♗xh3 22 cxd4 ♖f1+ 23 ♕xf1 ♗xf1 24 ♔xf1 ♕g4 25 ♖b8+ ♔f7 26 ♗e3 g5 27 ♘g2 ♕f3+ is unclear.

b) 16 ♖xb7!?, Cifuentes's suggestion, is an attempt to improve, but Black probably has nothing to worry about if he responds with 16...♖xb7 17 ♗xc6 ♕c8 18 ♗xb7 ♕xb7 19 ♕b5 ♕c8! (Cifuentes only gives 19...♕a8 20 ♖b1 ±; the text guards f5 and maintains the possibility of transferring the queen to either side) 20 ♗g5 ♗h3 when both 21 ♖e1 c6!? (planning ...♖e8; 21...a6!? is possible too) and 21 ♘g2 ♕a8! 22 ♕b2 ♖b8! promise a strong initiative.

c) After 16 ♖fe1 ♗h3, 17 ♗h1 ♖be8 is unclear, while 17 ♖xb7 is uninspiring in view of 17...♗xg2! 18 ♖xb8 ♖xb8 19 ♘xg2 ♘e5 20 ♕xa7 (20 ♕xd7 ♘fxd7 ∓) 20...♘f3+ 21 ♔h1 ♕c8 22 ♖f1 ♖a8! 23 ♕f2 ♘xh2! with a powerful attack on the light squares.

From the above analysis it becomes evident that the line starting with 6 g3 is very rich in thrust and counter-thrust. Although it is hard to exhaust all possibilities it seems that the way to secure counterplay lies in removing White's king's bishop, a most important piece in both attack and defence.

6...d6 7 0-0 ♗xc3 8 bxc3 ♘d7

Black can also play 8...♘e8!? and 8...♕e7 but the text looks fine.

9 ♘e1

Now the point behind 6 ♗e2 becomes clear: White wanted to save a tempo in order to open the game with f2-f4 as quickly as possible. Its drawbacks are also quite obvious as the bishop is restricting White's options along the e-file, and d5 is less well controlled than in 6 g3 lines.

9...♘c5 10 f4 exf4 11 ♗xf4 f5!

The correct reaction as it softens the enemy's central control. After the practically forced 12 exf5 White's pawn cluster d3-c3-c4 looks rather awkward.

12 exf5 ♗xf5 13 ♘c2 ♕e7!

This and the next move are evidence of Patrick Wolff's positional understanding. If the white knight were ever to reach d5 then Rohde's strategy would have paid dividends. The text combines development and prophylaxis since 14 ♘e3? would be now met by 14...♗xd3! 15 ♗xd3 ♖xf4! and Black wins.

14 ♕d2 ♖ae8 15 ♖ae1 *(D)*

15 ♘e3 was less bad than in the previous note but still not fully adequate: 15...♗xd3!? 16 ♗xd3 ♖xf4 17 ♖xf4 ♕xe3+ 18 ♕xe3 ♖xe3 is given as ∓ by Wolff but I think that after 19 ♖af1 the position is just unclear. I prefer instead the more solid 15...♗g6! with an excellent game for Black.

15...♘e5!

Move by move Black steps up the pressure. White's pair of bishops is

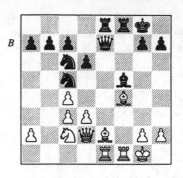

rather inactive as the pawn structure restricts its mobility.

16 ♘b4 ♕d7 17 ♗xe5

After this White falls on the defensive, but what else is there? Black was threatening to evict the white knight by ...a5 and win the shaky d-pawn.

17...dxe5 18 ♕e3 ♕d6 19 ♗f3 c6 20 d4 ♘d7?!

Missing his chance. 20...exd4! was better since Black need not be afraid of 21 ♕xe8: 21...♖xe8 22 ♖xe8+ ♔f7 23 ♖ee1 (23 ♗h5+ g6 24 ♖xf5+ ♔e8 −+) and now both 23...dxc3 and 23...♔g6 guarantee Black a clear advantage. I think that White's chances of salvation lie with 21 ♕xd4, a move dismissed by Wolff as clearly bad in view of 21...♖d8. This evaluation is open to discussion after the further 22 ♖e5!? so I suggest instead the centralizing 21...♕xd4+!? 22 cxd4 ♘e4 in order to take advantage of the strange position of White's knight on b4.

21 c5 ♕g6 22 ♗e2 exd4

Black would like to play 22...a5 but as Wolff points out White can defend himself in the nick of time. 23

$\mathbf{\hat{2}}$c4+! (23 $\mathbf{\hat{2}}$d3? exd4 24 $\mathbf{\ddot{w}}$xd4 $\mathbf{\Xi}$xe2! −+) 23...$\mathbf{\dot{z}}$h8 24 $\mathbf{\hat{2}}$d3 and now 24...b5? fails to 25 cxb6 $\mathbf{\hat{2}}$xb6 26 $\mathbf{\hat{2}}$xe5 $\mathbf{\Xi}$xe5 27 $\mathbf{\ddot{w}}$xe5 $\mathbf{\hat{2}}$xc4 28 $\mathbf{\Xi}$xf5. The text maintains Black's slight pull.

23 $\mathbf{\ddot{w}}$xd4 $\mathbf{\dot{z}}$h8?! *(D)*

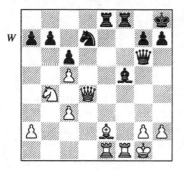

But not this! 23...$\mathbf{\hat{2}}$e5!? is natural and strong. Now Rohde, aided by Black's dilatory play, obtains good drawing chances.

24 $\mathbf{\hat{2}}$d3! $\mathbf{\Xi}$xe1 25 $\mathbf{\Xi}$xe1 a5 26 $\mathbf{\hat{2}}$xf5

More sensible is 26 $\mathbf{\ddot{w}}$xd7! $\mathbf{\hat{2}}$xd7 27 $\mathbf{\hat{2}}$xg6 axb4 (27...hxg6?! 28 $\mathbf{\hat{2}}$d3 ±) 28 $\mathbf{\hat{2}}$c2 bxc3 29 $\mathbf{\Xi}$e3 (Wolff) and the game peters out to a draw.

26...$\mathbf{\ddot{w}}$xf5 27 $\mathbf{\hat{2}}$d3 h6 28 h3 $\mathbf{\Xi}$f7 29 $\mathbf{\dot{z}}$h2 $\mathbf{\dot{z}}$h7 30 $\mathbf{\Xi}$e3 $\mathbf{\hat{2}}$f6

The character of the game is still basically drawish, but if anyone has to be careful it is White due to his pawn weaknesses. Rohde fails to sense the danger and starts vacillating only to slip into a lost position.

31 $\mathbf{\Xi}$f3?! $\mathbf{\ddot{w}}$d5 32 $\mathbf{\ddot{w}}$xd5? cxd5

This endgame is just what White should have avoided. The slight exposure of Black's a-pawn does not offer Rohde real compensation for his numerous weaknesses.

33 $\mathbf{\Xi}$f5 $\mathbf{\hat{2}}$c7 34 $\mathbf{\Xi}$e5 $\mathbf{\dot{z}}$g6 35 $\mathbf{\Xi}$e6 $\mathbf{\dot{z}}$f7 36 $\mathbf{\Xi}$b6?

White's rook seems excellently placed here, but in fact hits thin air. White should have endeavoured to prevent the centralization of Black's knight by 36 $\mathbf{\Xi}$d6!? when Wolff would have still had several technical difficulties to overcome. Now the end is near.

36...$\mathbf{\hat{2}}$e4 37 $\mathbf{\Xi}$b5 a4! 38 c4 dxc4 39 $\mathbf{\hat{2}}$e5+ $\mathbf{\dot{z}}$e8 40 $\mathbf{\hat{2}}$xc4 $\mathbf{\Xi}$xc5 41 $\mathbf{\Xi}$b4 b5

The game is practically over. In addition to his extra pawn Black enjoys a more active king and strongly centralized pieces. Still, by assuming that everything wins, Wolff manages to introduce complications into this highly advantageous position.

42 $\mathbf{\hat{2}}$e3 $\mathbf{\hat{2}}$d6

The first slip. Better was 42...$\mathbf{\hat{2}}$c3.

43 $\mathbf{\dot{z}}$g3 $\mathbf{\dot{z}}$d7 44 $\mathbf{\dot{z}}$f4 $\mathbf{\dot{z}}$c6 45 h4 $\mathbf{\hat{2}}$c4?

Wasting time. The simple 45...$\mathbf{\Xi}$c3 (Wolff) would have paralysed White.

46 $\mathbf{\hat{2}}$f5 $\mathbf{\hat{2}}$e5 47 $\mathbf{\dot{z}}$e4 $\mathbf{\hat{2}}$d7 48 $\mathbf{\hat{2}}$xg7

Now it's a fight again. Realizing that his carelessness may cost him dearly, Wolff makes optimum use of his abilities and concludes the game efficiently.

48...$\mathbf{\Xi}$c2 49 $\mathbf{\hat{2}}$f5 $\mathbf{\Xi}$xa2 50 $\mathbf{\hat{2}}$d4+ $\mathbf{\dot{z}}$c5 51 $\mathbf{\Xi}$xb5+ $\mathbf{\dot{z}}$c4 52 $\mathbf{\Xi}$b1 $\mathbf{\hat{2}}$c5+ 53 $\mathbf{\dot{z}}$e5 $\mathbf{\hat{2}}$d3+ 54 $\mathbf{\dot{z}}$e4 $\mathbf{\Xi}$xg2 55 $\mathbf{\hat{2}}$f5 $\mathbf{\Xi}$g4+ 56 $\mathbf{\dot{z}}$e3 $\mathbf{\dot{z}}$c3 57 $\mathbf{\hat{2}}$d6

On 57 $\mathbf{\hat{2}}$xh6 Wolff gives 57...$\mathbf{\Xi}$xh4 58 $\mathbf{\hat{2}}$f5 $\mathbf{\Xi}$h3+ 59 $\mathbf{\dot{z}}$e2 a3 −+.

57...♘b2!

Allowing the black king to support the advance of his passed pawn. The rest requires no further comments.

58 ♘b5+ ♔c2 59 ♖h1 ♘c4+ 60 ♔f3 h5 61 ♖h2+ ♔b3 62 ♖h1 ♔c2 63 ♖h2+ ♔d3 64 ♔f2 ♖f4+ 65 ♔e1 ♖e4+ 66 ♔d1 ♘e3+ 67 ♔c1 ♖c4+ 68 ♔b1 ♖b4+ 69 ♖b2 ♖xh4 70 ♘c7 ♘d1 71 ♖g2 ♘c3+ 72 ♔b2 ♖b4+ 0-1

3) Four Knights Variation: 4 d3/4 d4!?

Game 3
Serper – Salov
Tilburg 1994

1 c4 ♘f6 2 ♘c3 e5 3 ♘f3 ♘c6 4 d3

A logical build-up. White invites transposition to a Scheveningen Sicilian with colours reversed and a valuable extra tempo. This fact does not necessarily mean that White gets the upper hand after 4...d5, but it would be rather tiresome to work out all the ramifications deriving from this difference in such an elaborate system. Thus I suggest the calmer 4...♗b4, which also has its points.

The other move with the d-pawn, namely 4 d4!?, is not to be dismissed lightly since it was a Botvinnik speciality. Although only sporadically used nowadays, it can be dangerous against the unprepared. Black has two main replies :

a) 4...e4!? (this aims at a pitched battle) 5 ♘d2 (5 ♘g5 h6!? 6 ♘gxe4 ♘xe4 7 ♘xe4 ♕h4 and now White should opt for 8 ♘c3 ♕xd4 = since 8 ♕d3?! d5 9 cxd5?! ♘b4 risks disaster: 10 ♕b5+ ♔d8! ∓; 10 ♕b1 is met strongly by 10...♗f5 11 ♘d6+ cxd6! 12 ♕xf5 g6 −+, e.g. 13 ♕b1 ♖c8) 5...♗b4! (reaching an interesting position which bears a close resemblance to a Nimzo-Indian; the other choice 5...♘xd4 6 ♘dxe4 ♘xe4 7 ♘xe4 leaves White slightly better) 6 e3 ♗xc3! (it is best to capture the knight at once; after 6...0-0 7 ♕c2! I think that White has good chances to get an advantage) 7 bxc3 d6 8 ♗e2 0-0 9 0-0 ♕e7!? (a move stemming from Petrosian; on 9...♖e8 White may try the gambit 10 f3!? exf3 11 ♗xf3! ♖xe3 12 ♘b3 ♖xc3 13 ♗g5 when the position is unclear but White has certain attacking chances, as in Adamski-Knaak, E.Germany-Poland 1973) 10 ♔h1!? (threatening f3 or f4 as the black queen would then be unable to capture on e3 after ...exf3) 10...♗f5 11 f4 (11 f3 ♕d7 to be followed by ...♖ae8) 11...♕d7 and Black maintains the blockade on the light squares as 12 ♖g1 can be met by 12...♗g4!, while 12 h3? ♗xh3 is no good at all.

b) 4...exd4 (the most common choice) 5 ♘xd4 ♗b4 6 ♗g5 h6 7 ♗h4 ♗xc3+ 8 bxc3 d6 and now:

b1) 9 f3 ♘e5 10 e4 ♘g6 11 ♗f2 0-0 12 ♕d2 c6 13 ♗e2 d5 14 exd5 cxd5 15 0-0 (15 c5?! ♘h5 16 0-0 ♘hf4 threatened the unpleasant 17...♗h3 in Raičević-Gipslis, Vrnjačka Banja 1975) 15...dxc4 16 ♗xc4 ♗d7 17 ♗b3 ♖c8 (planning ...♘e5 or ...♕a5) 18 c4 a6 19 ♖fd1 ♕e7 20 ♖e1 ♕d6 21 ♕c2 ♘f4 was unclear in the game Tal-Dvoretsky, Wijk aan Zee 1976.

b2) 9 ♘xc6!? (a new idea which cannot change the evaluation that the black position is rock-solid) 9...bxc6 10 c5 ♕e7 11 e3 (11 cxd6 cxd6 12 ♕d4 c5 is unclear) 11...♕e5 (better than 11...dxc5?! 12 ♕f3 ±) 12 ♕d4 ♘e4 13 cxd6 cxd6 14 ♖c1 g5! (in Smirin-Tiviakov, Rostov 1993, Black played the faulty 14...♗e6? when after 15 ♗d3! {15 f3?! g5!} 15...♘c5 16 ♗b1 ♔d7 White could have obtained the advantage by the simple 17 0-0, threatening f4) 15 ♗g3 ♘xg3 16 hxg3 ♗e6 =.

Therefore, we may conclude that Black has enough play in the 4 d4!? variation, so let's return to our main line.

4...♗b4!? 5 ♗d2

The only move encountered in practice. White should prevent the doubling of his pawns when granted the possibility.

5...0-0 6 g3

Serper elects to fianchetto his king's bishop. At this point White has some interesting alternatives:

a) 6 a3!? is an attempt at clarification. Black is now forced to part with his bishop as the retreat ...♗f8 is not available. The continuation is 6...♗xc3 7 ♗xc3 (D).

7...e4!? (I consider this superior to 7...♖e8 8 e4!? d6 9 h3 a6 10 ♗e2 b5 11 cxb5 axb5 12 0-0 ♖b8 13 b4 ♘e7 14 ♖e1 ♘g6 15 ♗f1 ♗b7 16 ♘d2 c5 17 ♖c1 ♗a8 18 ♘b3 which should

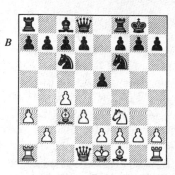

be worse for Black, though he eventually won in Sunye Neto-Christiansen, Wijk aan Zee 1982) and now White has the following choice:

a1) 8 ♘d4 exd3 with a further branch:

a11) 9 exd3 ♖e8+ 10 ♗e2 ♘xd4 11 ♗xd4 d5! gives Black the initiative. 12 0-0? is well met by 12...dxc4 13 dxc4 ♖xe2! 14 ♕xe2 ♕xd4 15 ♖ad1 ♗g4! −+.

a12) 9 ♕xd3 ♘c5 10 ♕c2! (10 ♕g3 d6! threatens both ...♘xc4 and ...♘e4) 10...d5! with counterplay. Not 10...♘xc4? 11 ♗b4 ♘d6 12 ♖c1! with a clear advantage for White.

a13) 9 e3 ♘e4 is at least equal for Black.

a2) 8 ♘e5 ♘xe5 9 ♗xe5 d6 (alternatively 9...♖e8!?) 10 ♗f4 (10 ♗c3 ♖e8 =) 10...exd3 11 ♕xd3!? (11 e3 ♗f5 12 ♗xd3 ♗xd3 13 ♕xd3 ♘h5 14 ♗g3 ♕f6 =) 11...♘d7 12 e3 a5 13 b3 ♘c5 14 ♕c3 b6 15 ♗e2 ♗b7 16 0-0 f5 is unclear. Black has reached a favourable version of a Budapest Gambit.

a3) 8 dxe4 ♘xe4 9 ♖c1 ♘xc3 10 ♖xc3 d6 11 g3 ♕f6 12 ♗g2 ♖e8 13 0-0 when 13...♗g4!, followed by doubling rooks on the e-file should be comfortable for Black.

b) 6 e3 ♖e8 7 ♗e2!? (for the continuation 7 ♕c2 ♗xc3 8 ♗xc3 d5 refer to Game 5, Ehlvest-Kasparov) 7...♗f8!? (White's build-up is slow and queenside expansion with b4 is rather harmless for Black with the bishop standing on e2; therefore keeping the position closed seems more logical than 7...d5 as in that case White gets play on the half-open c-file) 8 0-0 d6 and White has tried from this position:

b1) 9 ♘g5 ♘d7 10 f4 exf4 11 exf4 ♘d4! was at least equal for Black in Möhring-Gipslis, Hradec Kralove 1977/8. Nevertheless, the continuation of the game proved a nightmare for the Latvian grandmaster: 12 ♗h5 g6 13 f5 ♘f6! 14 fxg6 fxg6 15 ♘e2 ♘f5 (15...♘h5!?) 16 ♗f3 c6 17 ♘c3 d5?? (17...♘e3! 18 ♗xe3 ♖xe3 is slightly better for Black according to Gipslis, while 17...♗g7!? is also possible) 18 cxd5 cxd5 19 ♕b3 ♔g7 20 ♘xd5 ♗c5+ 21 ♔h1 ♗d4 22 ♘f4 ♕b6 23 ♕f7+ ♔h8 24 ♘d5 and 1-0. Chess blindness?

b2) 9 a3 (showing his hand too early; now Black may ignore b4 and try for play in the centre) 9...♘e7!? 10 b4 ♘g6 11 ♕c2 c6 12 b5 ♗d7 13 bxc6 bxc6 14 ♖fb1 ♕c7 15 ♖b2 d5 16 cxd5 cxd5 17 d4 ♖ab8 18 dxe5 ♘xe5 19 ♘e4 ♕xc2 20 ♘xf6+ gxf6 21 ♖xc2 ♖ec8 22 ♖xc8 ♗xc8 23 ♘d4 ♘c4 24 ♗xc4 dxc4 = Rivas-P.Nikolić, Manila OL 1992 (by transposition).

b3) 9 ♖c1 g6 10 ♘d5 ♗g7 11 ♘xf6+ ♕xf6 12 ♗c3 ♕e7 13 ♖e1 a5 14 b3 ♗f5 15 a3 (15 d4?! ♘b4) 15...g5!? 16 ♘d2 ♗g6 17 ♕c2?! (17 e4! is unclear) 17...f5 18 ♕b2 h5 19 b4 axb4 20 axb4 g4 gave Black an impressive game in Spraggett-Eslon, Seville 1993.

b4) 9 ♕c2!? (perhaps the most critical of White's ninth move alternatives; the idea is to save a tempo on Rivas-Nikolić) 9...g6!? (9...♘e7 10 b4! ±) 10 a3 a5 11 ♖ab1 ♗f5! (D).

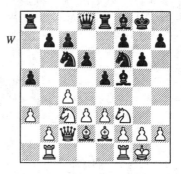

An important move, threatening ...e4. The following brief analysis serves to illustrate that Black is doing OK here:

b41) 12 ♘e4 a4.

b42) 12 ♘h4 ♗d7 13 b4 axb4 14 axb4 can be answered by 14...d5!? or 14...♘d4 =.

b43) 12 ♘g5! ♘d7! 13 ♘ge4 (13 e4!? ♘d4 14 ♕d1 ♗e6 15 ♘xe6 =) 13...♗e6 14 b4 (14 ♘d5 f5 15 ♘ec3? ♘a7! threatening ...c6) 14...axb4 15 axb4 f5 16 ♘g3 ♘f6 with an unclear position as White's knight is awkwardly placed on g3.

6...♖e8

The most common path, but the alternative 6...♘d4!? is also good enough. The game Vasiukov-Kochiev, USSR 1981 continued 7 ♗g2 (7 ♘xe5? ♕e7 ∓) 7...♘xf3+ 8 ♗xf3 ♖e8 9 0-0 c6 10 ♗g2 h6 11 ♖c1 (11 f4!?) 11...♗xc3 12 ♖xc3 d5 13 cxd5 cxd5 14 ♕b3 d4 15 ♗d2 and now 15...♗e6! would have yielded equal chances according to Vasiukov.

7 ♗g2 ♗xc3 8 ♗xc3 d5 9 0-0!?

Practical experience has nominated this as main line but in my opinion 9 cxd5 is the critical reply. After 9...♘xd5 White has:

a) 10 ♗d2 (given as ± in *ECO*, but this assessment is not particularly convincing) 10...♘d4! 11 0-0 ♗g4 12 ♘xd4 exd4 13 ♖e1 and now 13...c6! with a balanced position. 13...♕d7?! would be inferior as 14 ♕b3! gives Black problems.

b) 10 0-0! brings Black to a critical cross-road:

b1) 10...♖b8 11 ♖c1 (11 ♗d2!?) 11...♘xc3 12 bxc3 b6 13 d4 ♗g4 14 h3 ♗xf3 15 ♗xf3 ♘a5 16 ♕a4 ♕f6 17 dxe5 ♕xe5 18 ♖fd1 ♕e6 (Savchenko-Romanishin, Helsinki 1992) 19 ♖d7! ±. It is evident that Black hasn't got any winning chances if he continues in this fashion.

b2) 10...b6!? is an unusual idea but it might well be palatable in this position:

b21) 11 ♗d2!? deserves attention.

b22) On the slightly odd 11 e4, there follows 11...♘xc3 12 bxc3 ♗a6!, intending to meet 13 ♕a4 with 13...♘a5 14 ♖fd1 c5 15 d4 ♗e2! 16

♖d2 ♗xf3 17 ♗xf3 ♕f6 with unclear play.

b23) After 11 ♖c1 ♗b7 12 a3 (12 e4?! ♘db4 13 ♕b3 a5) 12...a5! (stifling White's aims of queenside expansion by means of b4; 12...♖e7?! is inferior in view of 13 ♘h4! with an initiative for White) 13 ♕a4 (13 ♖e1 is met by 13...a4, while 13 e4 ♘xc3 14 ♖xc3 ♖e7! plans ...♘d4) 13...♘d4! gives Black good chances for equality as the following variations show *(D)*:

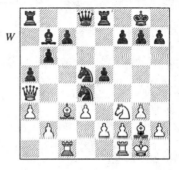

b231) 14 ♘xd4 exd4 15 ♗xd4 and here 15...c5! with good counterplay. Instead Black must avoid 15...♖xe2? 16 ♗xg7! with a big plus for White.

b232) 14 ♗xd4 exd4 15 ♘xd4 c5 16 ♘f5 (16 c4!? is also unclear) 16...g6! with a new subdivision:

b2321) 17 ♘h6+ ♔g7 18 ♘g4 ♖xe2! (18...h5? 19 ♘e3 ♘xe3 20 fxe3 ♗xg2 21 ♔xg2 ♖xe3 22 ♖xf7+! ±) 19 d4 c4! (only move) results in an unclear position.

b2322) 17 ♘e3?! ♘xe3 18 ♗xb7 ♘xf1 19 ♗xa8 ♕xa8 20 ♖xf1 ♖xe2 ∓.

b2323) 17 e4!? gxf5 18 exd5 ♗xd5 with an approximately equal position. Black's king is not in danger in view of the reduced material and the excellent centralization of his forces.

9...d4 10 ♗d2 h6

Two alternatives are also quite attractive for Black:

a) 10...e4!? was played in the game Koblack-Jansson, Denmark-Sweden, 1975 and is given as ∓ in *ECO*. This assessment is probably exaggerated, but in any case Black is not worse.

b) 10...a5 11 ♗g5 h6 12 ♗xf6 ♕xf6 13 ♘d2 is equal according to Salov.

Nevertheless, the game continuation is well worth following as it makes a fine aesthetic impression. Black's little pawn move prevents White from exchanging his awkwardly placed bishop and postpones the ...e4 advance until a more appropriate moment.

11 b4!

Expanding on the queenside is the logical sequel to White's previous play. Serper intends to activate his bishop by placing it on b4 whereupon co-ordination among his pieces would be restored.

11...♕d6 12 ♕b3

12 c5!? is an alternative.

12...♗f5 13 b5 ♘d8 14 ♗b4 ♕d7 15 ♖fe1 *(D)*

A good idea. White prevents the exchange of his light-squared bishop and prepares to play e3 to take advantage of the temporary reticence of Black's e-pawn.

15...♖c8!

Salov's feeling for strategy allows him to spot White's threat. In his notes to the game he criticizes the text, proposing instead 15...♗h3 16 ♗h1 ♖c8 as a way to carry out ...c5 under ideal conditions but I believe that his intuition was wiser since White is not forced to retreat with 16 ♗h1. 16 e3!? ♗xg2 17 ♔xg2 looks better as after 17...dxe3 18 ♖xe3 Black has problems defending his e-pawn.

16 e3

Salov pointed out the interesting alternative 16 ♕a3!? a6! 17 bxa6 bxa6 18 ♕xa6 c5. Black seems to have excellent compensation for the sacrificed pawn.

16...c5 17 ♗a3 ♗h3 18 ♗h1?

This strategic mistake swings the balance clearly towards Black's side. 18 e4 was imperative but Serper probably overlooked that after this mechanical retreat a knight's position on g4 would be unassailable. This factor enables Salov to saddle White with a backward d-pawn and at the same time strengthen his own position in the centre.

18...dxe3! 19 ♖xe3 ♘g4 20 ♖e4 f6! *(D)*

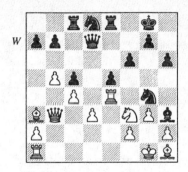

W

Here lies the difference! With h3 firmly under control Black has this solidifying manoeuvre at his disposal, leaving White without counterplay. This could hardly have been possible, for instance, after 18 &xe3 in the note to Black's 15th, since 18...&g4 19 &e2 f6?? simply loses a piece to 20 h3.

21 &g2

After his error on the 18th move there is not really much that White can do. It is obviously unattractive to exchange bishops now, but what else is there?

21...&xg2 22 &xg2 h5 23 &ae1

The white rooks are biting on granite on the e-file, but White had to make a move.

23...&f7 24 &c1 &cd8 25 &d1 &e6

Time is of the essence. Black has reorganized his troops and is ready to direct his fire against the impotent d-pawn. The rest is a witness to Scrper's agonizing efforts at counterattack, ending up in a rook trap.

26 h3 &gh6 27 &xh6 &xh6 28 &c2 &d6 29 &h4 &xd3 30 &xd3 &xd3 31 &xd3 &xd3 32 &xh5 b6

33 g4 &f7 34 &f5 &d6 35 &h5 g6! 36 &h4 &f7! 0-1

4) Anti-&b4 systems: Introduction to Four Knights 4 e3

Game 4
Goldin – Yakovich
Moscow 1992

1 c4 e5 2 &c3 &f6 3 &f3

A trickier move-order is 3 e3, in order to meet 3...&b4 by 4 &ge2. I think that in this case Black's best is the non-committal 3...&c6, maintaining the option of transposing to the main variation after 4 &f3 &b4. On other moves Black should, in general, follow Bagirov's advice and fianchetto his king's bishop. For example:

a) 4 d3 g6! is equal.

b) 4 &c2 g6 5 a3 &g7 6 b4 0-0 and now:

b1) 7 &b2 &e8 8 b5 &a5 9 &f3 c6 and here:

b11) After 10 d4, 10...exd4!? 11 &xd4 d5 is unclear, while 10...c4 11 &d2 d5 is assessed as ∓ by Ljubojević, but I'm not sure about this evaluation as the knight might end up out of play after 12 c5.

b12) 10 &e2 d5 11 cxd5 cxd5 12 d4 e4 13 &e5 &d7! 14 &xd7 (but not 14 &xd5? &xe5 15 &c7 &d3+ 16 &xd3 exd3 17 &c3 d2+! –+; 14 &xf7!? &xf7 15 &xd5 &b6 16 &c7 &f5 ∓ Ljubojević) 14...&xd7 15 &a4 b6 16 &a2 &b7 17 &c3 &c4 18

♕b3 a6 ∓ Miles-Ljubojević, Linares 1985.

b2) 7 ♘f3 e4 8 ♘g5 ♖e8 9 ♗b2 d6 and now *(D)*:

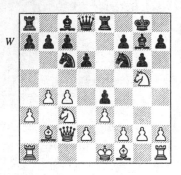

b21) 10 b5 ♘a5 (10...♘b8!?) 11 f3 exf3 12 ♘xf3 is unclear according to Karpov.

b22) 10 h4?! ♗f5 11 ♘e2 h6 12 ♘h3 a5 was again slightly better for Black in Sunye Neto-Karpov, Amsterdam 1985.

c) 4 ♘ge2 d5!? 5 cxd5 ♘xd5 6 ♘xd5 ♕xd5 7 ♘c3 ♕d8 8 ♗e2 ♗e6 9 0-0 ♗e7 10 a3 a5 11 d3 0-0 12 b3 ♕d7 13 ♗b2 ♖fd8 14 ♕c2 f6 15 ♖fd1 ♗f8 16 ♘e4 ♕f7 17 ♘d2 was unclear in Ivanchuk-Kamsky, Tilburg 1992.

d) 4 a3 g6 5 b4 (5 ♘f3 transposes to the 4 a3 line of the Four Knights, examined below, while White should probably avoid 5 d4 exd4 6 exd4 ♗g7 7 d5 ♘e7 8 ♗e2 d6 9 ♗f4 0-0 10 h3 ♖e8 11 ♘f3 ♘f5 12 0-0 ♘e4 13 ♘xe4 ♖xe4 14 ♗g5 ♗f6 15 ♗d3 ♖e8 ∓ Conquest-Howell, Oakham 1994) 5...♗g7 6 ♗b2 0-0 7 d3 d5 8 cxd5 ♘xd5 9 ♘ge2 ♘b6 10 g3? (10 ♘c1) 10...♗f5 11 c4 ♗g4 12 ♗g2 a5

13 f3? (13 b5 ♘d4, with initiative for Black, was the lesser evil) 13...axb4! 14 fxg4 bxc3 15 ♘xc3 ♕d7 16 0-0 ♖ad8 17 ♘d5 ♘xd5 18 exd5 ♘e7 19 ♖e1 ♘xd5 20 ♗xe5 ♘c3! 0-1 was Rivas-Anand, Madrid 1993.

3...♘c6 4 e3

Besides 4 g3 this is the most popular continuation in the Four Knights System. White intends simple development followed by the advance d4, a plan which should offer him a slight edge if Black reacts with the solid but passive 4...♗e7.

4 a3!? is an important alternative, a useful waiting move, with an additional point in preventing ....♗b4 lines. After the most logical reply, 4...g6, White's game is very flexible so I suggest that readers take a good look at the following examples *(D)*:

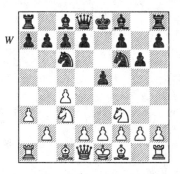

a) 5 e3 ♗g7 6 ♗e2 0-0 7 0-0 ♖e8 8 ♕c2 gives rise to a position similar to the ones arising in the variation 4 d3 ♗b4 5 ♗d2. Black has won several tempi over these lines but in view of the closed nature of the position this difference does not show too much. I can only claim that

Black is at least equal here, a point convincingly verified by the following games:

a1) 8...d6 9 d3 &f5 10 ♘d2 a6 11 ♖b1 (11 b4 e4 12 dxe4 ♘xe4 13 ♘dxe4 &xc4 with counterplay for Black) 11...h5 12 b4 ♘h7 13 ♘d5 (13 a4 a5!?) 13...&e6 14 a4 ♘b8! 15 b5 axb5 16 axb5 c6 17 bxc6 bxc6 was unclear in M.Gurevich-Karpov, Hilversum 1993.

a2) 8...a5 9 d3 d6 10 h3 h6 11 ♖b1 e4!? (a recurring tactical theme in this variation; if White wanted to prevent 11...e4 he should play 11 ♘d2, but then Black might strive for ...d5 by 11...&e6) 12 dxe4 ♘xe4 13 ♘xe4 ♖xe4 14 b3 ♖e8 15 &b2 &f5 16 &d3 &xd3 and here a draw was agreed in the game Illescas-Dorfman, Logroño 1991.

b) 5 b4 d6 6 &b2 &g7 7 e3 0-0 *(D)* and then:

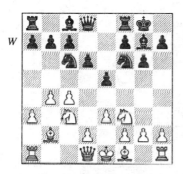

b1) 8 d3 ♖e8 9 &e2 (9 ♘d2?! ♘e7 10 &e2 c6 11 0-0 d5 12 b5 d4 ∓ Ree-Smyslov, Amsterdam Donner mem 1994) 9...e4!? 10 ♘xe4 ♘xe4 11 &xg7 ♘xf2 12 ♔xf2 ♔xg7 13 d4 (otherwise Black plays ...♘e5 with a

satisfactory game) 13...♘e7! 14 e4 f5 with good counterplay.

b2) 8 b5 ♘e7!? (8...♘b8 9 &e2 e4 10 ♘d4 c5 11 bxc6 ♘xc6 12 ♘xc6 bxc6 13 0-0, Vaganian-Eingorn, USSR Ch 1989, 13...♖b8! = Vaganian) 9 &e2 e4 10 ♘d4 c5 11 ♘b3?! (11 bxc6 =) 11...b6 12 ♕c2 &b7 13 0-0 ♘f5 14 a4 ♘h4 15 a5 ♖b8 16 ♖fd1 ♘f3+! led to a strong attack for Black in the game Santos-P.Schlosser, Clichy 1993.

c) 5 d4!? (this is an interesting recent idea) 5...exd4 6 ♘xd4 &g7 7 ♘xc6 bxc6 8 g3 and now:

c1) 8...d5? 9 &g2 &e6 10 ♕a4! and, surprisingly, Black is already in trouble as 10...&d7 can be met strongly by 11 ♕a5!.

c2) 8...♕e7?! 9 &g2 ♘g4 10 0-0 ♘e5 11 ♕a4 ♕c5 12 &f4! 0-0 (and not 12...♕xc4?? 13 &xe5 ♕xa4 14 &xg7! which leads to a disaster for Black) 13 b3 ±.

c3) 8...0-0 9 &g2 ♖b8 10 0-0 (10 ♕a4!? needs testing; Black may then react by 10...d5 with unclear consequences) 10...c5 11 ♕a4 d6! (this is an improvement over 11...a6 12 ♖b1 d6 13 b4 which was very slightly better for White in G.Horvath-Tolnai, Budapest 1995) 12 ♕xa7 &e6! gives Black excellent Benko Gambit-style positional compensation.

d) 5 g3 d5!? 6 cxd5 ♘xd5 7 &g2 ♘xc3 (or 7...♘de7!? Tukmakov) 8 bxc3 &g7 9 0-0 0-0 10 ♕c2 is Korchnoi-Tukmakov, Groningen 1993. Tukmakov now suggests 10...♖b8 with the idea of playing ...b6, followed by ...♘a5 and ...c5, enhancing

Black's central control. This plan seems to yield an even game, e.g. 11 d3 (11 ♖d1 e4!? is very interesting) 11...d6 12 ♖d1 ♕e8!? 13 d4 (13 a4 ♘a5 and 14...c5) 13...exd4 14 cxd4 ♗f5 15 ♕a2 ♗e4 with good fighting chances.

4...♗b4!

Reaching a reversed 3 ♗b5 Sicilian with a tempo less. Nevertheless Black has good chances for a complicated struggle here as he develops fast and in many cases inflicts damage on the opponent's pawn formation.

5 ♘d5!?

This is the most common alternative to 5 ♕c2, which is the subject of discussion in our next two illustrative games. Less respected continuations include:

a) 5 d3?! (this cannot be good) 5...e4 6 dxe4 ♘xe4 7 ♕c2 ♗xc3+ 8 bxc3 ♕e7 9 ♗e2 (9 ♘d2 ♘c5 {9...♘xd2!?} 10 ♘b3 d6 11 ♗e2 ♗e6 12 0-0 planning e4 gives equal play according to Ambrož, but I find it hard to believe this evaluation) 9...d6 10 ♘d4 0-0 11 0-0 f5 12 f3 ♘c5 ∓ Xu Jun-P.Nikolić, Biel IZ 1993.

b) 5 d4 exd4 6 ♘xd4 0-0 7 ♗e2 ♘e4 8 ♕c2 ♖e8 9 0-0 ♘xc3!? (the normal recapture, 9...♗xc3, is also playable but not as convincing as in the above-mentioned game) 10 bxc3 ♗c5 11 ♖d1 ♕f6 12 ♘b5 ♕d8 13 ♗a3? (White should have gone for the repetition of moves by 13 ♘d4, although I'm not certain whether Vaganian would have acquiesced

to it) 13...♗xa3 14 ♘xa3 ♕e7 and White had no compensation for his weaknesses in S.Garcia-Vaganian, Hastings 1974/5.

c) 5 ♗e2 e4 6 ♘d4 0-0 7 0-0 ♖e8 8 f3?! (thematic in analogous positions, but here it does not turn out well; the alternative 8 d3 is also uninspiring after 8...♗xc3 9 bxc3 exd3 10 ♗xd3 ♘e5 11 ♗e2 d6 12 f3 b6 so perhaps White should investigate 8 a3!?) 8...d5! 9 ♘xc6 bxc6 10 ♕a4 a5 11 a3 ♗d6 12 b4 exf3 13 ♗xf3 ♘g4! (the start of a remarkable combination) 14 ♗xg4 ♗xg4 15 c5 ♗e5 16 d4 axb4 17 ♕xb4 ♗xh2+! 18 ♔xh2 ♕h4+ 19 ♔g1 ♖eb8 20 ♘xd5 ♖xb4 21 ♘xb4 ♗e2 22 ♖f2 ♗b5 and White did not have enough for the queen in Larsen-C.Hansen, Odense 1988.

d) 5 ♕b3!? is an old idea of Korchnoi's that was recently revived *(D)*:

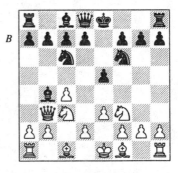

d1) 5...a5 6 ♗e2 0-0 7 0-0 ♖e8 8 d3 d6 9 ♕c2 ♗g4 10 b3 occurred in the original game, Korchnoi-Lehmann, Palma de Mallorca 1968, and now Black should have played

10...♗xc3 11 ♕xc3 e4 12 dxe4 ♘xe4
13 ♕c2 a4 with good counterplay.

d2) 5...e4!? seems more in the
spirit of Black's chosen variation:

d21) 6 ♘g5 ♗xc3! (this looks
better than Savon's recommendation
6...♕e7 7 ♘d5 ♘xd5 8 cxd5 ♘a5 9
♕a4 ♕xg5 10 ♕xb4 ♕xd5 as White
then has 11 ♕c3! with excellent
chances, e.g. 11...0-0?! 12 b4! ♘c6
13 ♗b2 with a strong attack) 7 ♕xc3
d5!? ∓.

d22) 6 ♘e5?! ♘xe5 7 ♕xb4 d6 8
♕a4+ c6 9 h3 0-0 10 ♕c2? ♗f5 11
f4 ♘d3+ 12 ♗xd3 exd3 13 ♕d1 d5 ∓
Banas-Savon, Trnava 1989.

d23) 6 ♘d4! is the only move to
create some problems:

d231) 6...♗c5 seems plausible,
but after 7 ♘f5! 0-0 8 ♘g3 ♖e8 9 d3
exd3 10 ♗xd3 White is slightly better.

d232) 6...♘xd4 also seems inferior: 7 exd4 a5 8 a3 ♗xc3 (= Savon)
9 dxc3 when White has an edge
thanks to his pair of bishops.

d233) 6...♕e7!? 7 ♘db5! (7 ♘f5
♕e5 8 ♘xg7+? ♔f8 9 ♘d5 ♗c7 −+;
7 ♘d5 ♘xd4! 8 ♘xf6+ ♕xf6 9 exd4
♗e7 =) 7...♗a5 8 ♘d5 ♕e5 9 ♕a3!!
♘xd5 (9...a6 10 ♘d4 ♘xd5 11
♘xc6 dxc6 12 ♕xa5 b6 13 ♕a4 ±)
10 cxd5 a6! (10...♕xd5?? 11 ♕xa5!
+−) 11 ♘c3! ♗xc3 12 ♕xc3 ♕xd5
13 ♕xg7 ♖f8 14 ♗e2 d6 with counterplay.

5...e4! 6 ♘g1

The alternative move, 6 ♘xb4, is
weaker because it lets Black generate play in the centre while White is
still undeveloped. After 6...♘xb4

White has tried the following continuations *(D)*:

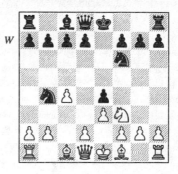

a) 7 ♘g5?! h6 (7...d5?! 8 ♕b3!) 8
♘h3 d5 9 ♕a4+ ♘c6 10 cxd5 ♕xd5
11 ♘f4 ♕d6 12 b3 (12 d3 ♕b4+ is
good for Black) 12...0-0 13 ♗a3 ♕c5
14 ♖c1 ♖d8 (Sunye Neto-C.Hansen,
Thessaloniki OL 1984) 15 ♗b5 (15
♗e2? g5 16 ♘h3 ♖d5 −+) 15...♗d7
∓. In the game White went quickly
downhill after 15 ♕b5?! ♘d5 16
♕c5 ♗f5 17 ♘xd5 (17 ♘e2!? was
the only chance) 17...♖xd5 18 ♕c2
♖ad8 19 ♗b2 ♕d6 20 ♗c3 b5!.

b) 7 ♘d4 c5 8 ♘b5 (8 ♘b3?! d6
9 d4 ♗g4 10 ♕d2 a5 11 a3 ♘c6 12
dxc5 dxc5 13 h3 ♕b6 14 hxg4 ♕xb3
15 ♗e2 ♖d8 was clearly better for
Black in G.Garcia-Knaak, Leipzig
1973) 8...d5 9 cxd5 0-0 10 a3 ♘d3+
11 ♗xd3 exd3 12 b3 (relatively best;
after 12 0-0 ♘xd5 13 b4?! ♗d7 14
♘c3 ♘xc3 15 dxc3 c4 16 e4 ♗c6 17
f3 f5 18 exf5 ♕b6+ 19 ♔h1 ♖ae8
Black had a strong initiative in the
game Granda-Eingorn, Zagreb IZ
1987) 12...♕xd5 13 0-0 g5 14 f3
♗d7 15 ♘c3 h5 ∓ Möhring-Knaak,
E.Germany 1973.

6...0-0 7 a3

The main line. The alternatives are most likely to transpose, for example 7 ♘e2 ♘xd5 8 cxd5 ♘e5 9 ♘g3 f5 10 a3 ♗d6 or 7 ♕c2 (this was the actual move-order of the present game) 7...♖e8 8 ♘e2 ♗d6 9 a3 b5!. In the last variation White may try 9 ♘ec3!? but Black has an adequate reply in 9...♘b4!, with equal chances.

7...♗d6 8 ♕c2

This move has superseded other continuations in tournament practice over the past few years, only to end up with a dismal score. In fact, the alternatives seem better:

a) 8 d3 is a solid response. In my opinion it is the best choice for White as he should already be looking for ways to equalize!

a1) 8...exd3 9 ♗xd3 ♘e5 10 ♗e2 c6 11 ♘c3?! (11 ♘xf6+ ♕xf6 12 ♕d4 is unclear according to Timman) 11...♗c7 12 ♘f3 d5 13 cxd5 cxd5 14 0-0 a6 15 ♘d4 ♕d6 16 g3 ♗h3 17 ♖e1 ♖ac8 18 ♗d2 (Petrosian-Timman, Nikšić 1983) 18...h5! and Black has good attacking chances.

b) 8 ♘e2 ♘xd5 9 cxd5 ♘e5 leads to a new parting of the ways:

b1) 10 ♘c3 f5 and now White should opt for 11 d3 ♕h4!? 12 g3 ♕e7 13 ♗e2, and although this is probably a little better for Black, the position is rather murky. Instead 11 d4?!, as played in the game Bischoff-Wirthensohn, Switzerland 1992, appears inferior in view of 11...♘g4! (11...exd3 12 ♗xd3 ♘xd3+ 13 ♕xd3 ♗e5 14 ♗d2 = was the meek game

continuation) 12 ♗e2 (12 h3? ♕h4!; 12 ♘xe4 ♘xe3 ∓) 12...♘f6 (planning ...b6 followed by ...♗b7 putting pressure on d5) 13 h3 b6 14 g4 ♗b7 15 ♕b3 fxg4 16 hxg4 h6 17 ♗d2 ♕e8! ∓.

b2) 10 ♘g3 (this is better than 10 ♘c3 because the white knight is needed on the kingside) 10...f5 11 d3 ♕h4!? (it is always thematic to put the queen on this square, but nevertheless 11...♘xd3+ 12 ♗xd3 exd3 13 ♕xd3 ♕f6 14 0-0, Agdestein-Hjartarson, Östersund Z 1992, 14...b6!? with ...a5 to follow also leads to interesting play) 12 dxe4 fxe4 13 ♗e2 ♘d3+ 14 ♗xd3 exd3 and here *(D)*:

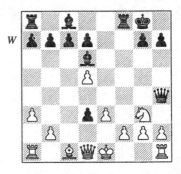

b21) 15 f4? b6 16 ♕xd3 a5 17 ♗d2? (17 0-0 ♗a6 18 ♕c2 ♗xf1 19 ♘xf1 was the lesser evil) 17...♗a6 18 ♕c2 ♕g4! 19 ♕d1 ♖xf4! −+ Seirawan-Sosonko, Tilburg 1983.

b22) 15 ♕xd3 ♗xg3 16 fxg3 ♕e7 gave Black compensation in Sokolin-Yakovich, Biel 1992. Black has other plausible queen moves as well.

8...♖e8 9 ♘e2 b5!

This fine move was invented by Romanishin. Apart from acceptance of the sacrifice, which is the subject of our featured game, White has unsuccessfully tried to ignore the pawn and further his development:

a) 10 ♘g3 bxc4 11 ♗xc4 ♗b7 12 b4 (12 ♘xf6+?! ♕xf6 13 ♘xe4? ♕g6+) 12...♘e5 13 ♘xf6+ ♕xf6 14 ♗b2 ♕g6 15 ♗e2 ♘d3+ 16 ♗xd3 exd3 17 ♕c4 a5! 18 0-0 ♕g5 19 ♗c3 axb4 20 axb4 ♕d5 21 ♕xd5 ♗xd5 22 f3 f6 23 ♖a5 c6 24 ♘f5 ♗f8 25 ♔f2 ♖ab8 26 ♖a7 ♖ed8 ∓ Adorjan-Romanishin, Riga IZ 1979.

b) 10 ♘ec3 bxc4 11 ♗xc4 ♗b7 12 b3 ♘xd5 13 ♗xd5 ♕g5 14 ♗b2 (14 ♗xe4? ♘d4 15 exd4 ♗xe4 16 ♘xe4 ♕xg2 −+) 14...♘d4! 15 exd4 ♗xd5 ∓ Rechlis-Soffer, Tel Aviv 1994.

10 ♘xf6+ ♕xf6 11 cxb5

Trying to keep the position closed by 11 c5 would be of no avail because Black's advantage in development is the key to the position. After 11...♗e5 12 ♘g3 (12 ♕xe4 d5! 13 cxd6 ♗d7 14 d4 ♗xd6 15 ♕d3 b4! is Gelfand's analysis) 12...♗b7 and now 13 ♗e2 ♗xg3 14 hxg3 ♘e5 gave Black a strong attack in the game Salov-Gelfand, Linares 1992. Instead 13 ♗xb5 ♗xg3 14 hxg3 ♘e5 (planning ...♗a6) 15 0-0 ♕h6 threatens ...♘g4 or ...♘f3+, while 13 ♘xe4!? ♕g6 looks extremely dangerous but it was probably a better chance for White than the game continuation.

11...♘e5 12 ♘g3

12 ♕xe4 has been unanimously condemned on account of 12...♗b7!. It is true that after 13 ♕c2 ♘g4! White seems unable to fend off the

attack but the incredible 13 ♕d4!?, centralizing the queen in spite of potential knight forks, may render the issue unclear. I can see good compensation for Black after, for instance, 13...a6!? 14 f4 ♕h4+ 15 ♘g3 ♘g4, but nothing like a forced win.

12...♗b7 *(D)*

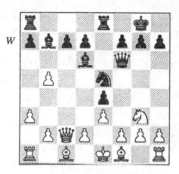

Yakovich has orchestrated his pieces in a very harmonious way. At the same time the pawn on c4 is severely cramping White's movements and encouraging several sacrificial motifs. These advantages seem to offer Black more than enough compensation for the pawn.

13 ♗e2

Now it's too late to take on c4: 13 ♘xe4? ♕g6 14 d3 (14 f3 ♘xf3+! 15 gxf3 ♖xe4! is a nice variation) 14...♘xd3+ 15 ♗xd3 ♕xg2 leaves Black with a clear plus.

13...♕h4!

Suppressing the white kingside even more and creating dual threats of ...♘d3+ and ...♘f3+. For example: 14 b4? ♘d3+! 15 ♗xd3 exd3 16 ♕xd3 ♗e5! 17 ♖b1 ♗xg2 −+ or 14 0-0? ♘f3+! −+ (Yakovich). Faced with this difficult situation Goldin finds a clever defence.

14 ♕a4!?

White wants to make use of an X-ray along the fourth rank to block the opponent's attack. Yakovich is alert to the situation and finds a good counterstroke.

14...a6! ∓

This move opens an offensive on all fronts, and ensures that White's king will not try to escape on the queenside.

15 f4

The alternatives offer White no relief either. Yakovich analyses:

a) 15 bxa6 ♗xa6! 16 ♗xa6 ♘d3+ 17 ♔e2 ♗xg3! 18 fxg3 ♕g4+ 19 ♔f1 ♕f5+ (I think that 19...♖xa6 is a simpler and nicer conclusion) 20 ♔e2 ♕f2+ 21 ♔d1 ♕xg2 22 ♖e1 ♕f3+ and Black wins.

b) 15 d4 axb5 16 ♕xb5 ♗a6 17 ♕b3 (17 ♕xa6 ♖xa6 18 dxe5 ♗b4+ wins) 17...♘d3+ is very good for Black.

15...axb5 16 ♕d4 *(D)*

On 16 ♕xb5 Black plays 16...♗c6! 17 ♕b3 ♘f3+! 18 ♔f2 (18 ♔d1?? loses to 18...♗a4) 18...♘xh2 with a continuing attack. The passive move 16 ♕d1 is even worse since after 16...♘d3+ 17 ♗xd3 exd3 White is totally suffocated.

16...♘f3+! 17 gxf3 exf3 18 ♗xf3

The best practical chance. After 18 ♗xb5 ♗xf4:

a) 19 ♔f1 ♕h3+ wins.

b) 19 0-0 ♗xg3 (19...♕h3? 20 ♖xf3! ♗xf3 21 ♗f1) 20 ♕xh4 ♗xh4 21 ♗xd7 ♖a5!.

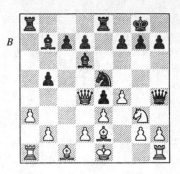

c) 19 ♔d1 and now Black wins easily by 19...♗xg3 20 ♕xh4 ♗xh4 21 ♗xd7 f2 22 ♖f1 ♗f3+ 23 ♔c2 ♗e2.

18...♗xf3 19 0-0

Goldin has averted immediate disaster but his weakness on the long diagonal doesn't promise him a bright future. With his next move Yakovich avoids White's last trap and takes over full control of the game.

19...♕g4!

But not 19...♗c6? 20 ♕xg7+! ♔xg7 21 ♘f5+ and the tables have been turned. The text prepares an advance of the h-pawn to which there is no defence.

20 b4 ♗e7 21 ♕d3 ♗f6 22 ♖a2 h5! 23 ♕xb5

Despair. On 23 ♕f5 Yakovich offers the following beautiful line: 23...♕xf5 24 ♘xf5 ♗d5 25 ♖c2 ♗e4 26 ♖c5 d6 27 ♖xb5 c6 and White loses a piece. But now the end is also not far away.

23...h4 24 ♖xf3 ♕xf3 25 ♘f1 ♖e6!

Also good is 25...h3 26 d4 ♕g4+ 27 ♘g3 ♗xd4 but the text is more elegant.

26 d3 ♗b2! 27 f5 ♖e5 28 ♕c4 ♖xf5 0-1

An important game for the evaluation of the 5 ♘d5 variation.

5) Four Knights 4 e3/ 5 ♕c2: Introduction

Game 5
Ehlvest – Kasparov
Reykjavik 1988

1 c4 ♘f6 2 ♘c3 e5 3 ♘f3 ♘c6 4 e3 ♗b4 5 ♕c2

The most fashionable variation. White avoids the doubling of his pawns and at the same time develops his queen to what is probably the best square for her in this opening. In fact White has not given up the ♘d5 idea, but simply maintains the option to realize it a move later without allowing his opponent the advance ...e4.

5...0-0 6 d3!?

From time to time White deviates from the universally recommended 6 ♘d5, the text move being his most usual choice. Other 6th move divergences have failed to achieve anything tangible:

a) 6 a3 ♗xc3 7 ♕xc3 ♖e8 8 d3 d5 9 cxd5 ♕xd5! 10 ♗e2 (for 10 e4 see Ljubojević-Illescas in the note to White's 7th move below) 10...e4 11 dxe4 ♘xe4 12 ♕c4 ♕f5 13 0-0 (13 ♗d3? ♘e5! ∓) 13...♗e6 14 ♕c2 ♗d5 and Black had the initiative in Bilecki-Smyslov, Havana 1964. Smyslov's opening play looks very strong.

It is hard to find improvements for White here.

b) 6 ♗d3 ♗xc3 7 dxc3 d6 8 0-0 ♕e7 9 ♘d2 (Korchnoi-Szabo, Amsterdam 1972) and now 9...h6!? with the idea ...♘d7-c5 seems to yield an unclear position. Korchnoi himself suggested 9...g6 as an alternative.

c) 6 ♗e2 ♖e8 7 0-0 is perhaps the most intriguing continuation available to White. After 7...e4 (D):

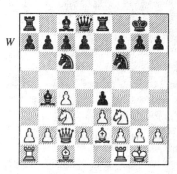

c1) 8 ♘d4?! ♘xd4 9 exd4 d5 10 cxd5 ♗f5 11 d3 (after 11 ♕b3 ♗d6 Black has good attacking chances) 11...exd3 12 ♗xd3 ♗xd3 13 ♕xd3 ♘xd5 14 ♕c4 ♗xc3 15 bxc3 b5! 16 ♕d3 ♕d7 17 a4 ♕c6! 18 ♗d2 ♕c4! was clearly better for Black in Bobotsov-Portisch, Siegen OL 1970.

c2) 8 ♘e1 ♗xc3 9 bxc3 d5 10 f3 (10 cxd5 ♕xd5 is also unclear) 10...dxc4! (10...d4 11 fxe4 ♘xe4 12 ♗d3!?) 11 ♗xc4 ♗f5 12 a4 ♘e5 13 ♗a2 ♕d7 14 ♗b1! ♖ad8 with an unclear game in Suba-Motwani, London 1989.

6...♖e8 7 ♗d2

In Ljubojević-Illescas, Groningen 1993, White attempted to improve on Bilecki-Smyslov above, by playing 7 a3 ♗xc3+ 8 ♕xc3 d5 9 cxd5 ♕xd5 (now we have transposed to that game) 10 e4!?. However, his experiment turned out to be extremely risky after 10...♕d6 11 ♗e3 ♗g4 12 ♘d2 ♘d4! (12...♖ad8 13 ♘c4 ±) 13 ♘c4 ♕c6 14 f3?! (Illescas suggested that 14 h3! would have been unclear) 14...♗e6 15 ♗xd4 exd4 16 ♕xd4 ♖ad8 17 ♕c3 ♗xc4 18 ♕xc4 ♕b6 19 ♕b4 ♕e3+ 20 ♔d1 ♘d7 when he was struggling to avoid immediate defeat in his miserably undeveloped state. Although Ljubojević failed to make the most of his chances I don't expect to see more of this line in the near future.

7...♗xc3!?

Black could have continued in the spirit of the 4 d3 line by 7...♗f8, followed by ...d6, ...♗g7, etc. However, the position of the queen on c2 suggests that an opening of the centre by ...d5 makes sense as White would have to lose time in order to meet the combined attack on his d-pawn by ...♗f5 and ...♘b4 when still trying to complete his development. Thus 7...♗xc3!? is the prelude to dynamic play with Black accelerating the development of his forces and White obtaining the pair of bishops and a central pawn preponderance.

8 ♗xc3 d5 9 cxd5 ♘xd5 10 ♗e2 ♗f5! *(D)*

The tactical justification of the black strategy. Although the move existed prior to this game it was considered inferior in view of 11 e4 ♘xc3 12 bxc3 ♗g4 13 0-0 ♘a5 14

♘e1! ♗xe2 15 ♕xe2 ♕d6 16 ♘c2 ♖ad8 17 ♖fd1 ♕c5 18 ♘e3!, which gave White the advantage in Taimanov-G.Kuzmin, Moscow 1974.

11 ♖d1

Ehlvest smells a rat and abstains from the theoretical 11 e4. Small wonder! After 11 e4?! Kasparov intended the stunning improvement 11...♘f4!! leading to a position with many tactical chances for Black. The main line runs 12 exf5 ♘d4 13 ♗xd4 exd4 14 ♘g1 ♕d5 15 0-0-0 ♕xa2 16 ♗f3 (after 16 g3 ♕a1+ 17 ♔d2 ♕a5+ 18 ♔c1, 18...♕a1+ leads to a draw by perpetual but obviously Black is not forced to go for it; Kasparov suggests 18...♘d5 as an interesting way to continue the attack) 16...♕a1+! 17 ♕b1 ♕a5 and despite being a piece up White is under tremendous pressure.

The text move is a solid way to take the sting out of ...♘b4 or ...e4, but has the disadvantage of committing the rook too early. No doubt, White would have preferred to post this rook on the c-file or even keep it on a1 for a while as the a-pawn is vulnerable in some variations. Thus, Kasparov's plan has been successful from the strategic point of view as it has managed to bring about a disharmony in White's ranks.

11...a5 12 0-0 ♕e7 13 a3

Preparing e4, since the immediate 13 e4 is weak in view of 13...♘db4 14 ♕b1 ♗g4.

13...a4

Grasping the opportunity to step up his control of the light squares. Black is still not afraid of 14 e4 as it would be met by 14...♘xc3 15 bxc3 ♗e6 (∓ Kasparov) pinpointing the weaknesses on White's queenside.

14 ♗e1?!

The start of an artificial manoeuvre. It is clear that White wants to bring his knight to d2 to prevent ...e4 once and for all, but the means he is using can hardly be recommended. The immediate 14 ♘d2 is also weak in view of the line 14...♘xc3 15 ♕xc3 ♘d4! but the preparatory 14 ♖fe1!? (Kasparov) seems to yield an even game. White's pieces are a bit congested but Black seems to have no clear plan to augment the pressure.

14...♗g6!

A tenacious way to keep up the pressure. Most players would have been carried away by 14...e4 which in fact is perfectly playable but does not really let White go wrong. Kasparov is obviously not willing to simplify and draw, even though he's playing one of the world's strongest players with the black pieces.

15 ♕c4?!

A move not bad in itself but coupled with the next one it spells disaster. It is apparent that the Estonian overlooked or underestimated Kasparov's 16th move.

15...♖ed8 16 ♘d2? *(D)*

After this Ehlvest is in for a big surprise. He had to play instead 16 d4! ♘b6 17 ♕c3 e4 18 ♘d2 ♕g5 19 ♘c4 ♘d5 20 ♕c1 when 20...♖e8 is only slightly better for Black according to Kasparov.

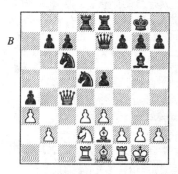

16...♘d4!

An excellent piece sacrifice, emphasizing the temporary lack of coordination among White's forces.

17 exd4 ♘f4 18 ♗f3 ♖xd4 19 ♕b5?!

Better was the continuation 19 ♕c3 ♖ad8! (19...♗xd3 20 g3 ♘e2+ 21 ♗xe2 ♗xe2 is also good for Black) 20 g3 ♖xd3 21 ♕h4 ♕xh4 22 axb4 ♖xf3 23 gxf4 ♖xf4 ∓ (Kasparov). After the text White goes under without a fight.

19...c6 20 ♗xc6

Not 20 ♕b6? because of the reply 20...♖a6.

20...bxc6 21 ♕xc6 ♕d8!

Kasparov considers 21...♖ad8 to be inaccurate due to 22 ♘f3 ♗e4 23 ♗b4!!, continuing 23...♕xb4 24 ♕xe4 ♖xe4 25 axb4 ♖xb4 with only a slight plus for Black, but I feel that the simple 23...♗xc6 24 ♗xe7 ♗xf3 25 gxf3 ♖8d5 should win. In any case, the move played is the most conclusive.

22 ♘f3 ♖d6 23 ♕b5 ♖d5 24 ♕b4 e4 25 ♗c3?

Losing a piece but his position was already hopeless in view of 25 ♘d2 ♕h4! 26 g3 (26 ♘xe4 ♘e2+ 27 ♔h1 ♕xh2+! 28 ♔xh2 ♖h5 mate) 26...♕h3 27 gxf4 ♖h5 with mate to follow.

25...♘e2+ 0-1

An impressive display of power from the World Champion.

6) Four Knights 4 e3/5 ♕c2: Main line

Game 6
G.Horvath – Sadler
Clichy 1993

1 c4 e5 2 ♘c3 ♘c6 3 ♘f3 ♘f6 4 e3 ♗b4 5 ♕c2 0-0 6 ♘d5!

The only continuation to pose Black some problems. The fight now assumes a sharp character because Black's kingside is most likely to be weakened but in return he gets fast development and counterplay in the centre.

6...♖e8 7 ♕f5!?

Normally moving the queen twice at such an early stage is bad, but in this case White's plan is tactically justified as Black cannot avoid the weakening of his pawn structure. Most alternatives result in positions of an amorphous nature where Black enjoys a good portion of space and chances to expand on the kingside:

a) 7 ♗e2? e4 ∓.

b) 7 a3 ♗f8 8 d3 should be met by 8...d6! = rather than 8...♘xd5?! 9 cxd5 ♘b8 10 d4 ±, Dorfman-Chabanon, Aix-les-Bains 1991.

c) 7 ♘g5 g6 should be an appropriate continuation for those who like to improvise, but as things stand Black's chances look bright. Witness the following cases *(D)*:

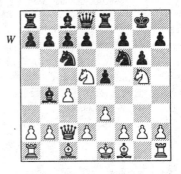

c1) 8 h4 ♗f8 9 a3 d6 10 b4 ♗g7 11 ♗b2 ♗f5 12 d3 ♘xd5 13 cxd5 ♘e7 14 ♗e2 h6 15 ♘f3 (Suba-Stefansson, Linares 1995) 15...♗d7!? 16 e4 c6 17 dxc6 ♘xc6 ∓.

c2) 8 ♘xb4!? ♘xb4 9 ♕b3 c5 10 a3 ♘c6 11 ♕c2? (11 d3! should be met by 11...a5!?, which is unclear; instaed after 11...d5?! 12 cxd5 ♘xd5 13 e4! the complications seem to favour White) h6 12 ♘e4 ♘xe4 13 ♕xe4 ♘d4! 14 ♕d3 d5 15 exd4

exd4+ 16 ♔d1 b5! 17 cxb5 ♗f5 led
to an overwhelming attack for Black
in the game Brinck-Claussen – Jak-
obsen, Stockholm 1971/2.

c3) 8 ♘xf6+ ♕xf6 9 ♘e4 ♕d8
10 a3 ♗f8 11 d3 ♗g7 12 ♗e2 ♘e7!?
13 0-0 d5 14 cxd5 ♘xd5 15 ♗d2 b6
16 b4 ♗b7 17 ♖ac1 ♕d7 18 ♖fd1
♖ac8 was unclear in Suba-Suetin,
Sochi 1977.

d) 7 ♗d3 is the only alternative
that has been employed at top level.
However, it looks rather artificial to
post the bishop on d3. After the universally adopted 7...g6 8 a3 (8 h4?!
♗f8 9 h5 ♘xd5 10 hxg6 ♘db4! 11
gxf7+ ♔xf7 12 ♖xh7+ ♔g8! –+
Karpov) 8...♗f8 Black has been getting very good positions:

d1) 9 ♖b1!? ♗g7 10 b4 d6 11 b5
♘d4 12 ♘xf6+ ♕xf6 13 ♘xd4 exd4
14 0-0 ♕h4 15 ♗b2 ♗d7 16 g3 ♕h5
17 ♗xd4 ♗h3 18 ♖fe1 ♕f3 19 ♗f1
♗xf1 20 ♖xf1 ♗xd4 21 exd4 ♕xa3
was equal in Ljubojević-Anand,
Monaco Amber (blindfold) 1993.

d2) 9 ♘xf6+ ♕xf6 10 ♗e4 d6 11
b3?! (11 b4 = would be similar to
Korchnoi-Nikolić below) 11...♘d8!
12 ♗b2 ♕e7 13 ♖c1 c6 14 ♕b1 ♗g7
15 0-0 ♗d7 (15...♗g4!?) 16 b4 f5 17
♗c2 ♘f7 18 ♘e1 c5 19 ♗c3 b6 20
♕b2 ♘g5 21 f3 ♗c6 22 ♗b3 ♘e6
23 ♘c2 ♕h4 was clumsy for White
in Ljubojević-Karpov, Linares 1993.

d3) 9 0-0 ♗g7 10 ♘xf6+ ♕xf6
11 ♗e4 ♕e7 12 b4 ♘d8 13 ♗b2 d6
14 d3?, Korchnoi-P.Nikolić, Amsterdam 1988, and now the surprising 14...d5 would have won a piece.

7...d6 8 ♘xf6+ gxf6 *(D)*

8...♕xf6 9 ♕xf6 gxf6 has also
been played but the move chosen is
more principled as White will have
to move his queen again. In any case
8...gxf6 complies with my policy to
offer interesting and complicated
lines whenever possible.

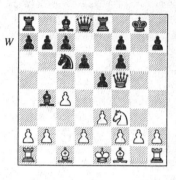

9 ♕h5

The only other serious possibility, namely 9 ♕c2, has been condemned by theory, rather unjustly.
After 9...e4 White has the following
continuations at his disposal:

a) 10 ♘h4 (the knight wants to
re-enter the fray via g2; Black must
react energetically) 10...f5 11 g3 d5
12 cxd5 and now:

a1) 12...♘e5?! was played in the
game Keene-Timman, Bad Lauter-
berg 1977, but it looks too hasty. After
13 ♗e2! (Timman's recommendation; the game continuation, 13 ♕b3?
♗c7 14 d4 exd3 15 ♗xd3 ♗xh4 16
gxh4 ♘f3+ 17 ♔d1 ♖e5, left Black
clearly better) 13...♕xd5 (Timman
suggests 13...c5!? as an improvement but I get the impression that
Black would be overreaching himself in trying to amend his previous

mistake) 14 ♕a4! Black has to play the awkward retreat 14...♘c6, which seriously compromises his chances.

a2) 12...♕xd5!. After this simple recapture Black may be even slightly better. It is important to develop quickly by ...♗e6 and then withdraw the other bishop to e7 in order to create the unpleasant threat ...♘b4.

b) 10 ♘g1!? d5 11 a3 (11 cxd5?! ♕xd5 12 a3 ♗d6 13 ♘e2 ♗f5 14 ♘c3 ♕e6 with an initiative for Black) 11...d4!? (11...♗f8 12 cxd5 ♕xd5 13 ♘e2 ♗f5 is unclear) 12 axb4 ♘xb4 13 ♕b3 c5 is proposed by Timman. His piece sacrifice is interesting, but in any case Black has safer ways to play the position.

9...d5 *(D)*

This is forced, in order to allow the stray bishop on b4 to join in the defence. At the same time Black opens up the centre to make use of his lead in development.

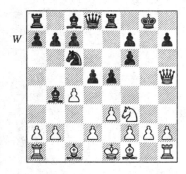

10 a3

10 ♗d3!? e4 11 cxd5 is a trickier move-order, hoping to entice Black into 11...exd3 12 dxc6 bxc6 13 b3!, when in comparison to the game continuation it's more difficult for Black to create counterplay on the queenside by pushing the a-pawn. However, after Bagirov's recommendation 11...♗f8!? White's most sensible move seems to be 12 a3 transposing to the main variation. The alternatives are risky: 12 ♗b5?! exf3 13 gxf3 and now rather than Bagirov's idea 13...♘d4, the reply 13...♖e5 seems even better; 12 ♗b1 ♘b4! ∓; 12 ♗xe4 ♖xe4 13 dxc6 ♕d3 is extremely dangerous for White as his king is stuck in the centre, but it deserves further investigation.

On the other hand, the older move 10 cxd5 is relatively harmless. After 10...♕xd5 11 ♗e2 ♗e6 12 0-0 (12 a3 ♗e7 13 d3 ♔h8 14 0-0 ♖g8 15 ♘e1 ♘a5 16 ♗d2 ♘b3 17 ♖d1 ♘xd2 18 ♖xd2 f5 was slightly better for Black in Timman-Portisch, Montreal 1979) 12...e4 13 ♕xd5 ♗xd5 14 ♘h4!? (14 ♘e1?! ♖ad8 15 d4 ♗xe1! 16 ♖xe1 ♘b4 led to insurmountable difficulties for White in the game Keene-Korchnoi, Montreux 1977) 14...♖ad8 15 f3 ♗e6 16 fxe4 ♗xd2 17 ♗b5! ♔g7 18 ♗xd2 ♖xd2 19 ♖f2 ♖d6 20 ♖c1 ♗d7 21 ♘f5+ ♗xf5 22 ♗xc6 bxc6 23 exf5 ♖xe3 24 ♖fc2 the ending was equal in Korchnoi-Karpov, Amsterdam 1987.

10...♗f8 11 ♗d3

Existing theory considers 11 d4!? to be more critical as it led to a beautiful win for White in Goodman-Nunn featured below. However, it appears that this view has been caused by this accidental loss by a strong player rather than to the move's objective merits. The following analysis should provide an antidote:

a) 11...exd4?! (this looks bad) 12 ♗d3 h6 13 0-0 ♘e5 14 ♘xe5 ♖xe5 and now instead of Bagirov's 15 ♕h4?! dxc4 16 exd4 (which can be met by 16...cxd3! 17 dxe5 d2 18 ♖d1 dxc1♕ 19 ♖axc1 ♕e8 with an unclear position) White should prefer 15 ♕f3! with good attacking chances in return for the pawn.

b) 11...e4 12 cxd5 ♘e7 is Bagirov's interesting recommendation. I think that Black has good chances in the ensuing struggle.

c) 11...♗e6! 12 ♗d3 e4 13 ♗c2 ♘e7! (unjustly criticized; 13...♗g7!? is also good) 14 ♘d2 f5 (planning ...♗g7 and ...c5) 15 cxd5 ♕xd5 16 f3 f4! (16...♕c6?? 17 ♘xe4!! ♕xc2 18 ♘f6+ ♔g7 19 e4! +− was the game Goodman-Nunn, England 1978) 17 ♘xe4 ♕xh5 18 ♘f6+ ♔h8 19 ♘xh5 fxe3 20 ♘f6 ♖ed8 21 ♗xe3 (21 ♘xh7 ♗h6 is unclear) 21...♗g7! (21 ♘f5? 22 ♗xf5 ♗xf5 23 g4! leaves Black struggling to draw) 22 ♘h5 (22 ♗g5?! h6 23 h4 ♖xd4; 22 ♘xh7?! f6! ∓) 22...♗xd4 −. Thus it seems that Black has good chances in this complicated variation.

11...e4 12 cxd5

Avoiding 12 ♗c2?! d4!, which leads to a strong initiative for Black.

12...exd3 13 dxc6 bxc6 14 b4!

Activating this bishop on the long diagonal as quickly as possible represents White's best chance for counterplay. 14 0-0 is inferior due to 14...♕d5!.

14...a5! *(D)*

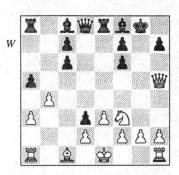

A rare picture in chess literature. We're just out of the opening and Black has no less than seven doubled or effectively isolated pawns. And yet, his position holds good prospects as all his pieces are tremendously active despite being still on their back rank!

15 ♗b2 axb4 16 ♕h4 ♗f5 17 axb4

On 17 ♗xf6 Ribli gives the continuation 17...♗e7 18 ♗xe7 ♕xe7 19 ♕xe7 ♖xe7 ∓.

17...♖xa1+ 18 ♗xa1 ♖e4 19 ♕xf6 ♕xf6 20 ♗xf6 ♗xb4 21 0-0? *(D)*

A bad mistake. Imperative was 21 ♘e5! preventing Black from driving away the powerfully placed bishop on f6. In that case chances would have remained balanced.

21...♖c6! 22 ♗b2 c5 23 ♖a1 f6 24 ♖a8+ ♔f7

Black is gradually taking over control of this endgame. With his king free to stroll he can now think about putting his pawn majority on the queenside to use.

25 h3?

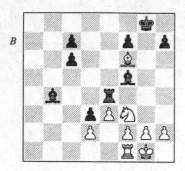

This accelerates White's downfall. By 25 ♖a7 (intending ♔f1-e1) he could have made a fight of it.

25...♗e4 26 ♖a7 ♖c6 27 ♗c1 ♗xf3

Removing this knight is the simplest way to victory. Without the aid of his king the incarcerated bishop on c1 cannot hope to face Black's dangerous pawns.

28 gxf3 c4 29 ♖a4 *(D)*

29 ♖a2 would have been also insufficient according to Ribli: 29...c3 30 dxc3 ♖xc3 31 ♗d2 ♖c2 32 ♖xc2 dxc2 33 ♗c1 ♔e6 34 ♔f1 ♔d5 35 ♔e2 ♔c4 and Black wins easily. The text move allows the young Englishman to finish the game with a small combination.

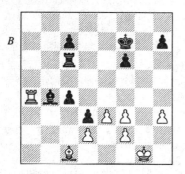

29...♗xd2! 30 ♗xd2 c3 31 ♗xc3 ♖xc3 32 ♖d4 c5 33 ♖d5 c4 34 ♔f1 ♖c1+ 0-1

7) Systems with 2 g3: White delays ♘c3

Game 7
Hertneck – M.Gurevich
Strasbourg 1994

1 c4 e5 2 g3!?

This move-order has many adherents. By playing 2 g3 White delays the development of his queen's knight, maintaining maximum flexibility. The knight might be developed on d2, giving White some extra possibilities after a potential opening of the c-file.

2...♘f6 3 ♗g2 d5

In the 4 d3 line of the Four Knights Variation I was reluctant to suggest a transposition to a Scheveningen with colours reversed because I considered it rather unnecessary to indulge in an elaborate theoretical treatise when a simpler alternative offered reasonable fighting chances. My attitude to g3 systems is based, however, on a less subconscious background: I believe that in these systems Black has no serious attacking chances whatsoever and should as a consequence focus his attention on the centre and queenside. Thus it seems logical to opt for ...d5, transposing to a reversed Dragon where the struggle revolves around positional matters, a fact often rendering

White's extra tempo relatively insignificant.

4 cxd5 ♘xd5 5 ♘f3 ♘c6 6 0-0 ♘b6!?

Practice indicates that White obtains an edge after 6...♗e7 7 d4! but I'm not so sure about it. In any case the text invites transposition to the Romanishin System (1 c4 e5 2 ♘c3 ♘f6 3 ♘f3 ♘c6 4 g3 d5 5 cxd5 ♘xd5 6 ♗g2 ♘b6 7 0-0 ♗e7) which is the backbone of our repertoire.

7 b3!?

White decides to fianchetto his queen's bishop to exert pressure on e5. A similar strategy could be initiated by 7 d3 ♗e7 8 a3 0-0 9 ♘bd2 (9 b4?! ♗f6! ∓) 9...a5 10 b3 when Black has the following choice *(D)*:

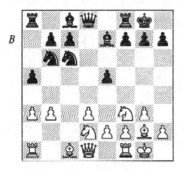

a) 10...♗e6 (the simplest route to equality) 11 ♗b2 f6 12 ♕c2 ♕d7 (12...♖f7 was successful in Speelman-Romanishin, Moscow 1985, which Black won in classical style: 13 ♖fd1 ♗f8 14 e3 ♗d5 15 ♖ac1 ♕e8 16 ♘c4 ♖d8 17 d4 a4 18 ♕b1 exd4 19 ♘xd4 ♗xg2 20 ♔xg2 ♘xd4 21 ♖xd4 ♖xd4 22 ♗xd4 ♘xc4 23 ♖xc4 c5! 24 ♗a1 axb3 25 ♕xb3 b5 26 ♖c3

c4 27 ♕b1 ♕c6+ 28 ♔g1 ♖d7 29 ♗b2 ♗c5 30 ♖c1 ♗xe3! 31 ♖e1 ♗d2 32 ♖e8+ ♔f7 33 ♖e2 ♗a5 34 ♖e3 ♗b6 35 ♖e2 ♕f3 36 ♕e1 h5 37 ♗c3 h4 38 gxh4 ♕g4+ 39 ♔f1 ♗c7 0-1; however, it is rather slow and by now it has been abandoned in favour of the more circumspect text move) 13 e3! (13 ♖fd1 ♖fd8 14 ♘c4 ♕e8! 15 ♘fd2 ♘d5 was excellent for Black in the game Dragomaretsky-Morozevich, Alushta 1993) 13...♖fd8 14 d4! exd4 15 ♘xd4 ♗d5 16 ♗xd5+ ♕xd5 17 ♘xc6 (17 ♖fd1 ♘xd4 18 ♗xd4 c5 intending ...♕d3 is unclear) 17...♕xc6 18 ♕xc6 bxc6 19 ♖fd1 a4! 20 b4 c5 21 bxc5 ♗xc5 and now:

a1) 22 ♖ac1?! ♖a5! 23 ♖c2 ♖b5 24 ♖a1 ♗e7 25 ♖a2 (Chernin-Smejkal, Altensteig 1991) and now Black should play 25...♖c5! ∓, as 25...c5 allows White an edge (Chernin).

a2) 22 ♔f1! ♖a5! 23 ♔e2 ♖b5 24 ♖a2 ♗e7 (with the idea ...♖e5-d5) 25 ♗d4!? (25 ♖c1? ♖xb2 ∓) 25...c5 26 ♗c3 g5!? to be followed by ...♔f7 and ...h5 is unclear.

b) 10...♖e8!? (a new plan devised by Romanishin) 11 ♗b2 ♗f8 12 ♖c1! (threatening ♖xc6; after 12 ♕c2?! ♗g4 13 e3 ♕d7 14 d4 exd4 15 ♘xd4 ♘xd4 16 ♗xd4 c5 Black was at least equal in Lalić-De Boer, Groningen 1992) 12...♘d4 results in a complicated position. White has the following choice:

b1) 13 e3 (this should cause Black no worries) 13...♘xf3+ 14 ♘xf3 f6 15 ♕c2 (15 d4 e4 16 ♘d2 f5 17 ♘c4 ♘d5 18 ♘e5 c6 =) 15...c5 16 ♘d2 a4

17 ♘c4 ♗e6 = Rotshtein-Gipslis, Minsk 1993.

b2) 13 ♘xe5!? introduces interesting play. After 13...♖xe5 14 e3 ♘xb3 15 ♘xb3!? (15 ♕xb3 was played in P.Schlosser-Romanishin, Altensteig 1992; then the natural 15...♗e6 would have left the situation totally unclear) 15...♖b5! 16 ♕c2 ♗d7!? (16...♘a4? 17 ♕c4 ±) 17 ♖a1!? (17 ♘d4 ♖c5) 17...♘a4 18 ♗c1 ♘c5 19 ♘d4 ♖b6 the odd-looking 20 a4!? (intending to answer 20...♖b4 or 20...♕e8 by 21 ♗a3!) produces an unclear position. Black's best seems the solid 20...♘a6, in order to exploit the newly created weakness on b4.

7...♗d6 8 ♗b2 0-0! *(D)*

The game's actual move-order was 8...♕e7 9 d3 0-0 but I consider it inferior because of 9 ♘c3!? when Black has to spend some time meeting meet the threat of ♘b5.

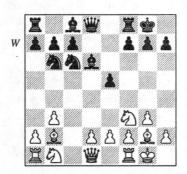

Gurevich's main objection to 8...0-0 is that White obtains a slight advantage after 9 d4 e4 10 ♘e5. True, but why is Black forced to react by 9...e4? After the correct 9...exd4 10 ♘xd4 ♗e5! it is White who has to start thinking about equalizing as both 11 ♗xc6 bxc6 and 11 e3 ♘xd4 12 ♗xd4 ♗xd4 13 exd4 c6 14 ♘c3 ♗e6 (Khramtsov-Nikolenko, Moscow 1990) look very promising for Black.

9 d3

9 ♘c3 can now be met by 9...♗g4 with an even game.

9...♕e7 10 ♘fd2?!

On 10 ♘c3 Black has a simple equalizing line in 10...♗a3 11 ♗xa3 ♕xa3 as 12 ♘b5 leads nowhere after 12...♕e7 (Gurevich). However, the text move makes an odd impression; I would prefer instead the natural 10 ♘bd2, with unclear play.

10...♗g4 11 ♘c3

Gurevich remarks that after 11 ♘e4 ♘d4 12 ♗xd4 exd4 13 ♘xd6 cxd6 Black has counterplay. This evaluation seems absurd at first glance as after 14 ♖e1 there is no pressure on e2 and White is threatening slowly to round up Black's weak pawn on d4, but closer inspection reveals a hidden tactical point on which Black's counterplay is based: 14...f5! 15 h3 (15 ♘d2 f4 16 ♘f3 ♘d5!? 17 ♘xd4 ♘e3 17 ♕d2 ♘xg2 18 ♔xg2 ♕e5 offers Black compensation) 15...f4! (15...♗h5?! 16 ♘d2 f4 17 g4 ±) and White has to weaken his king's position by 16 gxf4 as accepting the piece by 16 hxg4? fxg3 should lead to disaster.

11...♕d7!?

An efficient move. By threatening to exchange White's light-squared bishop Black gains time to carry out his plan, which consists of ...♖ae8 and ...f5, preparing to start a kingside attack. A further point of the move, indicated by Gurevich, lies in vacating e7 for his bishop in case of ♘de4.

12 ♖e1 ♖ae8 13 ♘c4 ♗c5 14 ♘e4

Purely temporary activity as the knight will be driven back. It seems that the German grandmaster, who is an expert of the black side of this opening, was already running out of ideas after his innocuous 10th move.

14...♗b4 15 ♘ed2?!

After 15 ♗c3 ♗xc3 16 ♘xc3 f5 Gurevich would have achieved his aim but White does not seem too badly off. The text results in an awkward pin on the a5-e1 diagonal.

15...♘xc4 16 bxc4 f5 *(D)*

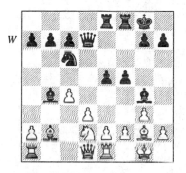

Black's position leaves little to be desired. All his pieces are finely placed with his two bishops, in particular, severely cramping White. With his last move Gurevich introduces a threat in ...e4, which his opponent is hard pressed to parry.

17 ♖b1

On 17 ♗d5+ ♔h8 18 ♖b1 Gurevich gives the following line: 18...e4 19 ♗xc6 bxc6 20 ♗xg7+ ♕xg7 21 ♖xb4 exd3 22 f3 dxe2 23 ♖xe2 ♕d4+ and then 24 ♔g2 ♗xf3+! 25 ♔xf3 ♕c3+ winning. However 24 ♖f2 is better – although after 24...f4! Black has a strong attack, the game is not over.

17...e4 18 d4 ♗a5!

The Russian grandmaster attaches an exclamation mark to this logical move and he is probably right. The alternative 18...f4 is not so clear after 19 d5!?. Note, however, that White should avoid Gurevich's 19 ♘xe4? ♗xe1 20 ♕xe1 ('with compensation') 20...♘xd4 when White is just dead lost. 21 ♖d1 ♘xe2+ 22 ♕xc2 ♕xd1+ is the end, while after 21 f3, 21...♖xe4! clinches the issue.

19 d5 ♘e5 20 ♗xe5 ♖xe5 21 ♖xb7!

Sacrificing an exchange to stay in the game. This is the only way to continue fighting as after 21 ♕c2 c6 White's position would rapidly disintegrate.

21...♗b6 22 ♘b3 ♕c8 23 ♖xb6 axb6 24 f4!?

24 ♕d4 was also possible.

24...cxf3 25 exf3 ♖xe1+ 26 ♕xe1 ♖e8 27 ♕c3 ♗h5 28 ♘d4 ♗f7 29 h4?!

Hertneck has defended well in the last dozen moves but his position would remain difficult even after the better 29 ♗h3!? g6 30 g4 f4 31 ♕d2 ♕a6! 32 ♗f1 ♖e3, which according to Gurevich is slightly better for Black.

29...♕d7 30 ♔f2 g6

Freeing the queen for action on the dark squares. Now Black has a technically won game and in the rest of the game he proceeds with care to bring his advantage home.

31 h5 ♕e7 32 hxg6 hxg6 33 ♗f1 ♕c5 34 ♕d2 *(D)*

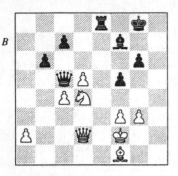

34...b5!

The final detail, winning a pawn.

35 cxb5 ♕xd5 36 ♕f4 ♕xa2+ 37 ♔g1 ♕a1 38 ♔f2 ♕b2+ 39 ♘e2 ♕e5 40 ♕xe5 ♖xe5 41 ♘d4 ♖c5 42 g4 fxg4 43 fxg4 ♗c4 44 ♗xc4+ ♖xc4 45 ♔e3 ♖c5 46 ♔f4 ♔f7 47 ♔e4 ♔f6 48 ♔f4 ♖e5 49 ♔f3 g5 0-1

8) Systems with 3 g3: White delays ♘f3

Game 8
Larsen – Arnason
Lone Pine 1980

1 c4 e5 2 ♘c3

The actual move-order was 2 g3.

2...♘f6 3 g3 d5 4 cxd5 ♘xd5 5 ♗g2 ♘b6 6 d3!?

White postpones the development of his king's knight in order to preserve the possibility of saddling Black with doubled pawns in case of ...♘c6. Alternatives include:

a) 6 a3 ♗e7 7 b4 0-0 8 ♘f3 ♘c6 9 b5!? (9 0-0 would transpose to one of the main lines in the Romanishin System) 9...♘d4 10 ♘xe5 ♗f6 11 f4 ♕e8!? (11...♖e8 is less flexible; after 12 0-0 ♗xe5 13 fxe5 ♖xe5 14 e3 ♘xb5 15 ♘xb5 ♖xb5 16 a4 ♖a5 17 ♗b2 White had good compensation for the pawn in Oney-Petursson, Komotini 1993) 12 ♘f3 ♘xb5 13 ♘xb5 ♕xb5 gave Black the initiative in Dragomaretsky-Beshukov, Moscow 1990.

b) 6 a4 a5 7 d3 ♗b4 is unclear.

c) 6 b3 ♗e7 7 ♗b2 0-0 8 ♖c1 c5 (an independent try; 8...♖e8 transposes into Serper-A.Sokolov discussed in Game 9, note to White's 8th) 9 ♘h3!? ♗e6 10 f4 ♕d7 11 ♘f2 exf4 12 gxf4 f5 13 ♖g1 ♗f6 14 d3 ♘c6 15 ♗xc6 ♕xc6 16 ♕d2 ♖ae8 was approximately even in Bischoff-Aseev, Krumbach 1991.

6...♗e7 7 ♗e3

The most useful if White insists on the strategy outlined above. There are, however, no less than four other interesting ways to play the position:

a) 7 f4 exf4 8 ♗xf4 0-0 9 ♘f3 c5 10 0-0 ♘c6 11 ♕d2 f6 12 ♗e3 ♗e6 with an unclear game, Miezis-Motwani, Bern 1992.

b) 7 ♘h3!? ♘c6 (7...0-0 8 0-0 ♘c6 9 f4 exf4 10 gxf4 ♘d4 11 e4 f5 12 ♔h1 c5 13 ♗e3 ♗e6 14 ♘g5! ♗xg5 15 fxg5 ♕d7 16 ♕d2 was slightly better for White in Van Wely-Brunner, Biel IZ 1993, mainly because of Black's displaced knight) 8 0-0 ♗e6 9 f4 ♕d7 10 ♘f2 (10 ♘g5 ♗xg5 11 fxg5 ♗h3 12 ♗xh3 ♕xh3 13 ♘e4 0-0 is unclear) 10...exf4 11 gxf4 f5 =.

c) 7 a3 0-0 8 b4 c5!? 9 bxc5 ♗xc5 10 ♗b2 ♖e8 11 ♘f3 ♘c6 12 0-0 ♗f8 13 a4 ♗e6 14 a5 ♘d7 15 a6 bxa6 16 ♖xa6 ♖b8 17 ♖xc6 ♖xb2 18 ♕c1 ♖b6 19 ♘g5 ♗b3 was slightly better for Black in Ubilava-A.Sokolov, New York Open 1990.

d) 7 a4 a5 8 ♗e3 can be met by 8...0-0 = or 8...♘c6!?, but 8...c6?! 9 ♘f3 ♘8d7 10 ♕b3! allows White an edge.

7...0-0 8 ♖c1 (D)

Still waiting! Another way to do so is by playing 8 ♕c1 but in my opinion that is rather harmless, unless Black weakens the g5-square by playing ...f5 prematurely. Then White may get the advantage by ♘f3, 0-0, ♖fd1 and an eventual d4, which is reminiscent of a typical Botvinnik manoeuvre from the Dragon. There two equally good lines after 8 ♕c1:

a) 8...♖e8 9 ♘f3 ♘c6 10 0-0 and then:

a1) 10...♗g4 11 ♖e1 ♗f8 12 ♘c4 (12 h3!?) 12...♗b4 13 ♗d2 f5 14 ♘c5 ♗xc5 15 ♕xc5 e4 16 ♘h4 ♖e5 was unclear in Benjamin-Miralles, Paris 1989.

a2) 10...♗f8!? (Poldauf-Savon, Podolsk 1991) 11 ♘e4 ♘d4 12 ♖e1 a5 13 ♘c5 a4 14 b4 axb3 15 ♘xb3 ♗a3 16 ♕b1 c5 ∓.

b) 8...♘c6!?. With the rook on c1 this would be somewhat inferior, but now it may be OK for Black to accept a weakened pawn formation in view of White's backward development, e.g. 9 ♗xc6 bxc6 10 ♘f3 f6 11 ♘e4 (11 0-0 ♗g4 12 ♖d1 ♘d5 gives Black counterplay) 11...♗h3!?.

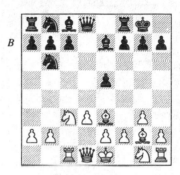

8...♔h8!

Black follows suit. Now White has no other useful move and finally decides to bring his knight into play.

9 ♘f3 ♘c6 10 0-0

The blunder 10 ♘a4? occurred in Csom-Liberzon, Palma de Mallorca 1989. After 10...e4! 11 ♘xb6 exf3 12 ♘xa8 fxg2 13 ♖g1 ♗h3 White's position was already ripe for resignation.

10...f5 11 ♘a4?!

As this has been proven ineffective for tactical reasons, attention has by now switched to 11 a3, waiting for Black to put his bishop on e6 before continuing with the manoeuvre ♘a4-c5. After 11...♗e6 White has tried other ideas as well but the general consensus seems to be that Black has a comfortable game here:

a) 12 ♘d2 f4!? (12...♘d5 =) 13 ♗xb6 cxb6! 14 ♗e4 ♗g5 15 ♗xc6 bxc6 16 ♘ce4 ♗d5 17 ♖c3 and a draw was agreed in Gavrikov-Tukmakov, Malgrat 1993. The final position seems, if anything, slightly better for Black.

b) 12 b4 a5! 13 b5 ♘d4 14 ♘xe5 ♗xa3 16 ♗xb7 ♗xc1 17 ♖xc1 ♘d5! 17 ♘xd5 ♗xd5 18 ♗xa8 ♗xa8 is slightly better for Black according to Romanishin.

c) 12 ♘a4 (the main line) when Black has a choice:

c1) 12...f4!? 13 ♘c5 ♗d5 14 ♗d2 ♗xc5 15 ♖xc5 ♕e7 16 ♕c1 (16 b4!? was played in Ibragimov-Schwartzmann, Odorheiu Secuiesc 1993; now, instead of the game continuation 16...♖f7?! 17 e4! fxe3 18 ♗xe3, which left White with an appreciably superior game as the rook is exposed to harassment on f7, Black should prefer 16...♖ad8 intending to meet 17 e4 by 17...♗g8! and 17 ♕c1 by 17...e4 18 dxe4 ♕xe4! when the threat of ...♘d4 promises some initiative) 16...♖f7 17 b4 ♗xf3 18 ♗xf3 ♘d4 19 ♕d1 c6 was unclear in the game Cebalo-Romanishin, Taxco IZ 1985.

c2) 12...♘xa4 (a simple route to equality) 13 ♕a4 ♗d5 14 ♖fe1 a6 15 ♗c5 e4 16 ♗xe7 ♕xe7 and although there is still some fight left in the position the players decided to call it a draw in Vaganian-Portisch, Moscow OL 1994.

An odd 11th move alternative is 11 ♕b3 (another idea of Larsen's) but it is rather pointless after the simple 11...♗f6, intending ...♖fe8 and ...♗e6.

11...f4 12 ♗c5 *(D)*

On 12 ♗xb6?! axb6 13 ♖xc6 bxc6 14 ♘xe5, Arnason gives 14...fxg3 15 hxg3 ♕d4! forking White's knights. Let's take this line a bit further: 16 ♘xe7 ♕xa4 17 b3!? ♕xa2 18 ♘xe7 and White has some drawing chances after either 18...♖a3 or 18...♗g4!?.

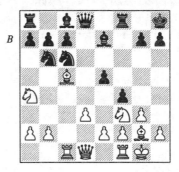

12...e4! 13 ♗xe7

13 ♘e1 does not solve White's problems either. After 13...♘xa4 14 ♕xa4 (14 ♗xe7 ♘xe7 15 ♕xa4 f3 16 exf3 exd3 is slightly better for Black according to Korchnoi) 14...♗xc5 (14...f3!?) 15 ♖xc5 ♘d4 16 dxe4? (16 ♗xe4!?) 16...♘xe2+ 17 ♔h1 ♗g4 Black had a big advantage in Spiridonov-Barbulescu, Polanica Zdroj 1984.

13...♘xe7 14 ♘e1

Subsequent efforts at improvement confirmed that White should merely be trying to equalize here:

a) 14 ♘g5 ♘xa4 15 ♕xa4 exd3 16 exd3 (16 ♖fd1 ♘g6 17 ♕a5 ♗f5 18 ♘f3 c6 19 ♕c3 fxg3 20 hxg3 ♕f6 ∓ Garcia Padron-Timman, Las

Palmas 1981) 16...♘g6 17 ♕a5 ♗f5
18 ♘e4 c6 19 ♕c3 ♕b6 20 ♘c5 ♖f6
21 ♖fe1 ♖af8 22 d4 ♗c8 gave Black
the initiative in Spiridonov-Tivia-
kov, Torcy 1991.

b) 14 dxe4!? ♕xd1 15 ♖fxd1
♘xa4 16 b3 ♘b6 17 ♖xc7 ♘g6 ∓
Kertesz-Barbulescu, Romania 1984.

14...fxg3 15 hxg3 e3! 16 ♘c3

16 fxe3? would have been unsound due to 16...♖xf1+ 17 ♗xf1
♘f5 with a strong attack. Larsen
realizes that the situation is getting
perilous and brings the exiled knight
closer to the threatened sector.

**16...exf2+ 17 ♖xf2 ♖xf2 18 ♖xf2
♗g4!** *(D)*

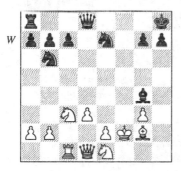

The Icelandic grandmaster is
well-known for his attacking spirit
and probably didn't doubt for a second whether he should sacrifice a
pawn here. Larsen's acceptance of
the sacrifice is no surprise as the
great Dane is an expert in the art of
living dangerously.

**19 ♗xb7?! ♕d4+ 20 e3 ♖f8+ 21
♗f3 ♕e5 22 ♘e4 ♕h5**

Black, naturally, scorns the pawn
on b2 as he is playing for higher

stakes. The text intensifies the pressure on the pinned bishop and ensures the penetration of his queen to
the vicinity of the white monarch.

23 ♘d2 ♘bd5

After 23...♘d7! White would be
teetering on the edge of a precipice.
For example: 24 d4 (to stop ...♘e5;
24 ♔g1 ♘e5 25 ♗xg4 ♘xg4 ∓)
24...♕h2+ 25 ♘g2 ♘f6! or 24 ♖xc7
♕h2+ 25 ♘g2 ♘e5 26 ♖xe7 ♗xf3
27 ♘xf3 ♘g4+ 28 ♔e1 ♕xg2 with
an unstoppable attack in both cases.
The text is also good, but requires
greater accuracy on Black's part.

24 ♘g2?

Arnason considers 24 e4 ♕h2+
25 ♘g2 ♗xf3 26 ♘xf3 ♘e3! 27
♔xe3 ♕xg2 ∓ to be the best defensive chance. The game continuation
should have led surprisingly quickly
to White's demise.

24...g5! 25 e4

After 25 ♖c5 the Icelander's suggestion 25...♗xf3 26 ♘xf3 g4 27
♘f4 ♘xf4 28 ♖xh5 ♘xh5 ∓ is good
enough but the most effective conclusion is 25...♕h2! when White is
totally defenceless.

25...♘b4?

Black has conducted the game in
great style but here he throws away
an easy win. The relatively simple
25...♗xf3 26 ♘xf3 g4 27 ♘h4 (27
exd5 ♕h2!) 27...♘g6! would have
removed the last obstacles on his
way to victory.

26 ♖xc7 ♘xd3+?

Arnason thought that his decisive
mistake was on the 25th move but I
think it really comes now. Instead of

driving the king to a better square by 26...♘xd3+? he should have played 26...♘g6! 27 ♕b3 (27 ♔g1 is met by 27...♘e5!, and not 27...♗xf3? 28 ♕b3!) 27...♘e5! 28 ♔g1 (what else?) 28...♘bxd3 when I cannot see a satisfactory defence for White.

27 ♔g1 *(D)*

Suddenly White is slightly better. the apparently strong 27...♘e5? is met by 28 ♗xg4 ♘xg4 29 ♘f3 with the devastating threat ♕d4+.

27...♗xf3 28 ♘xf3 ♕xf3 29 ♕xf3 ♖xf3 30 ♖xe7 ♘xb2 31 e5 ♔g8 32 e6 ♖xg3 33 ♖xa7?!

With time-trouble approaching Larsen misses a good winning chance in 33 ♖b7! ♘c4 34 ♖b8+ ♔g7 35 e7 ♘d6 36 e8♕ ♘xe8 37 ♖xe8 ♖a3 38 ♖e2. The other rook move, 33 ♖xh7, is not as good because of 33...♔f8 and Black holds.

33...♔f8 34 a4?! ♘c4 35 ♔f2 ♖g4 36 ♔f3? ♘e5+ 37 ♔f2 ♘d3+ 38 ♔e2 ♖xg2+?

The tale of woe continues. After 38...♘c5 Black draws easily.

39 ♔xd3 h5 40 a5 h4 41 a6 h3 42 ♖h7 ♖a2 43 a7 g4 44 ♔e3 h2??

And this is the tragic conclusion. Black misses his last chance to draw by playing 44...g3 45 ♖xh3 g2 46 ♖g3 ♖xa7.

45 e7+! ♔e8 46 ♖xh2 and Arnason resigned as he saw that after 46...♖a3+ 47 ♔f4 ♔xe7 48 ♖h8! his rook falls.

We will refer to the sequence 1 c4 e5 2 ♘c3 ♘f6 3 ♘f3 ♘c6 4 g3 d5 5 cxd5 ♘xd5 6 ♗g2 ♘b6 as the Romanishin System since the Ukrainian grandmaster has been one of its staunchest advocates.

9) Romanishin System: Introduction/Main line 8 ♖b1!?

Game 9
Serper – Korchnoi
Groningen 1993

1 c4 e5 2 ♘c3 ♘f6 3 ♘f3 ♘c6 4 g3 d5 5 cxd5 ♘xd5 6 ♗g2

The most exact move order. After 6 d3 Black may elect not to retreat his knight to b6. The main line goes as follows: 6...♗e7 7 ♗g2 (7 ♘xd5 ♕xd5 8 ♗g2 ♗e6 9 0-0 ♕d7 10 ♗e3 0-0 11 a3 a5 12 ♖c1 f6 13 ♘d2 a4 14 ♗xc6 bxc6 15 ♕c2 ♖a6 ½-½ was Andersson-Smyslov, Haninge 1989) 7...♗e6 (7...♘b6 transposes to the main line) 8 0-0 0-0 9 ♗d2 ♕d7 10 ♖c1 f6 11 a3 ♘xc3 12 ♗xc3 a5 13 ♘d2 a4 14 ♘e4 ♗d5 15 ♗d2 ♘d4 16 ♗b4 ♖fd8 17 ♗xe7 ♕xe7 18 e3 ♘b3 19 ♖c3 f5 20 ♘d2 ♗xg2 21

♔xg2 ♘c5 22 ♕c2 b6 and White had slightly the worse of it in Serper-Tal, USSR 1991, although he eventually managed to draw.

6...♘b6 *(D)*

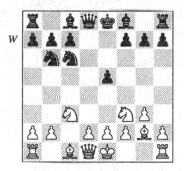

A typical position for the opening, popularized in the past two decades mainly due to the efforts of Oleg Romanishin. Viktor Korchnoi and Vladimir Tukmakov have also made important contributions to its theory, Korchnoi's being particularly noticeable as he has been practising the system with both colours.

It is not easy to sum up Black's ideas in a few lines but in general he should rely on sound development and centralization. The fight usually revolves around the desire of both players to gain territory in the centre and the queenside, which is only natural considering that the kings are very well sheltered after the opening stage. The present game is important from the theoretical point of view as it highlights a rather exceptional case with Black attacking on the kingside to counter White's early effort to develop a queenside initiative.

7 0-0

The most natural. Plans involving an early a4 are associated with the idea of forcing ...a5, but it is not clear in those cases who has been weakened more. Witness the following examples:

a) 7 b3 ♗e7 8 a4!? a5 9 ♗b2 0-0 10 ♘b5 f6 11 0-0 ♗e6 12 ♖c1!? (an interesting idea of Serper's; after 12 ♕b1?! ♘b4 13 d4 c6 14 ♘a3 e4! 15 ♘d2 {15 ♕xe4!? ♗xb3 16 ♗h3 ♗d5 17 ♗e6+ ♔h8 18 ♗xd5 cxd5 ∓} 15...f5 Black had the initiative in Chekhov-Vyzhmanavin, USSR Ch 1991) 12...♖c8 13 ♖xc6!? (13 e4 ♘b4 14 d4 c6 to be followed by ...♖c7-d7 offers Black good counterplay) 13...bxc6 14 ♘a7 ♖a8 15 ♘xc6 ♕e8 is unclear.

b) 7 a4 a5 8 d3 ♗b4 (8...♗e7 9 ♗e3 0-0 10 0-0 ♗g4 transposes to the illustrative game Korchnoi-Petursson) 9 0-0 0-0 10 ♗e3 occurred in Korchnoi-Eslon, Linares 1979. Now Korchnoi suggests 10...f5! 11 ♕b3+ (11 ♘g5 ♘d4 ∓) 11...♔h8 12 ♘g5 f4 13 ♗xb6 ♕xg5 14 ♗xc7 ♘d4 15 ♕d1 ♕h5 with compensation for the material.

7...♗c7 8 ♖b1!?

This plan has gained in popularity recently. The threat of b4 forces Black to commit himself rather early but this does not necessarily mean that his position is lacking in resources.

Apart from 8 d3 and 8 a3, which will be examined in subsequent illustrative games, White has a couple of alternatives here:

a) 8 b3 (this method of development is rather harmless for Black) 8...0-0 9 ♗b2 ♖e8 10 ♖c1 ♗f8 11 d3 ♘d4 12 ♘d2 c6 13 e3 ♘e6 14 ♘f3 ♘g5! 15 ♘xg5 ♕xg5 16 ♘e4 ♕g6 =. Black has comfortably equalized and went on to win in Serper-A.Sokolov, Moscow 1990.

b) 8 a4 a5 9 d4?! (it seems suspect to open up the position as the weakness on b4 becomes more significant; 9 d3 transposes once more to Korchnoi-Petursson) 9...exd4 10 ♘b5 and now:

b1) 10...♗f6!? (this move is adequate provided Black is content with a draw) 11 ♗f4 ♘d5 12 ♘fxd4 ♘xf4 13 ♘xc6 ♕xd1 14 ♖fxd1 ♘xe2+ 15 ♔f1 (15 ♔h1 0-0 16 ♘xc7 bxc6 17 ♘xa8 ♗xb2 with counterplay) 15...0-0 16 ♘ca7! (16 ♘xc7? bxc6 17 ♘xa8 ♗a6 18 ♘c7 ♗c4 ∓) 16...♗e6! 17 ♗xb7 (17 ♔xe2? fails to 17...♗c4+ to be followed by ...c6; 17 ♘xc7?! ♗c4 gives Black the initiative) 17...♗c4 18 ♔g2 ♗xb2 19 ♗xa8 ♗xa1 20 ♗d5 (Skembris-Seitaj, Varna 1994) 20...♗xb5! 21 ♘xb5 ♘c3 22 ♘xc3 ♗xc3 23 ♖c1 ♖d8! =.

b2) 10...0-0! 11 ♘bxd4 (or 11 ♘fxd4?! ♘b4! 12 e4 c6 13 ♘c3 ♗f6 14 ♘b3 ♘c4 15 ♕h5 ♕b6 and Black had strong pressure in the game Skembris-Kotronias, Athens 1994) 11...♘xd4 12 ♘xd4 c6 13 e3 ♗f6 14 ♕h5 ♕e7 15 ♗d2 ♖d8 16 ♖fc1 ♘d5 ∓ Hodgson-Bareev, Hastings 1991.

8...g5!?

A bold reaction. Normally Black would like to play 8...f6 in order to transpose to the main lines featured in the subsequent illustrative games, but the pawn sacrifice 9 d4!, introduced in Khalifman-Tiviakov, Linares 1995, casts doubt on this idea. After 9...exd4 10 ♘b5 there is not much choice:

a) 10...♗f5?. The bishop is exposed here and this factor proved decisive in the above-mentioned game, which continued 11 ♗f4! ♖c8 (11...♘d5 12 ♘fxd4 ±) 12 ♖c1 d3 13 exd3 ♘d5 14 ♘fd4 ♘xf4 15 ♘xf5 ♘xg2 (D).

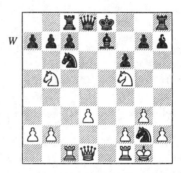

16 ♖xc6! bxc6 17 ♘xa7 ♕xd5 18 ♘xc8 ♕xf5 19 ♘xe7 ♔xe7 20 ♔xg2 ♕d5+ 21 ♔g1 ♕xa2 22 ♖e1+ ♔d8 23 ♕g4 and with his king wandering Black was doomed.

b) 10...d3 is an attempt to reduce the attacking force by closing the d-file. White has:

b1) 11 ♗f4?! and now, surprisingly, Black gets enough counterplay. 11...♘d5 12 ♕xd3 ♘xf4 13 ♕xd8+ ♗xd8 14 gxf4 and then:

b11) 14...a6?! 15 ♘bd4 ♘xd4 (15...♗d7 16 ♘xc6 ♗xc6 17 ♘d4! ±) 16 ♘xd4 ±.

b12) 14...♗d7?! should be met by 15 b4! ±, rather than 15 ♖fd1?! a6 16 ♘bd4 (16 ♘c3 ♗e7 followed by ...0-0-0 is equal) 16...♘xd4 17 ♘xd4 c6 =.

b13) 14 g5! (this seems extravagant but it complies with the principle of opening up the position when possessing the two bishops) 15 fxg5 a6!? (15...fxg5 intends to play ...a6 and ...g4, fighting for e5 and d4, e.g. 16 ♘d2!? ♗d7 17 ♘e4 a6 18 ♘bc3 ♗e7 19 ♘d5 0-0-0 is unclear) 16 ♘bd4 ♘xd4 17 ♘xd4 fxg5 18 f4! ♗f6 19 e3 0-0 results in approximate equality.

b2) 11 ♕xd3! ♕xd3 12 exd3 ♔d8 (12...♘d5 13 ♘e1! a6 14 ♘c3 ±; 12...♗d6 13 ♘d2!?) 13 ♗f4! (to disturb the co-ordination of Black's knights; after Khalifman's 13 ♗e3?! Black has 13...♘b4! when his control over d5 seems to neutralize White's advantage in development) 13...♘d5 14 ♗d2 ♗d7 (14...♗e6 15 ♘fd4 ♘xd4 16 ♘xd4 ♗f7 17 ♖fe1 to be followed by ♘e6+ is clearly better for White) 15 a3 ♖e8 16 ♖fe1 ±.

c) 10...0-0 is the lesser evil but at the same time an admission of strategic failure. After 11 ♘fxd4 ♘xd4 12 ♘xd4 White is slightly better.

8...f5!? seems to be a reliable new idea. Black manages to prevent b4 for a couple of moves and invests the time gained in bolstering his central position, d4 in particular. For example: 9 d3 (9 b4? e4 10 ♘e1 ♗xb4 11 ♗b2 ♘c4 12 d3 ♘xb2 13 ♕b3 ♗xc3 14 ♕xc3 ♘a4 15 ♕xg7 ♕d4 led to a disaster for White in Tabatadze-Smejkal, Brno 1994) 9...♗f6 10 ♗d2 0-0 11 b4 a6 12 ♗e3 ♘d4 13 ♘d2 c6 14 ♘b3 ♕e7 15 ♘c5 ♘d7 16 ♘3a4 ♘xc5 17 bxc5 ♗e6 18 ♗xd4 exd4 19 ♖b2 ♖ae8 20 ♕d2 ♕f7 21 ♖fb1 ♖e7 ∓ Kveinys-Smejkal, Lubniewice 1994. Black has solved the problem of defending his weakness at b7 and can look forward to attacking on the kingside. There is certainly a lot of room for investigation in this line.

Now we return to the main line after 8...g5!? *(D)*.

9 d3

The most critical test of Black's concept. The alternative move 9 d4 turned out to be rather innocuous in Claesen-M.Gurevich, Antwerp 1994, which continued 9...exd4 10 ♘b5 ♗f5 11 ♖a1 ♗e4! 12 ♘bxd4 (12 ♘fxd4 ♗xg2 13 ♔xg2 is a more exact move order) 12...♘xd4 13 ♕xd4 (after 13 ♘xd4 ♗xg2 14 ♔xg2, the reply 14...♕d7 is unclear – but not 14...♕d5+?! 15 e4! ♕xe4+ 16 f3 ♕d5 17 ♖e1 with an attack for White according to Gurevich) 13...♕xd4 14

♘xd4 ♗xg2 15 ♔xg2 0-0-0 16 ♘f3 (16 ♘f5 ♗f6 ∓) 16...♖hg8! with a good endgame for Black.

9...h5!?

Korchnoi shows that he is in a really aggressive mood. 9...g4!? 10 ♘e1 h5 is another continuation deserving attention, although after 11 ♘c2 h4 12 b4 hxg3 13 fxg3 ♘xb4? 14 ♘xb4 ♕d4+ 15 e3 ♕xc3 16 ♘d5 ♘xd5 17 ♗xd5 ♗e6 18 ♕a4+! (this was not played) Black should have bitten the dust in Hodgson-Bareev, Belgrade 1993.

10 a3

Perhaps 10 ♗e3!?, intending to meet 10...g4 by 11 ♘h4!? (11 ♘d2 h4 12 a3 hxg3 13 hxg3 ♗e6 is unclear) 11...♗xh4 12 gxh4 ♕xh4 13 ♘e4 (with compensation for the material – Korchnoi) would have posed more problems. I regard the position after 13 ♘e4 as unsatisfactory for Black, so an improvement is required on the 10th or 11th move (11...♘d4!?).

10...h4 11 b4 hxg3 12 hxg3

On 12 fxg3 the typical response 12...g4 13 ♘d2 a5 (not 13...♕d4+? 14 ♔h1 ♕xc3? 15 ♗b2 +–) 14 b5 ♘d4 produces a sharp position with chances for both sides. The text opens an avenue towards the white king, but everybody who has some experience with the Dragon knows that mating down the h-file is not as simple as it looks.

12...a6?!

Korchnoi gave a lot of analysis in *Informator 59*, concluding that Black could have done without this slow preparatory move. After 12...♕d6! 13 ♘b5 ♕h6 14 ♘xc7+ ♔f8 15 ♘xa8 ♘xa8 *(D)* the situation becomes extremely tense, so it is worth taking a deeper look:

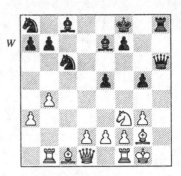

a) 16 e4 (this deserves a '?' in my opinion) 16...♘d4 17 ♖e1 ♗g4 18 ♗b2 (18 ♖e3 ♕h5) 18...♘xf3+ 19 ♗xf3 ♕h5! and then:

a1) 20 ♔g2 ♗xf3+ (Korchnoi apparently overlooked this simple win, suggesting instead 20...♕h3+ =) 21 ♕xf3 g4 and the game is decided.

a2) 20 ♖e3 ♗xf3 21 ♕xf3 ♕h2+ 22 ♔f1 ♕h1+ and Black wins.

b) 16 ♖e1? is no good at all since after 16...♗h3, although it would be easy to imagine that White could sidestep with 17 ♗h1, Black in fact has the killing 17...♗f5, picking off the b1-rook.

c) 16 b5 ♘d4 17 ♖e1 ♘xf3+ 18 exf3 ♗h3 19 f4 ♗xg2 20 ♔xg2 ♕h3+ 21 ♔f3 exf4 with compensation for the material – Korchnoi.

Thus, 12...♕d6! offered excellent chances, which is not the case with the text move.

13 b5!

An alternative was 13 ♘e4 g4 14 ♘fd2 f5 15 ♘c5 a5! with unclear play. Serper's choice is stronger because it keeps Black busy on the queenside.

13...♘d4 14 bxa6?!

After 14 ♘xe5! the complications turn out well for White: 14...♕d6 15 f4! and now:

a) 15...gxf4?! 16 ♘xf7! ♕c5 (or 16...♔xf7 17 ♗xf4 ♕c5 18 e3 ♘f5 19 ♘e4 ±) 17 e3 and now Korchnoi's 17...f3 18 ♘xh8 ♗g4 does not work because of 19 ♖f2, so Black has a sad choice between 17...♔xf7 18 ♖xf4+ ♔e8 19 exd4! ♕xc3 20 ♗b2 and 17...0-0 18 ♘h6+ with a clear advantage for White in each case.

b) Black can improve by trying 15...♘f5.

c) 15...♕h6 is also a better try. Black has the following variation in mind: 16 fxg5? (16 ♔f2! ±) 16...♕h2+ 17 ♔f2 ♗h3 18 ♖g1 ♘f5 19 ♘e4 ♗c5+! 20 e3 ♗xg2 21 ♘f6+ ♔e7 22 ♖xg2 ♗xe3+!! 23 ♔f3 (23 ♗xc3 ♕xg2+!) 23...♕h3 and White is in trouble.

However, I feel that in both 'b' and 'c' above White should be at least slightly better as his king is relatively safe.

14...♖xa6 15 ♘xd4?!

15 ♘xe5! is less good than it was in the previous note but still White's best chance. Now the scales tip in Black's favour.

15...exd4 16 ♘b5 ♘a4! 17 e3 c6 18 ♘xd4 ♘c3 19 ♕b3 ♘xb1 20 ♕xb1 ♕d6 21 ♕b3?

Stronger is 21 ♖e1 when the issue is not altogether clear. The loss of time entailed in Serper's move allows Black to demonstrate a forced win.

21...♕h6 22 ♖e1 c5!

Allowing his distant rook to join the attack with gain of tempo. The black king's position is not particularly endangered as he always has a square on f8 to which to flee.

23 ♘f3

On 23 ♘b5 Black has a deadly riposte in 23...♕f2+ 24 ♔f1 ♖f6! threatening ...♗h3. But now the end is also near as White lacks sufficient breathing space for his king.

23...♗h3 24 ♕xb7 ♗xg2 25 ♕c8+ ♗d8 26 ♔xg2 *(D)*

26...♖e6!

A nice move combining the motif of interference with a nasty potential discovery on the white queen.

27 ♘g1

Forced to meet the threat of mate in two. An attempt to escape with 27 ♔f1 succumbs to 27...♕h3+ 28 ♔e2 ♖xe3+ (the point of 26...♖e6) and the queen is lost.

27...♕h1+ 28 ♔f1 ♖f6 29 e4 ♖h2 30 ♔e2 ♖hxf2+ 31 ♔d1 ♖d6 32 ♗e3

An inglorious entrance to the game after 31 moves but at least White may die with a clear conscience having used the whole of his army.

32...♖xd3+ 33 ♔c1 ♖c3+ 34 ♔d1 ♕h6 0-1

35 ♗xf2 ♕d6+ 36 ♔e2 ♕d3 is mate. A game of wildly fluctuating fortunes.

10) Romanishin System: Main Line 8 d3 (Plans without an early a3 and b4)

Game 10
Korchnoi – Petursson
Lugano 1989

1 c4 ♘f6 2 ♘c3 e5 3 g3 d5 4 cxd5 ♘xd5 5 ♗g2 ♘b6 6 ♘f3 ♘c6 7 0-0 ♗e7 8 d3 0-0 9 a4!?

The most critical continuation, intending to force a weakening of the squares b6 and b5 and then lay siege to Black's queenside. The alternatives do not seem to put Black under such pressure:

a) 9 a3 ♗e6 10 ♘e4 (10 b4 is a direct transposition to 8 a3 lines) can be met by 10...f6 or 10...f5 11 ♘eg5 ♗d5 with equality in both cases (Korchnoi).

b) 9 ♗d2 ♖e8 10 ♖c1 ♗f8 11 ♗e3 ♘d4 12 ♘e4 ♗g4 13 ♗xd4 exd4 14 ♕d2 c6 15 a3 a5 ∓ Murey-Psakhis, Tel Aviv 1990. The loss of

time involved in moving the bishop twice is evident.

c) 9 ♗e3 (this natural move has been played a lot but it does not look dangerous) 9...♗e6 *(D)* and now White has a wide choice:

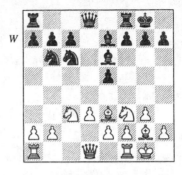

c1) 10 ♘a4 (this seems inferior) 10...e4! 11 ♘e1 exd3 12 ♘xd3 ♗d5 13 ♘xb6?! (13 ♗h3!?) 13...axb6 14 ♗xd5 ♕xd5 15 ♗f4 ♗d6 16 ♗xd6 ♕xd6 17 a3 ♖fe8 18 ♘b4 ♕xd1 19 ♖fxd1 ♘xb4 20 axb4 ♖xa1 21 ♖xa1 ♔f8 ∓ Uhlmann-Romanishin, Dresden 1988.

c2) 10 ♘e4!? and now:

c21) 10...♘d5 is the clear path to equality but probably no more than that: 11 ♗c5 f6 12 ♖c1 (12 ♗xe7 ♕xe7 13 ♖c1 ♖ad8 14 ♘c5 ♗c8 15 ♕b3 ♘a5 16 ♕a4 ♘c6 17 ♕b3 =; I do not see a satisfactory way to avoid the draw by repetition) 12...♗f7 13 ♗h3 (13 a3 a5 is unclear) 13...b6 14 ♗xe7 ♘dxe7 15 ♕c2 a5 16 a3 a4 with excellent Black counterplay in the game Beliavsky-Psakhis, Kislovodsk 1982.

c22) The old 10...f5!? may offer more fighting chances, e.g. 11 ♘c5

♗d5 12 ♖c1 (not 12 ♘xb7? ♕c8 13 ♘c5 f4 −+) 12...♖b8 13 a3 ♔h8 14 b4 a6 15 ♗d2 ♕e8 gave rise to an unclear position in Suetin-Flohr, Erevan 1955.

c3) 10 ♕d2 ♘d5 11 ♖fc1 f6 12 a3 ♕d7 13 ♘xd5 (13 b4!?) 13...♗xd5 14 b4 ♔h8 15 b5 (15 ♗c5!? b6 16 ♗xe7 ♘xe7 =) 15...♘d8 16 ♗c5 ♗xc5 17 ♖xc5 c6 18 e4 ♗g8 19 d4 ♘e6 (19...exd4!?) 20 bxc6 bxc6 21 ♗h3 was unclear in Ljubojević-Chernin, Wijk aan Zee 1986.

c4) 10 ♕c1 (this looks rather artificial when Black hasn't got ...f5 thrown in) 10...♘d5!? 11 ♖d1 (11 ♘g5 ♗xg5 12 ♗xg5 ♕d7 is unclear) 11...♖e8 12 ♘e4 ♘xe3 13 fxe3 (13 ♕xe3 ♘d4 14 ♖dc1 ♘xf3+ intending ...c6 with a slightly better position) 13...♖b8 14 ♘c5 ♗d5 15 ♕c3?! (15 e4 ♗xc5+ 16 ♕xc5 ♗e6 =) 15...♕d6! 16 ♖dc1 ♕h6 and Black had a strong initiative in Gabriel-Romanishin, Altensteig 1993.

c5) 10 ♖c1 ♘d5 11 ♘xd5 ♗xd5 12 ♕a4 ♖e8 13 h4?! a6 14 a3 ♖b8 15 ♖fe1 ♗f8 16 ♘g5 ♗xg2 17 ♔xg2 h6 18 ♘c4 f5 ∓ Oll-Romanishin, Debrecen 1990.

c6) 10 a3 f5 11 b4 (11 ♖c1 ♔h8 = − for this position refer to the games Vaganian-Portisch and Gavrikov-Tukmakov which may be found under lines without an early ♘f3) 11...♗f6 12 ♖c1 ♘d4 13 ♗xd4 (13 ♘d2 c6 14 ♗xd4 exd4 15 ♘a4 ♗f7 16 ♘c5 ♖b8 = Taimanov) 13...exd4 14 ♘a4 ♗d5 15 ♘c5 ♕e7 16 ♕d2 ♖ae8 17 a4 c6 18 ♖fe1 ♘c8 19 ♕f4 ♘d6 20 h4 b6 21 ♘a6 ♕d7 22 ♘d2

♗xg2 23 ♔xg2 (Ljubojević-Hjartarson, Reykjavik 1991) 23...♖e7 = (Hjartarson).

Now we return to the main line after 9 a4 *(D)*.

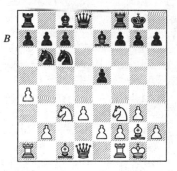

9...a5 10 ♗e3

In Geller-Flohr, USSR Ch 1954, White tried the immediate 10 ♘b5. After 10...♗e6 11 e4!? ♗f6 12 ♗e3 ♘h4 13 ♗c5 ♖e8 14 ♖a3 ♘d7 a complicated position was reached with good chances for Black.

10...♗g4

Best, as Black must fight for control of d4. His plan should be a rather simplistic one, namely ...♖e8, and ...♗f8, followed by an eventual ...♘d4.

11 ♖c1

Initiating pressure along the c-file which quite often culminates with an exchange sacrifice on c6. Efforts to do without this move have so far come to nought, e.g. 11 ♘d2 ♖b8 (this should be a standard reaction to ♘f3-d2) 12 ♗xb6 cxb6 13 ♘c4 f6 14 ♖e1 ♗c5 15 ♕b3 ♘d4 16 ♕a2 ♔h8 17 h3 ♗h5 ∓ Videki-Petursson, Vienna 1990 or 11 h3 ♗e6 12 ♕c1?!

(12 ♖c1 ♘d5 13 ♘xd5 ♗xd5 14 ♗c5 ♗d6 =) 12...♘d4 13 ♗xd4 exd4 14 ♘e4 ♗d5 ∓ E.Ragozin-A.Sokolov, Bern 1992.

11...♖e8

11...♖b8! is more precise, planning to meet 12 ♘d2 by 12...♘d4, relieving himself from pressure on c7. Still, there is nothing wrong with the text move if Black follows it up correctly.

12 ♘d2! *(D)*

A novelty at the time, this move is much stronger than the feeble 12 h3?! ♗e6 13 ♘e4 ♘d4 14 ♗xd4 exd4 15 ♘c5 ♗xc5 16 ♖xc5 c6 which left White worse in Bischoff-Suba, Dortmund 1983. Also not dangerous for Black is 12 ♘b5 in view of 12...♘d5 13 ♗c5 ♘db4 with easy equality.

12...♖b8 13 ♘b5 ♗b4?!

13...♕d7 also fails to equalize after Korchnoi's suggestion 14 ♘c4! ♘xc4 15 ♖xc4, which he very modestly assesses as =, but I think that 13...♗f8!? offers Black good prospects. For example: 14 ♗xc6 bxc6 15 ♘a7 ♕d5 16 ♘xc6 ♗h3 17 ♘f3

♗xf1 18 ♘xb8 e4! 19 ♕xf1 exf3 20 ♘a6! ♕b7! 21 ♘c5 (21 ♘xc7? ♖c8 ∓) 21...♕d5! (21...♗xc5?! 22 ♖xc5 ♘xa4 23 ♖xa5 ♘xb2 is less clear since the knight gets into difficulties) and now 22 d4 would be met by 22...♘c4. Instead 22 exf3 ♖xe3 23 fxe3 ♗xc5 is unclear, and 22 ♘a6 is a draw.

True, this variation leads to a draw by repetition, but the above improvement on Black's 11th move should offer him fully acceptable play.

14 ♗xc6!

14 ♖xc6 is tempting but leads to nothing special after 14...bxc6 15 ♘a7 ♗d7 16 ♘xc6 ♗xc6 17 ♗xc6 ♖e6 18 ♕c2 ♘d5!? 19 ♗xd5 (19 ♗a7? ♖xc6! 20 ♕xc6 ♖a8) 19...♕xd5 20 ♕xc7 ♕a8! =.

14...bxc6 15 ♘a7

The point of White's play. Black now loses a pawn, but in return gets some compensation in the form of light-square weaknesses around the white king.

15...♗h3 16 ♘xc6 ♕d5 17 ♘f3 ♖a8!

The only move! After the faulty 17...♗xf1? 18 ♘xb8 ♗xe2 19 ♕xe2 ♖xb8 20 ♗xb6 White has a clear advantage.

18 ♘xb4 axb4 19 ♖e1 ♘xa4 20 ♖xc7 b3!

This pawn is a valuable asset and certainly shouldn't be given away by 20...♘xb2? 21 ♕d2 when White enjoys an undisputed advantage. 20...♕a5 is also dangerous for Black in view of 21 ♖xf7!?.

21 ♕d2 ♖ec8 *(D)*

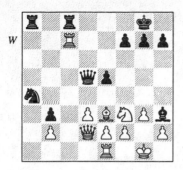

22 ♖xc8+!

Korchnoi is always tactically alert but this costs him dearly on the clock. With 22 ♖ec1? he could have fallen into a nasty trap: 22...♖xc7 23 ♖xc7 ♘xb2!! 24 ♕xb2 ♖a2 and it is already doubtful if White can save himself, for example 25 ♕c1/3 h6! or 25 ♕b1 ♖xe2 26 ♘h4 b2!.

22...♖xc8 23 ♖c1 ♖xc1+ 24 ♕xc1

The mass exchange of rooks has relieved White from his problems with the back rank but the presence of opposite-coloured bishops means that Black maintains certain drawing chances. With his next move Petursson begins a war of attrition in order to offset White's advantage.

24...h6! 25 ♘e1?!

There was still time to go wrong by 25 d4? ♕b5! 26 ♕d2 ♘c3!!, when White loses! However, 25 ♕d2! is best, to be followed by ♘e1 and f3, when Black would have had more difficulties in reaching the draw.

25...♕a5 26 ♗d2 ♕d5 27 ♗b4 e4 28 ♗a3 exd3 29 exd3

After Korchnoi has been forced to accept the splitting of his pawns the drawing process becomes much simplified in view of the insecure position of the white monarch.

29...♕h5 30 f3 ♕e5 31 ♔f2 ♗e6 32 ♘g2?! ♗f5 33 ♕e3?

An oversight, probably in time trouble. Fortunately for White the position is still a draw.

33...♘xb2! 34 ♕xe5 ♘xd3+ 35 ♔e2 ♘xe5 36 ♘e3 ♗d7 37 f4 ♗b5+ 38 ♔d2 ♘f3+ 39 ♔c3 ♘xh2 40 ♔xh3 ♔h7 41 ♔c3 ♘f3 42 ♘c2 and the players agreed to split the point as Black's extra pawn is meaningless.

11) Romanishin System: Main line 8 a3, 9 b4 without 10 ♖b1

Game 11
Portisch – Romanishin
Reggio Emilia 1985/6

1 c4 e5 2 ♘c3 ♘f6 3 g3 d5 4 cxd5 ♘xd5 5 ♗g2 ♘b6 6 ♘f3 ♘c6 7 0-0

The actual move-order was 7 d3 ♗e7 8 a3 0-0 9 0-0 ♗e6 10 b4.

7...♗e7 8 a3 0-0 9 b4 ♗e6 10 d3

It is generally considered more elastic to play 10 ♖b1 as White may decide to omit d3 and embark on a direct ♘e4-c5 manoeuvre. Most often, however, the choice between 10 d3 and 10 ♖b1 has no significance and will lead to the lines analysed under the next illustrative game.

Here we will deal with various efforts by White to avoid combining the text move with an early ♖b1.

10...a5

This is a typical thrust in this variation and Black's customary source of counterplay. It leads to a double-edged fight on the queenside since it gives rise to the creation of weak pawns and squares in that sector of the board.

11 b5 ♘d4 12 ♘d2 *(D)*

White has several other tries at his disposal but not one of them guarantees an advantage. Black should be able to generate interesting counterplay in the majority of these lines:

a) 12 ♘xe5? ♗f6 13 f4 ♘b3 ∓.

b) 12 ♘xd4?! exd4 13 ♘a4 ♗d5 14 ♘xb6 (14 ♗h3 ♖e8 ∓) 14...cxb6 15 a4 ♗xg2 16 ♔xg2 ♕d5+ 17 ♔g1 ♖ad8 (17...♗c5 ∓ Romanishin) 18 ♗a3 ♗c5 19 ♗xc5 bxc5 20 b6 h5! gave Black the initiative in H.Olafsson-Toshkov, Saint John 1988.

c) 12 ♗e3 ♘d5 13 ♘xd5 ♗xd5 14 ♗xd4 exd4 15 ♕a4 c5 (this leads to instant equality; 15...♖e8!?) 16 bxc6 ♗xc6 17 ♕xd4 ♕xd4 18 ♘xd4 ♗xg2 19 ♔xg2 ♗f6 = Ghitescu-Barbulescu, Baile Herculane 1984.

d) 12 ♗b2:

d1) 12...♗b3?! 13 ♕c1 ♗d5 14 ♘xd4 ♗xg2 15 ♘e6! fxe6 (15...♕d6, as in Miles-Steinbacher, Bundesliga 1983/4, is met by 16 ♘xc7! ±) 16 ♔xg2 a4 17 ♘e4 ♗d6 18 ♗c3 ♕e8 19 ♕b2 ♕h5 20 f3 ♘d5 21 ♗d2 ± Adorjan-Lücke, Altensteig 1989.

d2) 12...♘b3! 13 ♖b1 f6 14 ♘d2 ♘c5 15 a4 ♖f7 16 ♖a1 (16 ♗a3!? ♘cxa4 17 ♘xa4 ♗xa3 18 ♗xb7 ♖b8 19 ♗c6 ♗b4 is unclear) 16...♖c8 17 ♘ce4 ♘xe4 18 ♗xe4 c6 19 bxc6

bxc6 with complicated play was the game Cvetković-Cebalo, Yugoslavia 1986.

c) 12 ♖b1 f6 is considered under 10 ♖b1.

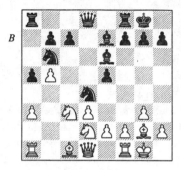

12...c6

A solid approach, offering equal chances. It has been for a long time a registered trademark of Grandmaster Oleg Romanishin.

The temporary sacrifice 12...a4!? is a more ambitious way of playing the position but is not considered very respectable in view of the following continuation: 13 ♗xb7 (13 e3? ♘b3 14 ♘xb3 ♗xb3 15 ♕e2 ♕d7 16 ♗xb7 ♖ad8 left Black in total control in the game Chabanon-Hertneck, Germany-France 1993) 13...♖a5 14 ♖b1 (14 ♗c6? ♘xc6 15 bxc6 ♕a8 ∓) and then:

a) 14...♕d7 15 ♘c4! ♘xc4 16 bxc4 ♗xc4 17 e3! ♗xf1 (17...♘e2+!? ±; 17...♗d3?! 18 exd4 ♗xb1 19 ♘xb1 ♖xb5 20 ♗e4 allows White to retain the initiative) 18 ♔xf1 ♖b8 19 ♗c6 ♕h3+ 20 ♗g2 ♕e6 21 exd4 ♕c4+ 22 ♘e2 ♖axb5 23 ♖xb5 ♖xb5 24 ♗e4 gave White a clear advantage in the game Portisch-Vaganian, Tilburg 1983.

b) However, it seems that the assessment is rather debatable as the relatively unknown improvement 14,.,♕e8!? prevents a pin along the d-file and recovers the pawn with a good game: 15 ♘f3 (15 ♗g2 ♘xb5 16 ♘xb5 ♖xb5 17 ♖xb5 ♕xb5 18 ♕c2 is unclear) 15...♘xb5 16 ♘xb5 ♖xb5 17 ♕c2 ♖c5 18 ♕b2 ♕b8 19 ♗e4 f5 20 ♗c3 fxe4 21 ♗xc5 ♗xc5 22 ♘g5 ♗d4 23 ♕c1 ♗a2 24 e3 ♗xb1 25 ♕xb1 ♗c5 26 d4 ♗e7 27 ♕a2+ ♔h8 28 ♘f7+ ♖xf7 29 ♕xf7 ♕f8 and Black emerged victorious from the complications in Dorfman-Guseinov, Kiev 1984.

13 bxc6

The alternative 13 a4 ♘d5 14 ♘xd5 was successful in Miles-Romanishin, Palma de Mallorca 1989 after 14...♗xd5?! 15 ♗xd5 cxd5 16 ♗b2 ♘e6? (16...♗f6 ±) 17 ♗xe5 d4 18 ♕b3! ♕d7 19 f4 ♖ad8 20 ♘f3, but Korchnoi's proposal 14...cxd5! looks like a good antidote, e.g. 15 ♗b2 ♕b6 16 e3 ♘f5 17 g4 (17 ♗xe5? ♘xe3!) 17...♘h6 18 ♗xe5 ♘xg4 or 16 ♗xd4 ♕xd4 (16...exd4!?) 17 ♘f3 ♕c3 18 ♖c1 ♕b2 19 ♖c7 ♗d8 20 ♖c2 ♕b4 21 ♘xe5 ♕xa4 with an unclear position in both cases.

13...♘xc6 14 ♗b2?!

A weird move, blocking the b-file for no apparent reason. Best seems to be 14 ♖b1!? a4 15 ♗xc6 bxc6 16 ♕c2 (Vladimirov-Savchenko, Helsinki 1992) although even here Black should be able to organize strong counterplay starting with 16...f5 or

even 16...h5!?. On the other hand rather worthless are 14 ♘a4 ♘xa4 15 ♕xa4 ♘d4 and 14 a4 ♕d7 15 ♘f3 ♖ac8 16 ♖b1 ♗b4 17 ♗d2 f6 18 ♘b5 ♖fd8 19 ♗xb4 axb4 20 ♘d2 ♕e7 21 ♖c1 ♘a5, which left White under pressure in C.Hansen-Romanishin, Tåstrup 1992.

14...a4! *(D)*

Of course! This is one of the main ideas of Black's system, combining restriction with the creation of a useful target on a3. With the b3- and c4-squares firmly under Black's control White's chances on the queenside are seriously hampered.

15 ♖c1 ♖a5!

The rook covers a lot of important squares here and may make its presence felt via b5 or c5 according to circumstance. For an analogous idea see Chernin-Smejkal mentioned under Illustrative Game 7.

16 ♖e1 ♕d7?

With 16...f5! Black would have completed the restriction theme by taking away the e4-square from the white knights. This is hardly the case after the text move as White is given the chance to obtain some breathing room by utilizing the unfortunate position of the black queen.

17 ♘c4! ♘xc4 18 dxc4 ♕xd1 *(D)*

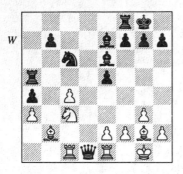

19 ♘xd1?

A passive recapture, leading to a difficult endgame for White. Portisch would have had excellent compensation for a pawn after the natural 19 ♖exd1 ♗xc4 20 ♖d7 ♗g5 21 e3 ♖b8 22 ♘d5 in view of his strong centralization and control of the seventh rank. A wiser response to 19 ♖exd1 is Romanishin's suggestion of 19...♘d4 but all the same Black's advantage is gone after his inexact 16th move.

19...♖c8 20 h4

White has to waste a tempo on this as the immediate 20 ♘e3 is well met by 20...♗g5! with a clear advantage for Black. Seeing that the knight is heading towards d5 Romanishin sets about shaking White's control of that square.

20...♘d4 21 ♘e3 b5! 22 ♘d5

The knight is doing nothing here but the alternative 22 ♗d5 doesn't help much either: 22...b4! (22...bxc4

23 ♗xe6 ♘xe6 ∓ Romanishin) 23 ♗xe6 fxe6 and Black's queenside pawns look very threatening. 22 ♗c3?! ♗xa3! 23 ♖a1 b4 24 ♖xa3 bxc3 is even worse as the a-pawn is unstoppable after 25 ♖xc3 a3.

22...♗f8 23 ♗c3??

This is a terrible mistake, rendering Black's task much easier. The best chance was probably 23 ♘b6!? ♖c7 24 e3 ♘b3 25 ♗xe5 ♖c5 26 ♗d4 (26 ♗c3? ♖a6 −+) 26...♘xc1 27 ♖xc1 with just a few chances of survival. What now follows is a complete massacre.

23...♖xc4!

Suddenly the game is decided as White will be left drastically behind in material, the obvious point being that 24 ♗xa5 loses immediately to 24...♖xc1. Annoyed by his colossal blunder Portisch prolongs the struggle for quite a while although the winning process would be straightforward even for an average club player.

24 e3 ♘b3 25 ♖cd1 ♗xd5 26 ♗xa5 ♗xg2 27 ♔xg2 ♘xa5 28 ♖d8 ♘c6 29 ♖a8 g6 30 ♖b1 ♔g7 31 ♖xb5 ♗xa3

Winning the a-pawn is usually the culmination of Black's strategy in this variation. In the present case it signals the final countdown for a game that was practically decided after a mere twenty moves.

32 ♖b6 ♗e7 33 ♖aa6 ♘d8 34 ♖a7 ♗f8 35 ♖a5 a3 36 ♖aa6 h5 37 ♖b5 e4! 38 ♖bb6 ♘e6 39 ♖b8 ♖c2 40 ♔g1 a2 41 ♔g2 ♘c5 42 ♖aa8 ♗d6 43 ♖c8 ♗e5 0-1

12) Romanishin System: Main line 8 a3, 9 b4 with 10 ♖b1

Game 12
Gulko – Tukmakov
New York 1994

1 c4 e5 2 ♘c3 ♘f6 3 ♘f3 ♘c6 4 g3
d5 5 cxd5 ♘xd5 6 ♗g2 ♘b6 7 0-0
♗e7 8 a3 0-0 9 b4 ♗e6 10 ♖b1 f6 11
d3 *(D)*

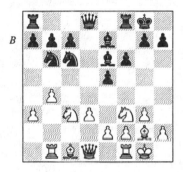

The opening set-up is almost identical to that of the previous game, the difference being the inclusion of the moves ♖b1 and ...f6 which should, in general, be favourable to White. Despite this positional nuance, practice has verified Black's game to be rock-solid and the customary plan with ...a5 is also appropriate here, albeit the ramifications differ. On the other hand, efforts to do without 11 d3 should come to nought if Black handles the position carefully:

a) 11 b5?! ♘d4 12 ♘e1 c6 13 a4
cxb5 14 axb5 ♕d7 15 e3 ♘f5 16
♕f3 ♘d6 17 ♕e2 ♗c4 18 d3 ♘xb5

and Black was a pawn to the good for nothing, although he eventually lost in Mirallès-Roos, France 1992.

b) 11 ♘e4 was for a long time considered to be the main line but in my opinion Black should be at least equal. 11...♗a2! 12 ♖b2 ♗d5 13 ♘c5 e4! 14 ♘e1 ♘c4 15 ♖b1 ♗xc5 16 bxc5 b6 17 d3 and now:

b1) 17...♘4e5!? 18 dxe4 ♗c4 19 ♕xd8 ♖axd8 20 f4 when Thorsteins suggests 20...♘d4!? or 20...♘d7.

b2) 17...exd3 18 e4 (18 ♘xd3 ♗xg2 19 ♔xg2 ♕d5+ is a little better for Black) 18...♗f7 19 ♘xd3 (Suba-Thorsteins, New York 1989) 19...bxc5!? 20 ♘xc5 ♕e7 21 ♘b3 ♖ad8 22 ♕c2 a5 with good counterplay for Black.

11...a5 12 b5

In Serper-Mainka, Vienna 1991, White tried the paradoxical idea 12 bxa5!? ♖xa5 13 ♘b5, which turned out well after 13...♕d7?! 14 ♗e3! ♘d5 15 ♗d2 ♖a6 16 ♕c2 ♘d8 17 e4 ♖c6 18 ♕d1 ♘b6 19 ♗e3 ♘f7 20 d4. However, it seems that Black's play was rather over-elaborate. With the simple 13...♘a7! (Korchnoi) he could have neutralized the dangerous knight, thereby obtaining excellent counterplay.

12...♘d4 13 ♘e1!?

Another subtle Korchnoi refinement. White is planning to answer 13...♗d5?! by 14 ♘xd5 ♗xd5 15 ♗d2! which should give him a steady plus. This is simply not possible in the 13 ♘d2 variation examined below, as d2 is occupied by the knight.

13 ♘d2 looks more natural and has been the subject of an interesting theoretical debate over the past decade. It seems to me that chances should be approximately even with best play, although there are still unexplored resources in the position as the following material indicates:

a) 13...♘d5?? 14 ♗xd5! ♗xd5 15 e3 and Black loses a piece.

b) 13...♗d5!? was a stunning discovery by Motwani and is currently regarded as the main line. It is indeed a rare occurrence in this type of position to surrender the powerful light-squared bishop, but as we have just seen, playing the knight to d5 is a terrible blunder. The usual continuation is 14 ♘xd5 (14 ♗h3 ♗f7 15 e3 ♘e6 16 ♘de4 g6! gives Black counterplay – Ftačnik) 14...♘xd5 *(D)*, when we reach a critical position:

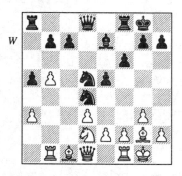

b1) 15 ♗b2 a4! 16 ♗xd4 exd4 17 ♗xd5+ ♕xd5 18 ♕c1 ♗c5 19 ♕c4 c6! ∓ Sunye Neto-L.Hansen, Novi Sad OL 1990. The pawn on a3 is, once more, extremely weak.

b2) 15 ♗xd5+ ♕xd5 16 a4 ♗b4 17 ♘b3 (17 ♘c4 e4 18 ♘c3 ♕h5 19 dxe4 ♘xe2+ 20 ♔g2 ♖ad8 21 ♕b3+ ♔h8 ∓ Ftačnik) 17...c6 (17...♘xb3 18 ♕xb3 ♖ad8 19 ♗e3 =; 17...c5 =) 18 e4?! (18 bxc6 bxc6 19 ♗e3 = Ftačnik) 18...♕d7 19 ♘xd4 exd4 20 ♗d2?! c5! ∓ Ftačnik-Torre, Bacolod 1991.

b3) 15 ♘e4! is the best try. According to my research Black faces a few problems here:

b31) 15...f5?! is interesting but probably inadequate for equality: 16 e3! fxe4 17 exd4 exd4 and now:

b311) 18 ♗xe4 ♘c3 19 ♕b3+ ♔h8 =.

b312) 18 dxe4 ♘c3 19 ♕b3+ ♔h8 20 ♖a1 and now 20...♘e2+ with equality or 20...a4 21 ♕c4 ♕d7!? (L.Hansen).

b313) 18 ♗b2! e3 (18...♘c3 19 ♗xc3 dxc3 20 ♗xe4 ♕d4!? 21 ♖c1! ±) 19 ♕b3 c6 20 ♗xd4 exf2+ and now 21 ♖xf2!? gives White a slight plus. Instead 21 ♗xf2 ♕d6 22 ♖bc1 ♖ad8 23 bxc6 bxc6 24 ♕b7!? ♖f6 25 ♖fe1 ♗f8 is less clear.

b32) 15...a4!? (this looks like an improvement) 16 e3 ♘b3 17 ♕c2 (17 ♖xb3!? axb3 18 ♕xb3 is unclear) 17...♔h8!? 18 ♘d2 (the most testing; White clarifies the situation on the queenside by exchanging Black's strong knight) 18...♘xc1 19 ♕xc1 ♕d6!? (better than 19...♕d7 20 ♘e4! with an edge for White). The position requires practical tests.

b) 13...♕c8! is complicated and appears the most logical. Black's slight weakness on the c-file is compensated by good piece play. 14 e3 ♘f5 15 ♕c2 ♖d8 16 ♘ce4 (16 ♗b2 a4 17 ♖fd1 ♘d6!? with a double-edged position) 16...♗d5! 17 ♗b2 (17 ♘c4!? ♕e6 =) 17...♘h6 18 ♖bc1 ♕e6 19 ♘c4 ♘d7!? 20 ♖fe1 ♘f7 21 ♕e2 was unclear in Vaulin-Tiviakov, St Petersburg 1993. Although Black eventually lost this game he is excellently centralized at the moment.

Besides 13 ♘d2, a secondary option for White is 13 ♘xd4. However, this shouldn't particularly worry Black: 13...exd4 14 ♘a4 (14 ♘e4?! a4 ∓ Feys-Yakovich, Ostend 1993) 14...♗d5 15 ♗h3! ♕e8 16 e4 (Contin-Kharlov, Bern 1992) is unclear and probably the best White can get after his feeble 13th move.

13...♕c8!

An important improvement over Korchnoi-Tukmakov, Wijk aan Zee 1993, in which White obtained a slight initiative after 13...c6 14 bxc6 ♘xc6 15 ♗e3! (the main idea behind Korchnoi's 13th is that this bishop can develop freely) 15...♘d5 16 ♘xd5 ♗xd5 17 ♖xb7 (17 ♖b5!?; 17 ♕a4!?). The text move clears d8 for the rook and prepares ...a4 or ...♗h3.

14 e3 ♘f5 15 ♘f3

White is experiencing some difficulties on account of the awkward placement of this knight. The chief problem with Gulko's position is that b3 lacks the useful protection this knight could afford but re-deploying it to d2 is out of the question as White would be two tempi behind compared to Vaulin-Tiviakov above.

15...♖d8 16 ♕c2 a4! *(D)*

After this move, White's a- and b-pawns are practically isolated, while

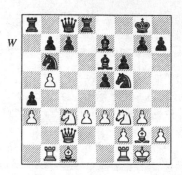

d3 also starts to feel the pressure. The opening has been a strategic success for Black, which is probably the reason for White's over-reaction in the next few moves.

17 e4?! ♘d4 18 ♘xd4 ♖xd4 19 ♖d1?

A logical follow-up to his 17th move, but an exchange sacrifice cannot be prosperous with the king's bishop shut in. For better or worse White had to try 19 f4 although it is not particularly appetizing either.

19...♗b3 20 ♖xb3 axb3 21 ♕xb3+ ♔h8 22 ♘e2 ♖da4

Tukmakov realizes that White has no attacking chances whatsoever and correctly decides to go after another pawn.

23 d4 ♗xa3 24 dxe5 fxe5 25 ♗e3 ♘c4 26 ♗h3 ♕f8

Of course not 26...♕xh3?? 27 ♕xa4 +−. This is the type of miracle White needs if he is to stave off defeat.

27 ♗c1 ♗xc1

27...♗c5 was probably better, but there is nothing wrong with the text move since every exchange brings Black closer to victory.

28 ♖xc1 ♖b4 29 ♕d3 ♖d8 30 ♕c3 ♖d2

The penetration of Black's rook to the seventh rank ensures a quick finale.

31 ♗f1 h6 32 ♖a1 ♔h7 33 ♖a8!? ♕xa8 34 ♕xb4 ♕g8! 35 ♘c3 ♕f7 36 f4?

A last mistake but White's position was absolutely hopeless anyway.

36...♕h5 37 ♘e2 ♖xe2 0-1

13) King's Indian Variation (Van Wely System): 10 ♘d2

Game 13
Renet – Van Wely
Brussels 1993

1 ♘f3 ♘f6 2 g3 g6 3 ♗g2 ♗g7 4 0-0 0-0 5 c4 d6 6 ♘c3 e5 7 d3 h6!? 8 ♖b1 a5 9 a3 ♖e8 10 ♘d2 c6

In contrast to the 7...♘c6 main line, here Black develops immediate central action. The plan of erecting a strong pawn centre looks healthier than a direct kingside attack as it provides space for free development and blocks the range of White's king's bishop.

11 b4 axb4 12 axb4 d5 13 ♕c2

In Vaganian-Van Wely, New York 1994, White decided on the traditional plan of challenging the a-file by 13 ♗b2. After the continuation 13...♗e6 14 ♖a1 ♘a6 15 b5 ♘c5 16 ♘a4 ♘fd7 17 ♘xc5 ♘xc5 18 ♕c2 ♖c8 19 bxc6 bxc6 20 ♖fc1 d4 21

♗a3! ♗f8 22 ♗xc5 ♗xc5 23 ♖cb1 ♗f8 24 ♖a6 c5 25 ♖bb6 ♔g7 26 ♕a2 the Armenian GM was on top, torturing his opponent for a long time before he finally achieved a draw on move 63 but obviously Van Wely was rather too ambitious in consistently avoiding a rook exchange. With 16...♘xa4 17 ♖xa4 cxb5! Black could have obtained excellent play.

13...♗e6 14 e4?

This is in effect the losing move. As the continuation proves, a combination of ♘fd2 and e4 is illogical. White should have continued his policy of attacking on the long diagonal by b5 which is similar to Vaganian-Van Wely and Zlotnikov-Van Wely mentioned in the Ideas Section.

14...d4 15 ♘d1 (D)

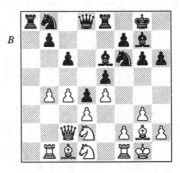

15...b5!

An important move, fixing the b4-pawn as a weakness. White will have insoluble problems in defending this pawn as his position is cut in two by the annoying wedge on d4.

16 f4

Trying to obtain breathing space on the kingside. Renet obviously realized that this move creates a glaring weakness on e3 but White seems to have no other way to stir up some counterplay.

16...♖a4 17 ♘f3 exf4 18 gxf4 ♘a6 19 ♗d2 ♘g4 20 ♘b2 ♘xb4! 21 ♕d1 ♘xd3!

Van Wely has broken into the heart of the enemy position, but has sacrificed almost nothing from the material point of view. White is practically obliged to take the rook as 22 ♘xd3 ♗xc4 forces capitulation.

22 ♘xa4 bxa4 23 ♕xa4 ♘e3! 24 ♕xc6 ♘xf4 25 ♗xe3 dxe3

A horrible position for White. Renet could have spared himself the rest by resigning here, but probably being short of time he continues to fight to the bitter end.

26 ♖fd1 ♕a8 27 ♕xa8 ♖xa8 28 c5 ♖a2 29 ♖d8+ ♔h7 30 ♘e1 ♗f6 31 ♖e8 ♗c3 32 ♗f3 ♖f2 33 c6 ♘h3+ 34 ♔h1 ♖f1+ 0-1

14) King's Indian Variation (Van Wely System): 10 e4

Game 14
Andrianov – Kotronias
Karditsa 1994

1 ♘f3 ♘f6 2 c4 g6 3 g3 ♗g7 4 ♗g2 0-0 5 0-0 d6 6 ♘c3 e5 7 d3 h6 8 ♖b1 a5 9 a3 ♖e8 10 e4!?

A logical response, because the moves ...h6 and ...♖e8 are not so useful in the Nimzowitsch/Botvinnik type of structure that has arisen on the board. The disadvantages of the move are also obvious since White's king's bishop is now hemmed in, which renders his preparations for b4 look rather silly. White hopes that he will be able to play the advance d4 later on, transposing to a sort of g3 King's Indian, in which the manoeuvre ♖b1 followed by b4 is commonly used.

10...c6 11 h3 ♘a6!

Prior to this encounter I had lost a game to Lirindzakis in which I developed my queen and bishop prematurely to the squares c7 and e6 respectively. My opponent opted for the simple plan of b3 and d4 after which I soon found myself without a constructive plan. The text is stronger, as it invites transposition to a King's Indian-type position without committing Black's pieces to squares that are unnatural for that opening.

12 ♗d2

An indication that White is not willing to play d4. 12 ♖e1 ♘d7!? 13 b4 axb4 (13...♘c7!?) 14 axb4 ♘c7 15 ♗c3 (15 d4?! exd4 16 ♘xd4 ♘c5 ∓) 15...♘e6 16 ♕d2 ♔h7 17 ♖a1 is also possible, though after 17...♖xa1 18 ♖xa1 f5! Black obtains strong counterplay.

12...♗d7 13 ♘e1 ♘c7 14 ♘c2 b5 15 cxb5 ♘xb5!

After 15...cxb5? 16 b4 White's position is better as the knight on c7 obstructs the development of Black's major pieces.

16 ♘xb5 cxb5 17 ♘e3 *(D)*

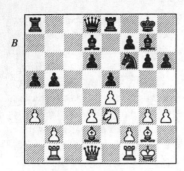

17...h5!

My best idea in the game. White was threatening to apply pressure on the queenside by means of ♖c1, ♕b3 followed by an eventual ♘d5 and I didn't like the prospect of constantly having to reckon with the possibility of the exchange sacrifice ♖c6 in the positions that would result after ...♘xd5, exd5. The text move intends to meet ♘d5 by ...♘xd5 and ...h4, creating counterplay on the kingside and also allowing the king's bishop to participate in the fight via h6.

18 h4

This was practically forced but now g4 has been weakened. As the game continuation shows, this is in Black's favour.

18...♕b6 19 ♖c1 a4!?

Played to keep the enemy queen out of b3 but concedes b4 to White's bishop. However, I thought that this was not so important as 20 ♗b4 can be met by 20...♖ac8 and if 21 ♕d2, then 21...♗h6!? is interesting.

20 ♕e2 ♗e6! 21 ♘d5?! ♘xd5 22 exd5 ♗g4!

The whole conception of 17...h5! has now been entirely justified. 23

♕e1 can be answered by 23...♕d4! 24 ♖c3 b4! 25 ♗e3? (25 axb4 ♕xb4 ∓) 25...bxc3! 26 ♗xd4 exd4 ∓ so White chose the only other playable continuation.

23 ♗f3 ♕d4! 24 ♗xg4

24 ♗c3! ♕xd5! is at least a little better for Black.

24...hxg4 25 ♗c3 ♕xd5 26 ♕xg4 ♖ac8

The situation has clarified. Black enjoys a slight plus in view of his superior pawn structure but it is not easy to take advantage of this factor as there are no agile minor pieces left to exploit White's weaknesses. Advancing the central pawns is the only alternative but this has to be done carefully, especially after White's next move.

27 h5!

This is not an attacking gesture, but White presumes that the lack of protective pawn cover around the king will make Black think twice before advancing in the centre.

27...gxh5 28 ♕xh5 ♖e6! 29 ♕g4 ♕b7 30 ♖ce1 ♖h6 31 ♕e4 d5 32 ♕g2 ♖e8 33 f4!? e4! 34 dxe4 dxe4 35 f5

35 ♗xg7?! is weaker as it helps Black double rooks on the h-file.

35...♗xc3 36 bxc3 ♕d5 37 ♖f4?

My opponent had conducted the defence well up to this point but here he faltered, in great time shortage. After 37 ♖e3 ♕c5 38 ♕e2 it is not clear if I could have won this game.

37...♕c5+

Not only winning a pawn, but also starting a fierce attack against the white king.

38 ♕f2 ♕xc3

38...e3 is stronger but for some reason I completely overlooked it!

39 ♖fxe4 ♖xe4 40 ♖xe4 ♕xa3

White's position is hopeless as Black can always force a winning endgame in view of his connected passed pawns on the queenside.

However, at this point I could never have guessed that I would lose these pawns in less than ten moves!

41 ♔g2 ♕c1 42 ♔f3 ♕d1+ 43 ♔f4 ♖h1 44 ♔e5 ♕a1+ 45 ♔d5 ♖d1+ 46 ♔c6 ♕f6+ 47 ♔xb5 ♖b1+ 48 ♖b4 ♕e5+ 49 ♔xa4 ♕e8+! 50 ♔a3 ♕a8+ 0-1

4 The Ideas Behind the Catalan Opening

1) The Fight on the Long Diagonal

The chief virtue of the Catalan system is the relatively smooth way in which White deploys his forces. This is a common advantage of most flank openings, particularly those in which White employs a kingside fianchetto, because the bishop exerts considerable influence on the centre, preventing Black from initiating complications at an early stage. In the Catalan this is always the case, since the kingside fianchetto constitutes a fundamental part of White's development. In fact, the longer the bishop remains unchallenged on the h1-a8 diagonal, the fewer Black's chances become of fighting on even terms. The first glimpse of counterplay will usually appear when the light-squared bishops cross swords on the long diagonal.

This position arose in the game **Karpov-Short**, *Tilburg 1988*. White seems to have a clear advantage on account of the backward c-pawn and the strange placement of the black pieces, yet as the game continuation proves, the important factor for a proper assessment of the chances is

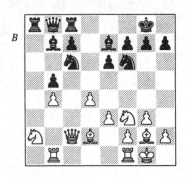

the unveiled force of Black's queen's bishop:

17...♖a6!

A strong preparatory move, freeing a8 for the black queen. From that square Her Majesty can support operations down the a-file, and, primarily, on the long diagonal.

18 ♘c1 ♕a8 19 ♕d1 ♖a3!!

This is an excellent geometrical motif, introducing the neat threat ...♘xd4! which, naturally, does not catch Karpov off guard. In retreating his knight though, he allows the English grandmaster to achieve a belated, yet effective, central thrust.

20 ♘e1 e5! 21 ♘c2 ♖a4 22 d5

After 22 ♗xc6? ♗xc6 23 dxe5 ♗f3 24 ♕e1 ♘g4 Black gets a tremendous attack for almost no material investment. Karpov correctly tries to keep the position closed, but the pawn on d5 provides Short with a new target for favourable liquidation.

22...♘d8 23 e4 c6! 24 dxc6 ♗xc6 25 f3 ♗d7 26 ♘d3 ♘c6 27 ♗e3 ♗e6

Black has comfortably equalized and perhaps a bit more than that. Karpov had to struggle until move 62 to achieve the draw.

In the above example the battery of queen and bishop worked well, but Black will not often have the possibility to set up a similar configuration. The following case shows a more usual type of this diagonal opposition, revealing that White's reluctance to exchange bishops can often be the source of serious trouble *(D)*.

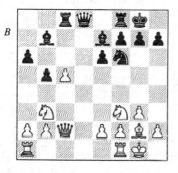

This is a well-known theoretical position, first reached in the game **Rogers-Geller**, *Vršac 1987* (the opening moves were 1 c4 e6 2 ♘f3 ♘f6 3 g3 ♗e7 4 ♗g2 d5 5 d4 0-0 6 0-0 dxc4 7 ♕c2 a6 8 ♕xc4 b5 9 ♕c2 ♗b7 10 ♗g5 ♘bd7 11 ♘bd2 ♖c8 12 ♗xf6 ♘xf6 13 ♘b3 c5 14 dxc5).

Black has sacrificed a pawn in order to free his game, and now proceeds to regain it by exploiting the superior activity of his pieces:

14...a5 15 ♖d1 ♕c7 16 ♕d3?!

Rogers failed to realize how perilous the situation was, for if he had, he would have tried to exchange light-squared bishops by 15 a4! ♗e4 16 ♕c3 b4 17 ♕e3 ♗d5 18 ♖fd1 ♕c7 19 ♘fd4 or 16 a4! with the same idea. It is to Black's advantage for the bishops to remain on the board, since their prescence makes it is impossible for White to gain access to his opponent's weaknesses on the queenside.

16...a4 17 ♘bd4 ♗xc5 18 ♕xb5?

Getting the queen out of the fork ...e5-e4, yet matters now take a turn for the worse as White's pieces are now totally uncoordinated. Geller remarks that 18 ♖ac1! would have made a fight of it because the apparently strong 18...e5 is answered by 19 b4!, equalizing the chances. Better is 18...b4!, when according to Geller Black can still boast of a slight initiative.

18...e5 19 ♘f5 ♗e4!

The bishop makes its presence felt, exploiting the awkward position of the enemy knight. After 20 ♗h3 ♖b8! 21 ♕xa4 ♖a8 22 ♕b3 ♗c2 the white game collapses into pieces so he has to allow the highly undesirable doubling of his e-pawns.

20 ♘e3 ♗xe3 21 fxe3 ♕a7 *(D)*

The shortcomings of White's play are more than obvious. His pawn structure has been torn apart, while

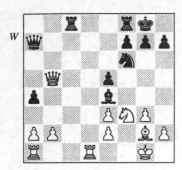

Black's pieces, led by the dominant e4-bishop (which White unwisely neglected to exchange a few moves ago), are closing in for the execution. Rogers is renowned for his skills in defending difficult positions but in the present case a miracle would be required.

22 h3 ♕xe3+ 23 ♔h2 ♖c2 24 ♖e1 ♗xf3

The bishop has done its duty and it is now given up to facilitate the winning process.

25 exf3 ♕xf3 26 ♖g1 a3?! 27 bxa3 ♕e3 28 ♖ge1 ♕f3 29 ♕f1??

Better was 29 ♖g1 e4 ∓, as now Black gets the opportunity to deliver a knock-out blow.

29...♖f2 0-1

White threw in the towel as 30 ♕g1 ♘h5 would be too much to withstand.

From the evidence presented so far (positions involving a queenside build-up with pawns on a6 and b5) one may easily draw the conclusion that Black's usual way of counterbalancing the pressure on the long diagonal involves a weakening of the square c6. This weakening is by no means easy to exploit, even after an exchange of the light-squared bishops, but this kind of simplification is rightly considered a strategic success for White as then he gets a concrete target to play for. Black is, in general, happy to postpone this exchange for as long as he can, but if it becomes inevitable he should always have in reserve some way to fortify the defence of the sensitive point. The following case is quite enlightening *(D)*:

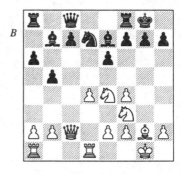

This is another standard position for the Geller system (arising after 1 d4 ♘f6 2 c4 e6 3 g3 d5 4 ♗g2 ♗e7 5 ♘f3 0-0 6 0-0 dxc4 7 ♕c2 a6 8 ♕xc4 b5 9 ♕c2 ♗b7 10 ♗f4 ♘d5 11 ♘c3 ♘xf4 12 gxf4 ♘d7 13 ♖fd1 ♕c8 14 ♘e4) but I have refrained from including it in our repertoire since it involves the time-consuming move ...♘d5xf4 which is not very much to my liking. Still, this particular situation is highly instructive, as Black has to take drastic measures to neutralize his opponent's pressure on the c-file. In **Ribli-Karpov**, *Amsterdam*

1980, the then World Champion eventually succumbed to the manyfold problems:

14...c5

The natural move, but it doesn't quite meet the requirements of the position. White is now able to capitalize on the weakness of c6, obtaining a long-term initiative.

15 dxc5 ♘xc5 16 ♘xc5 ♕xc5 17 ♕xc5 ♗xc5 18 ♖ac1 ♖fc8 19 ♘e5 ♗xg2 20 ♔xg2 *(D)*

20...f6

In the game Gavrikov-Azmaiparashvili, USSR 1981, Black chose the more refined 20...♖c7 but this didn't prevent White from maintaining a slight edge after 21 e3 ♖ac8 22 ♖d7 a5 23 b3 f6 24 ♖xc7 ♖xc7 25 ♘f3 ♔f7 26 ♘d4 h4 27 ♘b5 ♖c6 28 ♔f3 ♔e7 29 f5!. The combination of rook and knight is an ideal one for exploiting weaknesses on the light squares, and Black can at most hope to draw with resourceful defence.

21 ♘f3 ♗f8 22 e3 g6

Preferable was 22...♔f7, intending to approach as quickly as possible to the theatre of action.

23 b3 ♗b4 24 h3 ♔f8 25 ♘d4 ♔f7 26 a4! bxa4 27 bxa4 ♗c5?

A miscalculation, allowing the penetration of a white rook. After the logical 27...a5 it would have been extremely difficult for Ribli to break down Black's defences.

28 ♖c4! ♗a3

Karpov must have realized by now that his intended 28...♗xd4 doesn't solve Black's problems: 29 ♖cxd4 ♖e8 30 ♖b4 (to be followed by ♖b6 and ♖1d6) and a pawn is soon going to fall. The text is better in a practical sense as White has to demonstrate magnificent endgame technique in order to bring home his undisputed positional advantage.

29 ♖xc8 ♖xc8 30 ♖b1! ♖c4 31 ♖b7+ ♗e7 32 ♖a7 e5 33 fxe5 fxe5 34 ♘f3 ♖xa4 35 ♘xe5+ ♔f6 36 ♘c6 ♗c5 37 ♖xh7 ♖a2 38 ♔f3 a5

White has won a pawn, but the a5 pawn seems to guarantee Black sufficient counterplay for a draw. By utilizing a hidden tactical motif Ribli manages to restore the co-ordination of his pieces, destroying any illusions Black might have about splitting the point.

39 h4! a4 40 ♔e4! ♗f8

The pawn was immune because of 40...♖xf2? 41 ♘d8! and the black king is caught in a mating net. The end is now near as White's manoeuvre has gained him enough time to bring up the reserves.

41 ♖a7 ♗d6 42 f4 ♖h2

An attempt to maintain the a-pawn by 42...a3 would have failed to 43 ♘d4 ♗e7 (to prevent 44 ♖a6 ♔e7

45 f5) 44 ♘f3 ♖b2 45 ♘e5 a2 46
♖a6+ ♔g7 47 ♖xg6+ ♔h7 48 ♖a6
♗xh4 49 ♖a7+ ♔g8 50 ♘g4! and
the combined advance of White's
pawns will carry the day. Now, however, the end is much more prosaic.

**43 ♖a6 ♔f7 44 ♘e5+ ♗xe5 45
♔xe5 ♔g7 46 ♖a7+ ♔h6 47 ♖xa4
♖xh4 48 ♔f6 ♖h5 49 e4 ♖h4 50 e5
♖h5 51 e6 ♖f5+ 52 ♔e7 ♔g7 53
♔d6 ♖f8 54 ♖a7+ ♔f6 55 ♖d7! 1-0**

Returning to the diagram, what
should Black do? It seems that the
answer lies in the dynamic **14...f5!?**,
which was successfully tested in **Ricardi-Granda**, *Buenos Aires 1991*.
The merits of Granda's choice became immediately visible as White's
reply showed a lack of positional understanding:

15 ♘c5?!

This blocks White's own play on
the c-file. Correct was 15 ♘g3! c5 16
dxc5 ♘xc5 17 ♖ac1 a5!? (committal, but not without point) 18 e3 ♖d8,
with an interesting strategic battle
in prospect. White will sooner or
later force a favourable exchange of
bishops but Black has already taken
prophylactic measures (by solidifying the position of the knight on c5)
to cover the resulting light-square
weaknesses.

15...♘xc5 16 dxc5 ♗e4!

After this Black enjoys the freer
game. The creation of a strong-point
on d5 for the bishop denies White active play on the d-file as well.

**17 ♕b3 c6! 18 ♘e5 ♗d5 19 ♕e3
♗f6 20 ♖d2 ♕c7**

Introducing such ideas as ...g5 or
...♗xe5 followed by ...f4, according
to circumstances. It is not clear that
these ideas are valid at the moment
but the knight's hasty retreat con-
firms once more that the threat is
stronger than its execution.

**21 ♘f3 ♖fe8 22 ♘d4 ♔h8 23 a4
b4 24 ♖ad1 ♖ac8 25 b3 a5** *(D)*

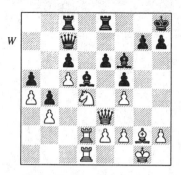

With careful play Granda has reduced his opponent to a state of complete passivity. White has no fewer
than three weak pawns (b3, c5 and
f4) to defend, not to mention that he
has to watch out constantly for ...e5
or ...g5. In his panicky anxiety to
clarify the situation White blunders
away an important pawn, after which
the game is essentially over.

26 ♗xd5? exd5 27 ♕h3

27 ♕f3 is met by 27...♕e7, with a
double attack on e2 and c5. The text
is no real improvement as Black can
now use the e-file for his attack.

**27...♗xd4 28 ♖xd4 ♖xe2 29
♕xf5 ♖ce8 30 ♖1d3 ♕e7 31 ♖h3 g6
32 ♕g5 ♖e1+ 33 ♔g2 ♕e2**

The queen's entrance signifies
the end of White's hopes. Black's

immediate threat is 34...♕f1+ 35 ♔g3 ♖(any)e3+, forcing mate.

34 ♕f6+ ♔g8 35 ♖f3 ♕f1+ 0-1

Ricardi resigned since 36 ♔g3 ♕h1! leaves White defenceless.

In several lines of the Geller System but, principally, in Korchnoi's Variation (1 d4 ♘f6 2 c4 e6 3 g3 d5 4 ♗g2 dxc4 5 ♘f3 ♗d7!?) Black employs the manoeuvre ...♗d7-c6 to neutralize the power of the fianchettoed bishop. This may often lead to a deterioration of Black's pawn structure, following a mass exchange of minor pieces on c6, but most notably, the exchange of bishops is here strategically desirable, as the whole operation is time-consuming for White and allows Black too much activity on the light squares. A typical example of what may befall White comes from the game **Liebert-Barczay**, *Szolnok 1975 (D)*:

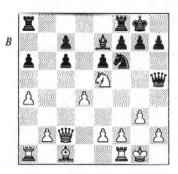

B

We join the game after White's 14th (the introductory moves were 1 c4 e6 2 ♘f3 d5 3 g3 ♘f6 4 ♗g2 ♗e7 5 0-0 0-0 6 d4 dxc4 7 ♕c2 a6 8 a4 ♗d7 9 ♘e5 ♗c6 10 ♘xc6 ♘xc6 11 ♗xc6 bxc6 12 ♘a3 ♕d5 13 ♘xc4 ♕h5 14 ♘e5). The casual onlooker would remark that the hostilities on the long diagonal have ended up in White's favour, in view of Black's weakened pawn structure, but as the game unfolds, the dynamic potential of Black's position becomes apparent.

14...c5 15 ♘f3

15 ♘c6 ♗d6 16 dxc5 ♗xc5 17 b4 looks tempting, for if Black were to play 17...♘g4 then White would obtain a significant edge after 18 h4 ♗d6 19 ♗b2. 17 b4 is in fact a mistake as Black has at his disposal the strong reply 17...♕h3!, when the deadly ...♘g4 is unstoppable.

15...♖ab8 16 ♗d2 cxd4 17 ♘xd4 ♘g4 18 h4 *(D)*

White, understandably, wanted to keep the enemy queen out of h3, but 18 ♘f3 was preferable.

B

18...♗c5 19 ♘f3 ♖fd8 20 ♗g5 ♖d5!

A wonderful centralizing manoeuvre, combining defence and attack. The rook seems exposed to the irritating e4 advance, but Barczay has calculated everything with precision.

21 e4? ♘xf2! 22 exd5 ♕xf3 23 ♖xf2 ♕xg3+ 24 ♔f1 ♕h3+!

The upshot of Black's combination, forcing the white king into the open. On 25 ♔g1?, 25...♖b4! is decisive.

25 ♔e1 ♗xf2+ 26 ♕xf2 h6 27 ♗e3 ♕h1+ 28 ♕g1 ♕xh4+ 29 ♕f2 ♕h1+ 30 ♕g1 ♕xd5 31 ♗xh6 ♕e5+ 32 ♗e3 ♖b3 33 ♖a3 ♖xb2 34 ♖d3 ♖b1+?

The simple 34...♕a5+ would have forced immediate resignation. The text led to a queen endgame where Black had five pawns for a bishop, winning eventually on move 59.

2) Piece Activity – Centralization

Centralization is the mother tongue of all great chess players and in this particular opening it is even more essential as a mean of exploiting a slight advantage. The margin between a win and a draw is smaller in the Catalan than most other openings as the nature of the struggle rarely leads to some kind of fixed central pawn structure. Thus, the player who usually prevails is the one with the better centralized pieces, since this allows him to take advantage of any temporary inconvenience in the enemy camp. The game **Reshevsky-Rogoff**, *Lone Pine 1978*, presents us with a primitive example on the power of centralization *(D)*:

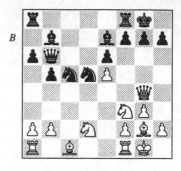

White has played the opening badly, allowing Rogoff to post his knights on the ideal squares c5 and d5. Still, the position needs care as the pawn structures are symmetrical and a slight mishandling is enough to throw away Black's advantage. Play proceeded:

15...♖ac8

Continuing to centralize. Instead of following suit Reshevsky resorts to a thoughtless move which merely worsens his position.

16 h4?

A flank attack cannot succeed when the opponent is in full control of the open centre. 16 ♘b3 was necessary, trying to relieve his position by exchanges. Now Black's advantage attains sizeable proportions.

16...♘d3 17 ♘b3 ♖c4

The consequences of White's play are starting to reflect on the mobility of his queen, which is running out of breathing space.

18 ♕h5 f5! *(D)*

Now Black is close to dominating the entire board. His positional superiority naturally gives rise to many tactical threats, the chief one being

19...♖xc1! followed by 20...♘5f4, trapping the lonely lady.

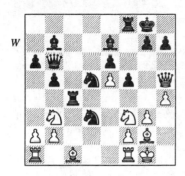

19 exf6?!

Reshevsky spots the threat, only to lose his queen in another way. Byrne and Mednis suggest 19 ♗g5!? as a better try, but after 19...♖g4! White has trouble finding an adequate reply.

19...♘xf6 20 ♕g5 ♗xf3 21 ♗xf3 ♘d5 22 ♕h5 g6 23 ♕xd5 exd5 24 ♗xd5+ ♔g7 and Black won easily.

In a almost all cases where Black is successful against the Catalan the key to his victory is a wonderfully centralized piece. The reader must have already noticed how strong a black bishop can be when effectively centralized at e4 or d5 (see Rogers-Geller and Ricardi-Granda) but no less important roles can be taken up by the rest of the pieces and, particularly, the black queen. After an exchange of light-squared bishops takes place, Her Majesty will often have the chance to seize control of the long diagonal – and then she can display her real powers.

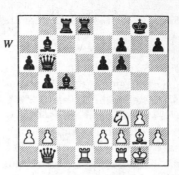

This position arose in the game **Khalifman-Aseev**, *Leningrad 1989*. The chances are approximately even since Black's weakened kingside is compensated by his bishop pair and excellent control of the centre. Probably thinking that 'everything draws' Khalifman played...

18 ♘e1?!

The manoeuvre ♘f3-e1-d3 is a standard idea in the Catalan but here it temporarily disrupts the communication of the white rooks, allowing Black a free hand on the c-file. Better was 18 ♘d2!, maintaining the option of trading rooks under more favourable circumstances as well as keeping an eye on e4.

18...♖xd1 19 ♕xd1 ♗xg2 20 ♔xg2 ♕c6+ 21 ♘f3?!

This knight belongs on d3, so 21 ♔g1! was called for. Now Aseev takes advantage of White's unfortunate play to create serious winning chances.

21...♗f8 22 ♕d2 ♕e4!

The queen is tremendously well placed here, creating a threat to win material by ...♖c2. Khalifman found nothing better than 23 ♕d3 ♕xd3 24

exd3 ♖c2 25 ♖b1 but this endgame proved untenable in the long run.

The creation of central outposts for one's knights is not an uncommon theme in the Catalan. Well-placed knights can often be used as restraining devices against White's central pawn preponderance. The games Vladimirov-Vaganian and Galdunts-Vaganian (see games section) will offer the reader further evidence of this but for the moment I will restrict myself to just one example, deriving from the game **Romanishin-Bryson**, *Manila OL 1992*.

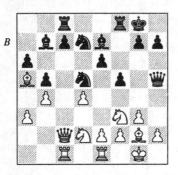

Black has fortified the position of the knight on d5 by playing ...f5, a typical way to control White's central expansion. The peculiarity of this particular variation (a5-bishop locked in) allows him to counterbalance the weakening of e6 by superior piece activity.

16...♖f6 17 e4!?

If White sits and waits he will slowly be smothered by a kingside attack. The text has the disadvantage of opening the f-file, but at the same time yields some pressure against the weak e6-pawn.

17...fxe4 18 ♖xe4 ♖cf8 19 ♖ce1 ♗d6! *(D)*

Romanishin's last move set a nasty trap: 19...♖xf3? 20 ♘xf3 ♖xf3 21 ♕e2 ♖f5 22 g4 ♕g5 23 h4! and White wins! Black rightly concentrates on increasing the mobility of his pieces, emphasizing the strength of his well-centralized knight.

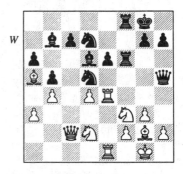

20 ♖xe6?!

Entering complications cannot be good with a piece out of play. White had to opt for the endgame resulting after 20 ♖h4 ♕f5 21 ♕xf5.

20...♖xf3 21 ♘xf3 ♖xf3 22 ♕e2 ♘5f6! 23 ♖xd6 cxd6 24 h3

The bishop has been extricated, yet the position is now lost as White is drastically behind in material.

24...h6! 25 g4 ♕d5 26 ♕e6+ ♔h7 27 ♕xd5 ♗xd5 28 ♗xf3 ♗xf3 29 ♖e6 ♘e4 30 ♗c7 ♘df6?

A bad mistake, throwing away the fruits of his labour. 30...♘f8! 31 ♖e8 ♘g6 32 ♖d8 ♘f4 would have reduced White to a state of helplessness.

31 ♗xd6 and Romanishin even managed to win after some more mistakes by his opponent.

Black's piece activity in the Catalan is based on a well-timed ...c5, allowing the black pieces to spring to life. The reader will find numerous examples in the Games Section involving this thematic thrust. However, note that strong players tend to postpone this possibility for as long as tactics demand without putting their chances in serious jeopardy. In the game **Budnikov-Pigusov**, *St Petersburg Z 1993*, Black had to wait 33 moves to make this pawn break most effective:

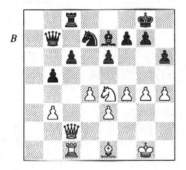

White's last was 33 h4, creating a huge empty space around his king. This weakening is by no means decisive but opening up the position is now undoubtedly much more pleasant for Black than it would have been with White's kingside pawns still on their original squares.

33...c5! 34 dxc5

34 ♗b4 fails in view of 34...f5! 35 gxf5 exf5 36 ♘xc5 ♕f3 37 ♕f2 ♕g4+ 38 ♕g2 ♘f6! and Black is clearly better despite the temporary pawn deficit (Belov).

34...♗xc5 35 ♗f2 ♖c7 36 ♕d3 b4!

Evgeny Pigusov is a deep strategist and here he correctly realized that the weakening of c4 is insignificant compared to White's corresponding weakness at c3. In fact White cannot profit from Black's 'concession', as his kingside is too open to allow him the luxury of positional considerations.

37 g5 ♗e7 38 ♖d1

Better was 38 ♖xc7 ♕xc7 39 gxh6 gxh6 although even then Black enjoys an edge.

38...♘b6 39 ♘g3 ♖d7 40 ♕e2 hxg5 41 hxg5 ♖xd1+ 42 ♕xd1 ♘d5 43 ♕c2 ♘c3 *(D)*

The situation has clarified and it is evident that all the black pieces are more active than their white counterparts. Although one cannot claim that Black has a winning advantage, White's collapse comes rather naturally as it is psychologically tiresome to defend this kind of position.

44 ♕d3 g6 45 e4 ♕c7 46 ♗e3?
♗xg5! 47 e5 ♗e7 48 ♗d2 ♕a7+ 49
♔f1 ♕a1+ 50 ♔g2 ♕d1 0-1

Piece activity and centralization
are closely connected in the Catalan,
as the player who controls the centre
inevitably acquires the best-placed
pieces. There are, however, a few exceptional cases where centralization
does not have the desired effect and
these relate to positions in which
Black has retained the wrong set of
minor pieces. A significant example
is the game **Gulko-Pigusov**, *Moscow 1990*:

1 d4 ♘f6 2 c4 e6 3 ♘f3 d5 4 g3
♗e7 5 ♗g2 0-0 6 0-0 dxc4 7 ♕c2 a6
8 a4 ♗d7 9 ♕xc4 ♗c6 10 ♗g5 ♗d5
11 ♕d3 c5 12 dxc5 ♘bd7 13 ♘c3
♘xc5 14 ♕e3 ♕a5 15 ♘xd5! ♘xd5
(D)

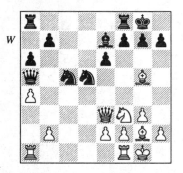

Black's cavalry looks imposing
and, in fact, the white queen doesn't
seem to have an entirely satisfactory
square to which to flee. Yet Gulko
proves by judicious manoeuvring
that his long-range bishop is stronger
than Black's centralized knights.

16 ♕a3! ♗xg5
Avoiding the main line of White's
calculations, which was 16...♗d6 17
♘d2! ♘e4 18 ♘c4! ♗xa3 19 ♘a5
♘xg5 20 ♖xa3 and all of a sudden
Black is totally disorganized. Now,
however, White's play has paid off
handsomely as he has extricated his
queen from its difficulties and can
look forward to an advantageous
middlegame.

17 ♘xg5 h6 18 ♖fc1! ♘d7 19
♘e4 b5! 20 b4?!
With 20 axb5! ♕xb5 21 ♘c3
♘xc3 22 ♖xc3 White would have
obtained a slight but permanent plus.
After the text Gulko was still able to
torture his opponent until move 86,
but without having realistic winning
chances.

3) The Art of Playing Simple Positions

The Catalan is not as boring as peo-
ple tend to think, but if White is only
interested in a draw then, admittedly,
that poses some technical problems
to the ambitious supporters of the
black side. The answer to these
problems is not a simple one, because playing for a win against
closed openings presupposes excellent theoretical preparation in combination with pure chess qualities
such as a sense of harmonious positional play or good endgame technique. I believe that the Games
Section will cover all questions of a
theoretical nature, but in my opinion

it is the development of other skills that will mostly help in scoring well against the Catalan. Hopefully, this section will give readers a hint of what I mean, by presenting fighting ways to treat positions that would normally be dismissed as 'easy draws'.

1 c4 e6 2 g3 ♘f6 3 ♗g2 d5 4 ♘f3 ♗e7 5 0-0 0-0 6 d4 dxc4 7 ♘a3 ♗xa3 8 bxa3 ♗d7 9 ♕c2 ♗c6 10 ♕xc4 ♘bd7 11 ♗g5 h6 12 ♗xf6 ♘xf6 13 ♖fc1 ♕d6 14 ♘e5 ♗xg2 15 ♔xg2 ♘d5 16 ♕b3 ♖ab8 17 ♖c2 c6 18 e3 ♖fd8 19 ♖ac1 ♘b6 20 ♕b4 *(D)*

The diagram arose in **Aseev-Rozentalis**, *USSR Ch 1990*. Black has solved his opening problems in a satisfactory way but the position seems to hold little promise for anything more in view of the reduced material and the apparent insignificance of the weakening of White's pawn structure. Rozentalis, however, believed otherwise:

20...♕d5+ 21 f3 ♘d7! 22 ♘xd7?

A positional error. White should have seized the chance to exchange

queens by 22 e4! ♕b5 23 ♕xb5 cxb5, although even then the resulting endgame is not an automatic draw. Now Black gets an enduring initiative as the presence of solely major pieces on the board facilitates the preparation of pawn breakthroughs in the centre.

22...♕xd7 23 a4 ♖e8 24 ♖c5 ♖bd8 25 ♖1c2 ♖e7!

Black is effectively manoeuvring in his interior lines, which is highly unpleasant for White whose static pawn structure reduces him to 'wait-and-see' tactics. The rook move frees the queen from the burden of protecting the b-pawn and prepares ...♕e8 followed by ...e5.

26 a5 a6 27 f4?

What could be more natural than bolstering e5? Yet this is probably the decisive error as White cannot prevent ...e5 in the long run, and when that happens, the newly created weaknesses around the white king will spell the end.

27...f6! 28 ♕c3 ♔h8 29 ♕b2 ♕e8 30 ♖2c4 ♖d5 31 ♕c2 ♕d8! *(D)*

The preparations for ...e5 are now complete.

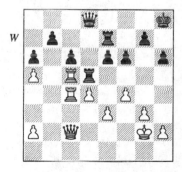

32 ♕e4 e5! 33 dxe5 ♖d2+!

Not 33...fxe5?, which would have spoilt everything: 34 ♖xd5! cxd5 35 ♕d3! and White stands well. The enemy monarch is now forced to wave goodbye to his headquarters as returning to the first rank would have been suicidal.

34 ♔h3 ♖xa2 35 ♕f5

35 e6 can be met by 35...♕d1 or 35...♕e8!?, in both cases with a substantial plus for Black.

35...fxe5 36 ♖xe5?

36 fxe5 was the only way to prolong resistance but that would have deprived us of a grandiose finale.

36...♖xe5 37 ♕xe5 ♖xa5 38 ♕e6 ♖h5+ 39 ♔g4

Choosing the most romantic way to lose although 39 ♔g2 ♕d2+ 40 ♔f3 ♕d1+ 41 ♔e4 ♕d5+! (Rozentalis) was just as beautiful.

39...♕d1 mate! (0-1) *(D)*

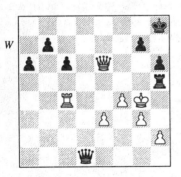

An engrossing finish.

The problem of somehow breaking the symmetry is a regular headache for Black in the Catalan but one shouldn't believe that symmetrical positions are necessarily devoid of winning chances. The following example shows in crystal-clear fashion that Black's chances of gathering small advantages can be considerable if White is too persistent in simplifying from a similar structure *(D)*:

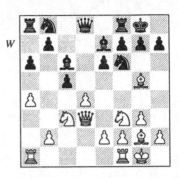

This is a well-known theoretical position arising after 1 d4 d5 2 c4 e6 3 ♘f3 ♘f6 4 g3 ♗e7 5 ♗g2 0-0 6 0-0 dxc4 7 ♕c2 a6 8 a4 ♗d7 9 ♕xc4 ♗c6 10 ♗g5 ♗d5 11 ♕d3 c5 12 ♘c3 ♗c6. Although it does not form part of the suggested repertoire, I consider that Black has very good chances here since the main continuation, 13 ♗xf6 ♗xf6 14 dxc5 ♘d7 15 ♕c4 (P.Nikolić-Bönsch, Munich 1990) 15...♖c8!, seems to offer him a slight initiative (16 b4 ♘b6! 17 ♕b3 ♘d5). In **Tsorbatzoglou-Wells**, *Aegina 1995* the Greek player preferred to go his own way:

13 e4?

A source of future trouble, as the move creates weaknesses along the d-line.

13...cxd4 14 ♕xd4 h6 15 ♗e3 ♘bd7 16 e5

White had pinned his hopes on this move, which appears to accomplish massive simplification. The English GM happily agrees to it as the e-pawn has by now become vulnerable.

16...♗c5 17 ♕d2 ♗xe3 18 ♕xe3 ♘d5 19 ♘xd5 ♗xd5 20 ♖fc1 ♖c8! 21 ♖xc8 ♕xc8 22 ♖c1 ♕b8 23 ♕c3 (D)

A superficial assessment would tell us that White has achieved his object, as he has even managed to control the c-file. This is in fact not the case as White has weaknesses on e5 and a4 and Black's next move merely serves to underline their existence.

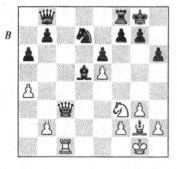

B

23...b6! 24 ♕c7 ♘c5!

The game is essentially decided. White loses a pawn, without having anything to show for it.

25 ♕xb8 ♖xb8 26 ♘d4 ♗xg2 27 ♔xg2 ♘xa4 28 b4 ♖d8 29 ♘c6 ♖d2 30 ♔f3 ♘b2 31 ♔e3? ♖xf2! and Black won on move 40.

The type of symmetrical pawn structure that arose in this game (i.e. a-, b-, e-, f-, g- and h-pawns for each side) occurs in several lines of the Geller Variation and we will focus on it for the rest of this chapter. In Tsorbatzoglou-Wells things went smoothly for Black because White voluntarily created several weaknesses in his effort to simplify, but this case hardly reflects the usual treatment of the particular formation by an experienced Catalan practitioner. In most cases Black has to work hard to create winning chances and this consists of first detecting a disharmony in the enemy camp and then transforming it into something tangible, such as a pair of bishops or a rook on the seventh. In the majority of cases where Black obtains the advantage it is a fragile one and consequently very exact moves are required to maintain it or enhance it. All this may sound a bit sophisticated so let's see how things work out in practice:

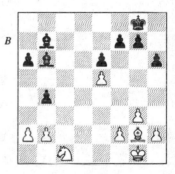

B

Our first example is a fragment from the game **Sosonko-Karpov**, *Waddinxveen 1979*. Karpov has obtained the advantage of the bishop pair and now proceeds to exploit it, aided by the open nature of the position.

28...♗c8!

But not 28...♗xg2? 29 ♔xg2 with an inferior ending for Black as his queenside pawns will be fixed on dark squares.

29 ♗e4 ♗d4 30 ♘d3 a5 31 ♔g2 f5!

The bishops need space to show their real strength. 31...♗a6?! 32 b3 ♗xd3?! 33 ♗xd3 ♗xe5 would have thrown away most of Black's advantage.

32 exf6 gxf6 33 g4 ♔f8 34 b3 ♔e7 35 ♔g3 (D)

35 f4!? f5 36 gxf5 exf5 37 ♗f3 would have been more difficult to break down as it is not easy for the black king to penetrate White's fortress. In the next few moves Sosonko plays without a plan, allowing Black to push ...f5 under much more favourable circumstances.

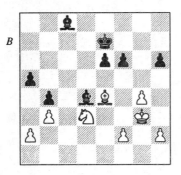

35...♔d6 36 ♔f4 ♗d7 37 h3 ♗b5 38 f3?

A serious mistake, not only depriving his king of an important

square (f3) but also increasing the scope of the d4-bishop.

38...♗d7! 39 ♔g3

39 ♗g6 would be answered by 39...♗g1! (threatening ...♔d5-d4) 40 ♗e4 ♗h2+ 41 ♔e3 f5 with a clear advantage, but still that was far superior to the game continuation. Now the white pieces will end up totally uncoordinated, providing an easy prey for the black bishops.

39...f5 40 gxf5 exf5 41 ♗b7 ♗b5 42 ♘e1 ♗c3 43 ♘c2 ♗d3 0-1

On 44 ♘e3 Black would reply 44...♗e1+ 45 ♔g2 (45 ♔f4 ♗d2) 45...♔e5! and the plan of ...♔d4 and ...♗b1 will be decisive.

Our next example is more complicated and comes from the game **Andersson-Petursson**, *Reggio Emilia 1989 (D)*:

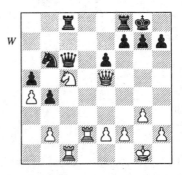

The game looks totally equal and at first I had my doubts as to whether it was the real Ulf Andersson who lost this position with White. In fact it is the real one so I suggest that readers take a good look at the proceedings:

27 ℤdc2

White gains nothing tangible by 27 ℤd6 ♕c7 28 ℤc2 in view of 28...♕a7!, so he settles for the logical doubling of rooks on the c-file.

27...ℤcd8!

Revealing a deep positional understanding. Contesting the c-file is not necessary here as White is tied to the defence of his a-pawn and cannot really use his rooks unless he plays b3. That move, however, would invite occupation of c3 by the black knight so Petursson is practically risking nothing by re-deploying his rook to the d-file.

28 ♘b3!?

Andersson senses the danger, refraining from 28 b3. The text is an effort to relieve the position by exchanges, even at the cost of a pawn.

28...ℤd1+! 29 ℤxd1 ♕xc2 30 ♕d4!?

White continues to rely on active play and his intuition is probably correct. Petursson gives the line 30 ℤd3 ♘c4 31 ♕c5 ♕b1+ 32 ♔g2 ♘xb2 33 ℤf3 ♘xa4 34 ♕xa5 ♘c3 35 ♕xb4 ♘xe2 36 ℤe3 as only slightly better for Black but in my opinion White is in big trouble after 36...♕g1+ 37 ♔f3 ♘c1! 38 ♘xc1 (38 ℤe1? ♕xf2+!) 38...♕h1+! 39 ♔g4 ♕xc1 because it is not easy for his king to return home.

30...♕xb3 31 ℤd3 ♕xa4 32 ♕xb6 ♕a1+ 33 ♔g2 ♕xb2 34 ♕xa5 g6

34...♕xe2 35 ℤd4 b3 36 ℤb4 ♕d1 was possible, but Black is playing for higher stakes than a mere 4 vs 3 pawn advantage on the kingside.

35 ♕b6! ℤc8?!

Black had to settle for 34...♕xe2 as it is by no means certain that White can save the ensuing position. The text merely loses time.

36 ♕b7! ♕c2 37 ℤf3 ℤf8 38 ♕b5?

Returning the favour. 38 ℤe3! (Petursson) would have drawn easily.

38...♕e4!

Now Black is in control again. The centralization of the queen ties down the white forces for a while, allowing the Icelander to improve his position.

39 h4 ℤd8 40 ♔h2 e5 41 ℤe3 ♕d4 42 ♕xe5 ♕xe5 43 ℤxe5 ℤb8

White has managed to restore material equality but the resulting rook endgame is difficult for him as the black rook is placed behind the dangerous passed pawn.

44 ℤd5 f5 *(D)*

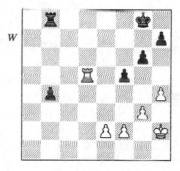

45 ℤd2?

After this time-pressure error the game cannot be saved. Petursson gives the study-like 45 ♔g2 ♔f7 46 ♔f3 ♔e6 47 ℤd1! b3 48 ♔e3 ♔e5

49 ♖b1 b2 50 ♔d3 f4 51 g4 f3! 52 e3 ♖b4! 53 h5! g5 54 h6! ♔f6 as slightly better for Black but I presume that even Andersson cannot find all this with his flag hovering.

45...♔f7 46 ♔g2 ♔e6 47 ♔f3 b3 48 ♖b2 ♔d5 49 ♔e3 ♔c4 50 ♔d2 ♖d8+ 0-1

Since 51...♔c3 will be terminal.

Our final example is a typical case of accumulating small advantages. It requires a lot of patience to turn them into account, but it can be done!

This position arose in **Mirallès-Vaganian**, *Haifa Echt 1989*. Black's pieces are slightly more active but the draw shouldn't be far away with careful play by White.

31...♗d5 32 ♘e1 ♗xg2 33 ♘xg2 ♘d5 34 ♕c5?

A pointless move. 34 ♘e1? was also bad due to 34...♕c6!, seizing control of the c-file, but after 34 ♘f4! (34 ♘e3 ♕b6 is slightly awkward) 34...♕b6 35 ♕xb6 ♘xb6 36 ♘d3 White would have won an important tempo over the game continuation.

34...♕b6! 35 ♕xb6 ♘xb6 36 ♘e1 ♘a4 37 a3 ♘c3 38 e3 ♔f8 39 ♔g2 ♔e7 40 ♔f3 f5!

This is where the tempo is important! Black exploits to the utmost the cramping position of the c3-knight to gain more space on the kingside. If the white knight had already been on d3, then the move ♘c5 would have equalized immediately.

41 ♘d3 ♘e4 42 g4

Necessary, as the threat ...♔d6-d5 can be met only by evicting the e4-knight from its present position. To achieve this White must play ♔e2 and then f3 but with the pawn on g3 this is impossible due to ...♘xg3+.

42...♔d6 43 gxf5 exf5 44 h4 g5! 45 hxg5 hxg5

White has managed to exchange some pawns, but now the knight on e4 will be almost impossible to chase away. The reason lies in the fact that the move f3 allows Black the possibility ...g4, creating an outside passed pawn.

46 ♘e1

Hurrying to put some pressure on f5 because 46 ♔e2 ♔d5 47 ♔d1 would have been hopeless due to 47...♘d6! followed by ...♘c4 and ...♔e4-f3.

46...♔d5 47 ♘c2 g4+ 48 ♔f4 ♘xf2 49 ♘d4 ♘h3+! 50 ♔xf5 g3 51 ♘f3 g2 52 e4+ ♔c6 53 e5 ♔d7 54 ♔f6 ♔e8 55 e6 g1♕ 56 ♘xg1 ♘xg1 57 ♔e5 ♘e2 58 ♔d6 ♘c3 59 ♔c6 ♘b1 60 ♔b6 ♘xa3 61 ♔xa6 ♔e7 0-1

A splendid positional achievement.

5 Beating the Catalan Opening

1) Geller's System: 6 ♕c2 and other White 6th move alternatives

Game 15
Korchnoi – Short
Lucerne Wcht 1989

1 c4 e6 2 g3 d5 3 ♗g2 ♘f6 4 ♘f3 ♗e7 5 d4 0-0 *(D)*

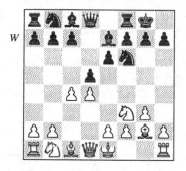

6 ♕c2

This is the main alternative to 6 0-0.

a) 6 ♘c3 is equally important. It is most likely to transpose to the next game or produce a hybrid of the line 6 0-0 dxc4 7 ♘e5 ♘c6 8 ♗xc6 bxc6 9 ♘xc6, discussed in Game 18. After the more or less accepted sequence 6...dxc4 7 ♘e5 ♘c6 8 ♗xc6 bxc6 9 ♘xc6 ♕e8 10 ♘xe7+ ♕xe7 11 ♕a4 c5 12 ♕xc4 cxd4 13 ♕xd4 e5 14

♕h4 I think that Black's best fighting chance is 14...♗b7 (14...♖b8 is the main line but this is merely a matter of fashion as the move has been introduced by Karpov) 15 0-0 ♕e6!? transposing into the game Gelfand-Aseev, Klaipeda 1988. The continuation of that game is worth examining in some detail as Black must play with the utmost precision to obtain sufficient counterchances: 16 e4 (16 ♗g5 ♘d5 17 ♗d2 ♖ac8 is fine for Black) and now *(D)*:

a1) 16...♖fc8?! 17 f3! (17 ♗g5? ♖xc3! 18 bxc3 ♘xe4 ∓) 17...♕b6+ and now:

a11) 18 ♖f2?! (inexact) 18...h6! 19 ♔g2 (19 g4?! ♖xc3! 20 bxc3 ♖d8! 21 ♗a3 ♖d3! 22 ♔g2 ♘xe4! and Black has a strong attack according to Gelfand and Kapengut) 19...♖d8 20 g4 ♖d3 21 g5 hxg5 22 ♗xg5 ♘h7 23 ♖g1 ♖e8! (by now

Black has strong counterplay) 24
♔h1 ♖e6 25 ♗c1 ♘f8 26 ♖fg2 ♖g6
with an annoying situation for White
as he has the more exposed king and
no clear plan. In the aforementioned
game Gelfand-Aseev, White lost on
move 37, after a blunder in a difficult
position.

a12) After 18 ♔g2! intending
g4 and ♕f2 White is better, e.g.
18...h6 19 g4 ♖xc3!? 20 bxc3 ♘xe4!
21 ♕e1! (21 fxe4!? ♗xe4+ 22 ♔h3
♖d8 23 ♕e7 ♖d3+ 24 ♔h4 ♕g6! is
tricky, e.g. 25 ♖f2? f6! ∓ or 25 ♕e8+
♔h7 26 ♖f2 ♗f3!, but the most attractive line is 25 ♖e1 ♗f5!! threatening 26...♕h5+!!, winning; White's
best is probably 25 ♕xe5 ♗g2 26
♗e3 ♕g5+! 27 ♕xg5 hxg5 28 ♔xg5
♗xf1 29 ♔f4! with a symbolic plus)
21...♘f6 22 ♕xe5! ♘xg4 23 ♕g3!
(otherwise 23...♕g6 will be dangerous) 23...♘e3+ 24 ♗xe3 ♕xe3 25
♖ab1! and Black has insufficient
play for the exchange.

Still, the question remains: what
should Black play on move 16?

a2) It seems to me that Black
should follow Gelfand's recommendation of 16...♖ac8!? in order to neutralize the plan with g4 and ♕f2.

a21) Indeed, after 17 f3 ♕b6+ 18
♔g2?! ♖fd8 19 g4 ♖d3! 20 ♕f2
♕e6! White's position looks difficult, with a variety of sacrificial possibilities hanging over his head.

a22) 17 ♗e3!? is a more critical
test, hitting the a-pawn. It is hard to
say who is better in the complications that follow after 17...♘g4 18
♗xa7 f5! and then 19 f3 ♕a6! or 19

h3 ♘f6 20 f3, but the certain thing is
that Black has a lot of practical
chances.

b) On the other hand, 6 ♘bd2 is
rather innocuous. After the principled 6...c5 7 dxc5 ♗xc5 8 0-0 ♘c6
Black gets free play for his pieces
and will usually (though hardly necessarily) reach an isolated d-pawn
position which compares favourably
with those arising from the Tarrasch
Defence in view of the inferior position of White's queen's knight. The
following examples seem to substantiate this opinion:

b1) 9 ♘b3 ♗e7 (9...♗b6!?) 10
cxd5 ♘xd5 (here Black adopts the
less committal option) 11 a3 b6 12
♕c2 ♗b7 13 e4 ♘f6 14 e5 ♘d5 15
♕e4 ♖c8 16 ♖e1 ♗a6 17 ♗d2 ♘b8!
18 ♖ac1 ♕d7 and Black gradually
assumed the initiative in Csom-
Espig, Berlin 1979.

b2) 9 a3 a5 10 cxd5 exd5 11 ♘b3
♗b6 12 ♘bd4 ♘e4 13 ♗e3 ♖e8 14
♖c1 ♗d7 was very double-edged in
Lima-M.Gomez, Salamanca 1989.

b3) 9 e3 ♕e7 10 a3 a5 11 b3 ♖d8
12 ♕c2 b6 13 ♗b2 ♗b7 14 cxd5
exd5 15 ♖fe1 ♖ac8 16 ♕f5 ♕d7 17
♕xd7 ♘xd7 18 ♗h3 ♖a8 19 ♖ed1
♘f8! with a balanced ending in Tuk-
makov-Kharitonov, Sochi 1987 as
White is unable to blockade the d-
pawn in a satisfactory way.

6...c5 *(D)*
The best reaction. The queen
move has weakened White's control
of the critical square d4 and Black is
rightly in a hurry to exploit this fact
as slower means would allow his

adversary to consolidate his position by bringing a rook on d1. White has now three continuations at his disposal but none of them promises him a great future.

7 dxc5

Korchnoi chooses to clarify the situation in the centre, an aim that would be carried out less successfully by the alternative capture 7 cxd5 in view of 7...cxd4! 8 ♘xd4 ♘xd5 9 ♕b3 ♘c6 10 ♘xc6 bxc6 11 e4 ♘b4 12 0-0 c5 13 ♘a3 ♘c6 14 ♗e3 ♖b8 15 ♕c3 ♘d4 and Black was already slightly better in Grigorian-Vyzhmanavin, Pinsk 1986. However, 7 0-0 is more critical, maintaining the tension while avoiding an early opening of the c-file when the queen's position might be prone to harassment. After 7...cxd4 8 ♘xd4 Black has two options:

a) 8...e5!? and now:

a1) 9 ♘f3?! ♘c6 10 cxd5 ♘xd5 11 ♘c3 ♘xc3 12 bxc3 ♗e6 13 ♖d1 ♕c7 14 ♘g5 ♗xg5 15 ♗xg5 (Salov-Kotronias, Haifa 1989) 15...♘d4!? 16 ♕d2 ♕xc3! is at least ∓. In the game the less incisive move 15...h6

allowed White to equalize after 16 ♗e3 ♖fd8 17 c4 ♘a5 18 ♖db1! ♕xc4 19 ♕xc4 ♗xc4 20 ♗xb7 ♘xb7 21 ♖xb7 and the players floundered for another 21 moves before agreeing to a draw.

a2) 9 ♘f5 d4 10 ♘xc7 ♕xe7 11 ♗g5 ♘c6 12 ♘d2 h6 13 ♗xf6 ♕xf6 14 c5 ♗f5 15 ♕a4 and now instead of 15...♕e7 16 b4 a5 17 b5, which led to a white initiative in Zilbershtein-A.Geller, Belgorod 1989, I like 15...♕g6!?, controlling the important h7-b1 diagonal and preparing to meet b4 with the simple ...a6. The position looks fairly unbalanced and in my opinion Black has excellent chances to play for a win here.

b) 8...♘c6 9 ♘xc6 bxc6 10 b3 ♗a6 11 ♗b2 ♖c8 12 e3 (12 ♘d2 d4!? 13 ♘f3 c5 14 ♖fe1 ♕c7 15 e3 e5 16 exd4 exd4 17 ♘e5 ♗d6 18 ♘d3 is unclear according to Karpov) 12...♕b6 13 ♘d2 ♖fd8 14 ♖fd1 ♘d7 15 ♖ac1 ♗b7 16 ♘f3 (16 e4 e5 and 16 ♕b1!? c5 17 ♕a1 are also evaluated as unclear by Karpov) 16...c5 and now 17 ♘e5? ♘xe5 18 ♗xe5 d4! 19 exd4 ♗xg2 20 ♔xg2 f6 21 ♗f4 cxd4 ∓ was Gulko-Karpov, Thessaloniki OL 1988. Instead of allowing his opponent a strong pawn centre, Gulko should have preferred 17 cxd5 exd5 18 ♕f5 ♘f6 19 ♘g5 with a sharp game, offering chances to both players.

7...♕a5+ 8 ♘c3

In the second game of his 1968 match against Tal in Moscow, Korchnoi tried 8 ♕c3 but I think the most White can hope for with this move is a laborious draw: 8...♕xc5 9 cxd5 ♘xd5 10 ♕xc5 ♗xc5 11 0-0 ♘c6 12 a3?! (12 ♖d1 looks better but Black still keeps a slight edge by 12...♗d7) 12...♗d7 13 ♘bd2 ♘d4! 14 ♘xd4 ♗xd4 15 ♘f3 and now instead of 15...♗b6, as played in the game, Black could have maintained uncomfortable pressure by 15...♗f6! 16 e4 ♘b6 17 e5 ♗e7, e.g. 18 ♘d4 ♘c4!.

8 ♘bd2 (better) 8...♕xc5 9 0-0 b5! 10 b3 and here it cannot be said with certainty that Black enjoys the advantage but at least he is assured that no early simplifications take place.

8...dxc4 9 ♘d2?!

In Romanishin-Shneider, Kherson 1989 White refrained from this dubious move in favour of the more natural 9 0-0!. After 9...♘c6 10 ♗g5 ♕xc5 (if Black is looking for the whole point then he should investigate the manoeuvre 10...♘b4!? 11 ♕c1 ♘bd5 which despite its artificial appearance can be more annoying for White than the game continuation) 11 ♗xf6 ♗xf6 12 ♘e4 ♕e7 13 ♖fd1 b5 14 a4 ♖b8 15 axb5 ♖xb5 16 ♕xc4 ♖b6 17 ♘xf6+ ♕xf6 18 ♘d2 ♗b7 19 b3 ♘e5 20 ♕d4 ♗xg2 21 ♔xg2 ♘c6 22 ♕e3 and then 22...♖fb8? 23 ♘e4 White obtained a slight advantage, but the simple 22...♖d8 would have yielded easy equality.

9...♕xc5 10 ♘a4

If White wants to regain his pawn he has to play this move immediately. On 10 0-0? there follows

10...♘c6 11 ♘a4 ♘d4! and Black remains a pawn up with the better position.

10...♕a5 11 ♕xc4 (D)

11...♗d7!

This must have been an unpleasant surprise for Korchnoi, who was probably counting on a normal developing move like 11...♘c6. Although such a move would have hardly been bad, Short's way has the advantage of disrupting the routine course of events a Catalan connoisseur would be fond of, by threatening immediately to neutralize White's powerful bishop.

12 ♘c3?!

White must have realized that taking on b7 is not as simple as it looks: After 12 ♗xb7 ♗b5! Black has a lot of tactical chances because the white queen lacks an entirely satisfactory flight square. For example: 13 ♕f4 e5! 14 ♕f3 (14 ♕xe5? ♘bd7!; 14 ♕h4 ♘c6! 15 ♗xa8 ♘d4! and Black has a strong initiative) 14...♕xa4 15 ♗xa8 ♘c6 or 13 ♕h4 ♘d5 14 ♕e4 ♗c6! 15 ♗xc6 (15 ♗xa8? ♗xa8 ∓) 15...♘xc6, in both cases with excellent compensation for the material, although White should probably entered the latter variation. The text move is tantamount to an admission that Black's opening has been a success as he is now able to achieve his strategic goal of opposing bishops on the long diagonal.

12...♖c8 13 ♘b3 ♕h5 14 ♕f4 ♗c6 15 0-0 h6 (*D*)

Short is in no hurry to trade bishops because that would improve the co-ordination of the white pieces. Moreover, the text move creates a bolt-hole for his king and at the same time highlights the awkward position of the enemy queen and the lack of any constructive plan on White's part.

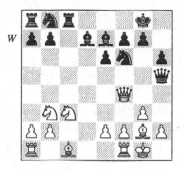

16 e4

This may seem anti-positional but Black was beginning to threaten ...e5.

16...♘bd7

Sosonko rates this position as equal in *ECO* but I have to disagree with his evaluation. The light-square weaknesses on White's queenside,

d3 in particular, guarantee Black an appreciably superior game.

17 f3 a5! 18 g4 ♕e5 19 ♕g3 ♕xg3 20 hxg3 ♘e5 (*D*)

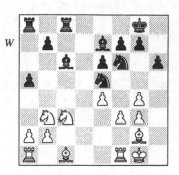

The exchange of queens has not relieved White from his troubles. His kingside pawn structure has been deprived of its mobility, his minor pieces are inactive and what is worse, the black knight is well on its way to invade on the weakened queenside. In retrospect it would seem that the only chances of survival lay in 21 g5, although it is hard to believe that this move would have saved White in the long run. The move played by Korchnoi allows the English grandmaster a swift demonstration of his undoubted technical skills.

21 ♖d1?! b5!

Preparing to evict the knight from c3 and then infiltrate with his rooks along the c-file. As it turns out White is powerless to prevent this plan.

22 ♘d4 ♗c5 23 ♔f1 ♗xd4

Time is precious! The bishop has served its duty and now is given up in order to ensure the penetration of the black rook to its seventh rank.

24 Rxd4 b4 25 ♘d1 ♗b5+ 26 ♔g1 Rc2 27 ♗f4?

This prepares a blunder, but White's position was already lost.

27...♘d3 28 ♗f1? ♘e1! 0-1

A stylish finish. This game is a perfect illustration of the dynamism concealed in such positions.

2) Geller's System: 6 0-0 dxc4 7 ♘c3 (plus lesser 7th moves)

Game 16
Lautier – Karpov
Dos Hermanas 1995

1 d4 ♘f6 2 c4 e6 3 g3 d5 4 ♗g2 ♗e7 5 ♘f3 0-0 6 0-0 dxc4 (D)

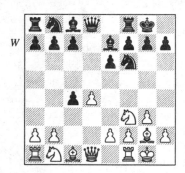

7 ♘c3

A logical continuation: White develops and at the same time increases his influence on the important central squares e4 and d5. The disadvantages are also obvious as the text move blocks the c-file, thus rendering recovery of the pawn time-consuming. If White scorns the pawn and plays for the attack then Black obtains excellent chances of victory in view of his sound defensive formation on the kingside.

Besides the double-edged text move and the important alternatives 7 ♘a3, 7 ♘e5 and 7 ♕c2 – all examined in following games – White has two lesser options:

a) 7 a4 (this idea shouldn't cause Black any worries) 7...♘c6 8 a5 Rb8 9 ♕c2 ♘xd4 10 ♘xd4 ♕xd4 11 ♗e3 (not 11 Rd1? ♕c5! 12 ♗e3 ♕h5 13 ♕xc4 ♘g4! 14 ♕xc7 ♕xh2+ 15 ♔f1 ♘xe3+ 16 fxe3 ♗h4!! 17 ♕xb8 {17 ♔f2 e5!} 17...♗xg3 18 ♕xa7 e5 19 e4 f5! with a strong attack for Black) and now:

a1) In the game Kožul-Kotronias, Bled/Rogaška Slatina 1991, I tried the adventurous 11...♕g4!? which should also be good enough. After 12 h3 ♕h5 13 ♕xc4 e5! 14 ♕xc7 ♗d7 15 g4 ♗xg4 16 ♕xe7 ♗xh3 17 f3 Rfe8 18 ♕a3 e4! 19 ♘d2 ♗xg2 20 ♔xg2 and now 20...♕g6+? was too enthusiastic, and after 21 ♔f2 exf3 22 Rg1! ♘g4+ 23 Rxg4 ♕xg4 24 ♘xf3 White was clearly better. With the simple 20...♘d5 21 ♘xe4 (there is nothing else) 21...Rxe4! Black would have assured himself of perpetual check.

a2) 11...♕d7 is another option: 12 ♕xc4 b6 13 axb6 axb6 14 Ra7 ♗d6 15 Rd1 b5 16 ♕b3 ♕e7 17 h3 ♘d5 18 ♗xd5 exd5 19 ♘c3 ♗xh3 20 ♕xd5 (Zhidkov-Ubilava, Krasnodar 1980) and now 20...Rfe8! would have been better for Black according to Neishtadt.

a3) 11...♕d6! and here:

a31) Kožul gives the continuation 12 ♗xa7 ♖a8 13 ♗e3, planning ♘d2xc4, as slightly better for White, but I find this comment incomprehensible in view of the simple 13...♘d5 when White would be hard-pressed to prove equality.

a32) 12 ♘a3 ♕a6 13 ♘xc4 (13 ♕xc4 ♘d5 ∓) 13...♗d7 when the slight space advantage enjoyed by White does not seem to outweigh the pawn minus.

a33) 12 ♕xc4! ♘d5 13 ♗xa7 ♖a8 14 ♗d4 and Black has a pleasant choice between 14...c5 15 ♗c3 b5!? 16 ♕xb5 ♗a6 and 14...e5!?, in both cases with a rather unclear game.

b) 7 ♘bd2!? b5! (if Black is playing for the win he must take everything on offer; the alternative 7...c5 does not promise more than equality) and now:

b1) 8 ♘e5 ♘d5 9 b3?! (this looks bad but 9 e4 ♘b6 10 d5 also fails after 10...exd5 11 exd5 ♗b7 12 ♘c6 ♘xc6 13 dxc6 ♗c8 14 a4 bxa4 with the better game for Black – Neishtadt) 9...c3 10 ♘b1 ♗b7 11 e4 ♘f6 12 ♘xc3 b4 ∓ F. Olafsson-Filip, Moscow 1959.

b2) 8 a4 c6 9 ♘e5!? (9 e4 ♗b7 10 e5 ♘d5 11 ♘e4 ♘d7 is unclear) 9...♘d5 10 e4 ♘f6 (Cvetković considers the alternatives 10...♘b6 and 10...♘b4 also to be interesting but I prefer the solid text move) 11 d5 ♕c7! 12 ♘xc6 ♘xc6 13 dxc6 ♕xc6 14 axb5 ♕xb5 15 e5 (15 ♕a4?! ♕xa4 16 ♖xa4 ♗d7 ∓) 15...♘d5 16

♕g4 ♗a6 17 ♘e4 ♔h8 18 ♘c3 ♘xc3! 19 ♗xa8 ♖xa8 20 bxc3 ♗b7 and Black had reasonable play for the exchange in V.Kostić-Cvetković, Yugoslavia 1993. However, I would like to point out that sacrificing material is not obligatory in this line as Black has interesting deviations in 13...♗a6!? or 17...♖fd8, both of which seem to offer a fully acceptable game.

7...♘c6 (D)

By putting pressure on d4 Black makes it difficult for his opponent to recover the pawn. Other moves are significantly inferior and clearly outside the spirit of Geller's System.

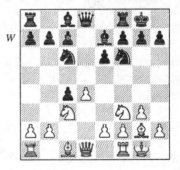

8 e3

8 e4 has never been popular, probably as a result of the game Kavalek-Geller, Wijk aan Zee 1977, where White's attack backfired quickly after 8...♖b8 9 ♖e1 (9 e5!?) 9...b5 10 e5 ♘d5 11 ♘e4 ♘cb4 12 ♘fg5 h6 13 ♘h3 ♘d3 14 ♗xh6 gxh6 15 ♕g4+ ♔h7 16 f4 f5 17 exf6 ♘xf6 18 ♘hg5+ hxg5 19 ♘xf6+ ♗xf6 20 ♕h5+ ♔g7 –+, as there are no more checks or pieces to sacrifice. 9 ♗e3

is more rational, when Filippov-Kiriakov, Moscow 1995 continued 9...b5 10 a3 ♘a5 (10...a5 11 ♕e2!?) 11 ♕c2 ♗b7 12 ♖ad1 a6 13 d5!? exd5 14 exd5 ♘b3 15 ♘e5 ♖e8 16 ♘c6 ♗xc6 17 dxc6 ♕c8 with an unclear position. It seems that this line holds good prospects for further investigation by both sides.

8...♗d6!

Now that ♗g5 is no longer possible, Black may afford the luxury of playing for ...e5! This strong novelty by Korchnoi seems to have displaced the older main line 8...♖b8 9 ♕a4 ♘b4 10 ♕xa7 ♗d7 11 ♘e5 ♘fd5 12 ♕xb8! ♕xb8 13 ♘xd7 ♕a7 14 ♘xf8 ♗xf8 15 ♘xd5 exd5 16 ♗d2 c6 17 a3 ♘d3 18 ♗c3 b5 19 ♖fd1 ♕d7!? 20 ♗f1 ♕f5 (planning ...h5-h4) with an unbalanced position, requiring extreme accuracy on Black's part.

9 ♘d2

An attempt to improve over Lautier-Korchnoi, Moscow OL 1994 (the stem game of this variation), in which the young Frenchman suffered a catastrophic defeat with 9 ♕a4: 9...e5 10 d5 (after 10 ♕xc4 exd4 11 exd4, both 11...h6!? and 11...♘b4 12 a3 ♗e6 13 ♕e2 ♘bd5 are satisfactory for Black; 10 dxe5 ♘xe5 11 ♘xe5 ♗xe5 12 ♖d1 ♕e7 13 ♕xc4 c6 is slightly worse for White because his kingside pawn majority is not as useful as his opponent's on the queenside) 10...♘b4 11 ♘xe5 a6! and now:

a) 12 ♘f3?? (this is equivalent to suicide) 12...♗f5 13 ♘d4 ♗d3 14

♖e1 ♗c5 15 e4 ♘bxd5 16 ♘f5 ♘xc3 17 bxc3 ♘g4 18 ♘e3 *(D)*.

18...♘xf2! 19 e5 (19 ♔xf2 ♕f6+ 20 ♗f3 ♕xc3) 19...b5 20 ♕a5 ♘g4 21 ♔h1 ♘xe5 and Lautier played on for another dozen moves before acquiescing to the inevitable.

b) 12 ♘xc4 b5 13 ♘xb5 axb5 14 ♕xa8 bxc4 ∓.

c) 12 e4 b5!? (Korchnoi gives only 12...♘bxd5 13 ♘xc4 ♘xc3 14 bxc3 b5 15 ♕c2 bxc4 16 e5 ♖b8 17 exd6 cxd6 =) 13 ♕a5 ♗b7! 14 ♗f4 and now rather than 14...♘c2?! 15 ♖ac1 ♗b4 16 ♘c6! ♗xc6 17 ♕xc7, which is unclear, or 14...♘h5!?, Black has 14...♖e8! ∓.

d) 12 a3 b5 13 ♘xb5 (13 ♕a5 ♗xe5 14 ♕xb4 ♖e8 ∓) 13...♗xe5 14 f4! (14 ♕xb4? ♖b8 ∓; 14 axb4? ♗d7 ∓) 14...♘fxd5 15 axb4 ♗d7 16 ♗xd5 ♗xb5 17 ♕d1 c6 = (Korchnoi).

e) 12 f4!? ♘bxd5 13 ♘xc4 ♘xc3 14 bxc3 ♗c5 would have been unclear according to Korchnoi.

Considering that 9 ♘d2 comes to nought in the present game, I don't expect to see much of 7 ♘c3 in the near future.

9...e5 10 ♘xc4

On 10 d5 there follows 10...♘a5 11 ♕e2 (11 ♕a4?! b6 12 ♘xc4? ♗d7 −+) 11...♗g4! 12 f3 ♗d7 13 ♘xc4 ♘xc4 14 ♕xc4 c6, and if anyone is for choice, it has to be Black.

10...exd4 11 exd4 ♗g4 12 ♕b3!?

The most principled. White may also strive for a draw with 12 ♕a4 ♘xd4 13 ♘xd6 ♕xd6 14 ♗f4, but I'm not sure whether he is in full control of the situation: 14...♕c5!? (Karpov gives only 14...♕b6 =) 15 ♗e3 (15 ♗xb7 ♖ab8; 15 ♖ac1 b5!? 16 ♕a5 ♗f3! ∓) 15...♖ad8! (not 15...♖fd8? 16 ♖ad1! ±) 16 ♗xb7 (Black is threatening ....♗f3; on 16 ♖ad1? there follows 16...♗xd1 17 ♖xd1 b5! −+) 16...♕b6! (and not 16...♗f3?! 17 ♗xd4 ♖xd4 18 ♕b5!) manages to keep some tension in the game.

12...♘xd4 13 ♕xb7 *(D)*

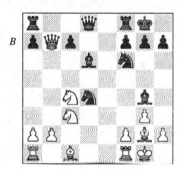

13...♗f3!

A powerful way to neutralize White's initiative. Lautier was probably counting only on 13...♖b8?! 14 ♕xa7 ♘e2+ 15 ♔h1! (15 ♘xe2 ♗xe2 16 ♘xd6 ♗xf1 17 ♘b7 ♕d1

18 ♗xf1 ♕d5 19 ♘c5 ♖a8 20 ♕xc7 is also better for White) 15...♘xc3 16 ♘xd6! ±, but Karpov's move is far superior as it accomplishes the positionally desirable exchange of light-squared bishops.

14 ♕a6?

A sign of panic. 14 ♗xf3! ♖b8 15 ♕xa7 ♘xf3+ 16 ♔g2 is much better, with a highly interesting situation:

a) 16...♗b4?! 17 ♖d1! gives Black problems: 17...♕c8 18 ♔xf3! ♗xc3 (18...♕f5+? 19 ♔g2 ♗c5 20 ♘e3! +−) 19 ♔g2! ± or 17...♕e8 18 ♕e3! ♘h4+ 19 gxh4 ♕c6+ 20 ♕f3 ♕xc4 21 ♗f4 ±.

b) 16...♕d7!! (Karpov) 17 ♘xd6! (17 ♘e3? ♘g5! ∓) and now Black can choose between a safe and a risky continuation (the alternatives 17...♕c6? 18 ♘de4! ♘xc4 19 ♕a4! ± and 17...♖b4? 18 ♕e3! ♖h4 19 ♖h1!! +− are not viable):

b1) 17...♘h4+ 18 gxh4 ♕g4+ 19 ♔h1 ♕f3+ with a draw – objectively the sounder continuation, and a logical conclusion to a well-conducted game.

b2) 17...♕xd6!? 18 ♕a4! (not 18 ♔xf3? ♕c6+) 18...♖b4 19 ♕d1 ♘d4 20 f3 (20 ♖c1!?) 20...c5 to be followed by ...♕c6 gives rise to a difficult position, in which Black appears to have some compensation for the pawn deficit.

The text move surrenders the initiative to Black without anything tangible in return.

14...♗b4 15 ♗e3!

White has lost the opening battle but from now on he puts up a stout resistance. The alternatives 15 ♗g5? ♗xc3 16 ♗xf6 ♘e2+ 17 ♔h1 ♗xg2+ and 15 ♗xf3? ♘xf3+ 16 ♔g2 ♗xc3 17 bxc3 ♕d3! 18 ♗e3 (18 ♕a4 ♘xh2) 18...♕e4 both lose quickly as this analysis (by Karpov) convincingly demonstrates.

15...♗xg2 16 ♖fd1!

Centralization is White's main trump in his efforts to salvage a draw. With 16 ♔xg2? he could have fallen into the nasty trap 16...♗xc3 17 bxc3 ♕d5+ 18 f3 ♘c2 19 ♖ad1 ♕xc4!, forcing immediate resignation.

16...c5 17 ♗xd4 cxd4 18 ♔xg2 ♖c8!

An attempt to force matters by 18...♗xc3?! would have squandered a great part of Black's advantage, e.g. 19 bxc3 ♕d5+ 20 ♔g1 ♕f5 21 ♖xd4 ♘e4 22 ♖f1 ♘xc3 23 ♘d6. Karpov rightly prefers to centralize his rooks before resorting to drastic operations.

19 ♔g1 ♖e8 20 ♖ac1 ♕d7 21 ♘b5?

A most critical moment in the game. Karpov's last move has revealed his intention of following up with ...♕h3 and ...♘g4, but 21 ♘b5? is hardly an appropriate answer to the threat because it neglects the blockade of the dangerous passed d-pawn.

After 21 ♘e3! Black's task of proving a significant advantage would have been rendered considerably more difficult: 21...♗e6 22 ♕d3 and now 22...♖d6?! 23 ♘f5!? (instead of Karpov's 23 ♘c4 ♖xc4 24

♕xc4 dxc3 25 ♖xd6 ♕xd6 26 ♕c8+ ♕f8 27 ♕xf8+ ♔xf8 28 bxc3 ♗c5 ∓) 23...dxc3 24 ♘xd6 ♖d8 25 ♕b5!? is just unclear, so Black ought to try 22...♕e8!? 23 ♕xd4 ♗c5 24 ♕d3 ♖xe3! 25 fxe3 ♗xe3+ 26 ♔f1 ♗xc1 27 ♖xf1 ♕c6 28 ♕d4 h5!? when the exposed position of the enemy king offers him chances of ultimate success.

21...d3!

21...♕h3 22 ♘xd4 ♘g4 23 ♘f3 ♘xf2!? was not out of the question but the game continuation is clearer. As it turns out, White's uncoordinated pieces are unable to stave off the numerous threats.

22 ♘e3 ♖xc1 23 ♖xc1 d2 24 ♖d1 ♘d5! 25 ♕a4

In case of 25 ♘g2 Black would have won nicely by 25...♘f4! (26 gxf4 ♕g4 −+). The position abounds in neat tactical possibilities.

25...a6! 26 ♕xa6 ♘xe3 27 fxe3 ♕d3 28 ♕c6 ♕xe3+ 29 ♔g2 ♕e2+ 30 ♔h3 ♕h5+ 0-1

3) Geller's System: 6 0-0 dxc4 7 ♘a3!?

Game 17
Alburt – Geller
New York 1990

1 d4 d5 2 c4 e6 3 ♘f3 ♘f6 4 g3 ♗e7 5 ♗g2 0-0 6 0-0 dxc4 7 ♘a3!?

An important line. White is in effect playing a gambit as Black is practically forced to take on a3 and try to hold on to the extra pawn.

7...♗xa3 8 bxa3 ♗d7!

There are several reasonable alternatives (8...♘bd7, 8...♘c6, 8...b5) but Geller's move seems to offer the best prospects for an active deployment of the minor pieces. Although Black will, most likely, end up with two knights vs two far-ranging bishops, his chances in the resulting middlegame are not to be underestimated as he has a pawn more and possibilities to exploit his opponent's weaknesses on the queenside.

9 ♘e5

Accepting the challenge. The alternative 9 ♗g5 led to an approximately even game in Murey-Geller, Moscow IZ 1982, after 9...♗c6 10 ♗xf6 ♕xf6 11 ♕c2 ♘d7 12 ♕xc4 ♖fd8 13 ♖fd1 ♕e7 14 ♕d3 ♘f6. In this type of position Black's main aim should be to swap off the remaining minor pieces as that would significantly accentuate the weakness of the doubled a-pawns.

9...♗c6 10 ♘xc6 ♘xc6 11 ♗b2 *(D)*

11 ♗g5?! is weaker, since after 11...h6 12 ♗xf6 ♕xf6 Black enjoys a slight advantage according to Geller.

11...♕d6!?

An interesting move. Black not only connects his rooks, but, most importantly, guards his queen's knight in order to play ...b5. The queen is actively placed on d6, eyeing a3 and preparing to meet e4 by ...e5. Thus, Black is hoping to block the activity of the ever-dangerous enemy bishops.

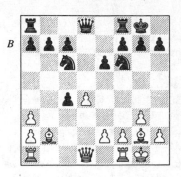

a) A more conservative approach consists of 11...♘d5 intending to play ...♘b6 to be followed by such typical moves as ...♖ab8, ...♕d7/6 and ...♖fd8. This policy is by no means inferior, but the fact that White also has time to organize his troops forces Black to curb his ambitions. Some examples:

a1) 12 ♖b1 ♘b6 13 e3! (after 13 e4?! ♕d7 14 ♕d2 ♖ad8 15 ♖fd1 ♖fe8!, 16 ♗a1 e5 17 d5 ♕d6! was fine for Black in Morozov-Tsaturian, corr. 1989, while 16 ♕c3 e5 17 dxe5 ♕xd1+ 18 ♖xd1 ♖xd1+ 19 ♗xf1 ♘xe5! 20 ♕c2 ♖e1 ∓ is analysis by Kasparov and Tsaturian) 13...♕d6 14 ♕c2 ♖fd8 15 ♖fd1 ♖ab8 16 e4 e5 17 d5 ♘d4! 18 ♗xd4 exd4 19 ♖xd4 c6 20 a4! ♕c5! 21 ♕c3 cxd5 22 cxd5 ♖bc8 23 ♖b5 (Khalifman-Portisch, Reykjavik 1991) and now 23...♘xa4 24 ♖xc5 ♘xc3 25 ♖dxc4 ♖xc5 26 ♖xc5 ♘xa2 would have yielded an immediate draw.

a2) 12 ♖c1 ♘b6 and now:

a21) 13 e4!? ♘e7 (13...♕d6!? is more advisable) 14 ♕c2 ♕d7 15 ♗a1 when 15...♖ad8?! 16 ♕c3 f6 17 ♖cd1! ± was Illescas-Kosashvili,

Holon 1986, but 15...f5!? (Illescas) seems better, e.g. 16 exf5 ♘ed5! 17 fxe6 ♕xe6 18 ♖fe1 ♕d6 19 ♖e5 c6 20 ♖ce1!? (20 ♗b2 ♘6d7 21 ♖e2 b5 22 ♖ce1 ♘7f6) 20...♕xa3 21 ♗e4 h6 22 ♗f5 ♔h8, when the extent of White's compensation is unclear.

a22) 13 e3 ♕d7 14 ♕c2 ♖ab8 15 ♖fd1 ♘e7 16 ♗f1 ♖fd8 17 ♗xc4 ♘xc4 18 ♕xc4 ♕d5!? 19 ♕xc7 ♘c6 20 ♕f4 ♕xa2 21 ♖d2 e5 22 ♕g4 ♕e6 23 ♕d1 and in this position the players agreed to a draw in Glek-Yarkov, corr. 1988.

b) On the other hand, 11...♕d7 is less good. This move bears close similarity to the text, but the difference lies in 12 ♕a4! ♘xd4 13 ♕xc4 ±, a variation that would not be possible with the black queen on d6 in view of the simple reply 13...c5 (and if 14 e3? then 14...b5! −+).

Taking all the above-mentioned into consideration one may arrive at the unsurprising conclusion that 11...♕d6 represents Black's best winning chance in the line under discussion.

12 ♖c1

In the game Krasenkov-Bönsch, Wattens 1990, White opted for the direct 12 e4 and soon came out on top after Black's reply: 12...c3?! 13 ♗xc3 ♕xa3 14 ♕c2 ♖fd8 15 ♖fd1 ♘b4 16 ♗xb4 ♕xb4 17 ♖ab1 ♕a5 18 ♖xb7 ♖ac8 19 ♕c4 h6 20 ♖b5 ♕a6 21 ♖c5 ♕xc4 22 ♖xc4 and the Russian turned his slight advantage into a win on move 53. Instead of the feeble 12...c3?! Black should follow Geller's recommendation of 12...e5

13 d5 ♘e7, reaching a position which compares favourably with the one he attains in our main game.

12...b5 13 e4 e5 14 f4!

A powerful move, opening up the game for his pair of bishops. Alburt's position makes a strong impression, but as the game continuation proves Black has considerable defensive resources.

14...♖ad8! 15 d5 exf4! 16 gxf4

White prudently restricted himself to this natural recapture. The 'clever' 16 ♔h1? fails to 16...f3! and Black obtains a practically won game as he gets e5 for his knights.

16...♖fe8 17 ♕c2

A critical moment. Besides the logical game continuation White had several interesting alternatives at his disposal:

a) 17 ♔h1 ♘xe4! 18 ♗xe4 ♖xe4 19 dxc6 ♕xc6 20 ♕f3 (20 ♕xd8+?? loses to 20...♖e8+) 20...♖d3 21 ♕g2 ♕g6! and Black is slightly better according to Geller.

b) 17 ♗xf6 ♕xf6 18 ♔h1!?.

c) 17 ♕f3!? ♘xe4! 18 dxc6 ♕c5+ 19 ♔h1 f6! and despite the extra piece White faces serious problems.

17...♘e7 18 ♕f2!

Black is planning to undermine the white centre by means of ...♘g4 and ...f5. Having realized that, Alburt switches his queen over to the kingside to increase the pressure on g7.

In Ortega-Lagumina, Forli 1991, White deviated from our featured game by 18 ♔h1. After the thematic response 18...♘g4! 19 ♗h3 h5 20

♗xg4 hxg4 21 f5 c6! Black should be clearly better but the outcome of the fight didn't confirm this evaluation: 22 ♖g1 cxd5 23 ♖xg4 d4 24 ♖cg1 g6 25 ♕f2 and then Black made a serious mistake: 25...♕f6 26 ♗c1 d3 27 ♗g5 ♕e5 28 ♕h4 ♘xf5 29 exf5 ♕d5+ 30 ♖4g2 ♖e4 31 ♕h6 ♖e2 1-0. After the correct 25...c3 26 ♗c1 d3 27 ♗f4 ♕b6! (27...♕c6? 28 ♗e5!) 28 ♕h4! (28 ♗e3 ♕c6) 28...♘xf5 29 exf5 ♕c6+ 30 ♖4g2 d2 31 fxg6 fxg6 32 ♗e5 ♖xe5! 33 ♕xd8+ ♖e8 34 ♕d3/g5 ♖e1 the game would have reached its natural conclusion.

White can try to prevent Black's idea in other ways as well but all of them seem to be tactically flawed. A characteristic episode is 18 ♕c3 (intending to tie Black up on the long diagonal) 18...♕b6+! 19 ♔h1 c6! and it suddenly turns out that 20 d6? is out of the question because of 20...♖xd6 21 e5 ♖d3 while 20 ♕g3 is convincingly answered by 20...cxd5!, protecting the knight on f6. Therefore, White does best to follow the game continuation.

18...♘g4 19 ♕g3 f5 20 ♖cd1

20 exf5 h5! (Geller) is good for Black.

20...♕b6+ 21 ♗d4? (*D*)

This impulsive move is a decisive mistake because it loosens White's control on d5, after which his pawn centre quickly disintegrates. Geller's suggestion of 21 ♔h1! ♕e3!? 22 ♗f3 (22 ♖f3? ♕e2) 22...c3 23 ♗c1 ♕c5 24 ♗xg4 (24 exf5 ♘f6) 24...fxg4 25 ♕xg4 ♘g6 would have created a

total mess, while now the balance swings irremediably towards Black.

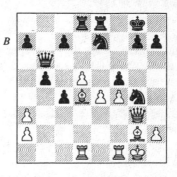

21...♕g6! 22 ♗f3 h5!

A witty rejoinder, allowing Black to secure a tremendous outpost on f5 for his knights. The shortcomings of 21 ♗d4? are already evident, and, unfortunately for White, there is little he can do to repair the damage.

23 ♕g2 fxe4 24 ♗xe4 ♘f5

Geller considered Black to be already winning at this point, an evaluation that can hardly be challenged. White's position has been deprived of his dynamism, and despite his stubborn resistance in the rest of the game he never comes close to drawing.

25 ♗xf5

A sad choice, but there was nothing better. 25 h3? loses to 25...♖xe4!.

25...♕xf5 26 h3 ♘f6 27 ♗e5 ♖d7 28 ♖f3 h4 29 ♔h2 ♖ed8 30 ♖ff1 ♘e4 31 ♖d4 ♘g3

The knight is well on its way to f5. In the mean time White remains a passive spectator as he cannot take advantage of any weaknesses in the black camp.

**32 Zfd1 Wh5 33 Z4d2 Wf5 34
Wf3 Wf7 35 Wg4 Wh5 36 Zd4 a6
37 a4 Wf7 38 Z4d2 ۩f5**

The long-awaited change of the
guard finally takes place. Having
organized his forces in the best possible way Black is now ready to mo-
bilize his dangerous pawns on the
queenside.

**39 Wg5 b4 40 a5 c3 41 Ze2 Zxd5
42 Wxd8+ Zxd8 43 Zxd8+ ۩h7 44
Zg2 Wc4 45 Zd1 c5 46 Zdg1 ۩g3**

White's position is hopeless, but
the motto 'everything can happen in
an American open' guides him for
another twelve moves.

47 Zd1 We4 48 Zd7 ۩f5?!

48...Wb1 was quicker.

**49 ۩xg7 Wxf4+ 50 ۩g1 We3+ 51
۩h2 We6 52 Za7 ۩e7 53 Zb7**

53 ۩f8 Wd6+ 54 ۩h1 c2 –+.

**53...We4 54 Zb6 ۩f5 55 ۩f6 c2
56 ۩g5 We5+ 57 ۩g1 c1W+ 58
۩xc1 We1+ 0-1**

An artistic achievement by Geller.

4) Geller's System: 6 0-0 dxc4 7 ۩e5 ۩c6! 8 ۩xc6!?

Game 18
Stohl – Polak
Czechoslovakia 1990

**1 ۩f3 ۩f6 2 d4 d5 3 c4 e6 4 g3 ۩e7
5 ۩g2 0-0 6 0-0 dxc4 7 ۩e5** *(D)*

A popular continuation. It allows
the fianchettoed bishop to exert an
immediate influence to the centre in
the interest of recovering the pawn as

quickly as possible. White also hopes
that in this way he will discourage
his opponent from freeing his game
on the queenside.

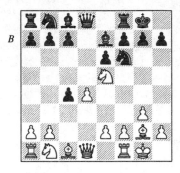

7...۩c6!

This bold discovery by the Aus-
trian GM Karl Robatsch has estab-
lished itself as a key move in Black's
system. It may appear weird at first
sight, but a deeper look reveals its
logical background: Black proposes to trade his as yet undeveloped
knight for the well-posted e5-knight,
which has already moved twice. Of
course, the text ruins his pawn structure on the queenside, but Black
trusts that the opening of the b-file
in conjunction with the avenues
opened for his queen's bishop will
offer him sufficient compensation.

8 ۩xc6!?

The start of a pawn-snatching operation. White hopes to show that the
absence of this bishop from the defence is less important than a pawn,
but the analysis included in the present game contradicts this reasoning.
The main line, 8 ۩xc6, is dealt with
in our next illustrative game.

8...bxc6 9 ②xc6

In Korchnoi-Petrosian, Il Ciocco Ct (1) 1977 (one of the first games with this variation), White experimented with 9 ②c3. After 9...c5 10 dxc5 ♗xc5 11 ♕a4 ②d5! 12 ②e4 (12 ♕xc4 ②xc3 ∓; 12 ♕c6 ②xc3 13 ♕xa8 ②xe2+ gives Black excellent chances) 12...②b6 13 ♕c2 ♗e7 14 ②xc4 ②xc4 15 ♕xc4 ♕d5 16 ♕c2 ♗b7 17 f3 ♕d4+ 18 ♔g2 ♗xe4 19 ♕xe4 ♕xe4 20 fxe4 the game quickly petered out to a draw, but it seems to me that instead of 13...♗e7, Petrosian could have been more ambitious with 13...♕d5!?, e.g. 14 ②g5 f5 15 ♗f4 ♗d6! when I don't believe in White's compensation.

9...♕e8 10 ②xe7+

An attempt to get more out of the position by 10 ♕a4?! would be asking for trouble: 10...♗d6 11 ♕xc4 a5! and now:

a) 12 ②c3 ♗a6 13 ②b5 (13 ♕a4 ②d5 ∓) 13...a4! ∓ Pigusov.

b) 12 ♗g5 ②e4 13 ♗e3 f5 14 f3 ②f6 15 ♗f2 ♔h8 16 ♕c2 ♗b7 17 ♖c1 ♖a6 18 ②e5 ♕h5 19 ②d2 ♕h3 20 ♕d3 g5 gave Black reasonable attacking chances for the pawn in Kurasev-Dziuban, USSR 1980.

c) 12 ②e5 c5 13 ②f3 ♗a6 14 ♕c2 ♖c8 15 ②c3 cxd4 16 ②xd4 and Black has a pleasant choice between 16...♗c5! and 16...♗e5!? 17 ♖d1 ♖c4 (17...②d5 ∓ Pigusov) 18 ②f3 ♗xc3 19 bxc3 ♕c8 20 ♗b2 ♕c5, which amounted to good compensation for Black in Pigusov-Naumkin, Belgrade 1988.

10...♕xe7 11 ♕a4 (D)

On 11 b3 there follows 11...cxb3 12 ♗a3 b2! 13 ♗xb2 ♖d8 with an even game. A line worth investigating is 11 ②a3!? c5 12 ②xc4 ♖d8 13 ♗e3 (Sokolowski-Marcussi, corr. 1991), and now, instead of the game continuation 13...②g4?! 14 ♕d3!, which left White on top, the rook centralization 13...♖d5!? (intending ...♕d8 or ...♗b7) successfully combines pressure on d4 with play on the light squares.

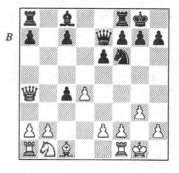

11...a5!?

11...c5 12 ♕xc4 cxd4 13 ♕xd4 e5 14 ♕h4 ♕e6 15 ②c3 ♗b7 16 e4 was the actual move-order of Gelfand-Aseev, examined in note 'a' to White's 6th move in Game 15, but nobody seems to have noticed the unpleasant 12 ♕a3!? when Black is struggling to achieve equality.

The older continuation, 11...e5, is more reliable, but the reader should keep in mind that Black then gets realistic chances to play for a win only if White presses too hard. After 12 dxe5 (12 ♕xc4?! exd4 ∓ Garcia Gonzales-Geller, Bogota 1978) 12...♕xe5 we have a branch:

a) 13 ♕xc4 ♗e6 14 ♕d3!? (14 ♕a6? ♗h3 15 ♖e1 ♕d5 16 f3 ♘g4 17 ♘c3 ♕c5+ 18 e3 ♘e5 19 ♕e2 ♖ad8 20 ♖d1 h6 21 ♗d2 f5 22 ♗e1 ♕c6 23 ♖xd8 ♖xd8 24 ♔f2 f4! led to a disaster for White in Spiridonov-Geller, Novi Sad 1978; 14 ♕c2 invites a draw by repetition after 14...♗f5 15 ♕c4 ♗e6, as in Kirov-Geller, Sochi 1976) 14...♖ad8 15 ♕e3 ♕h5 16 f3 ♗c4! (this is superior to 16...♖fe8? 17 ♕g5 ♕h3 18 ♕c5!, which allowed White a clear advantage in Gelfand-Timoshchenko, Sverdlovsk 1987) 17 ♘c3 ♖fe8 and now:

a1) 18 ♕g5 ♕h3! 19 ♗e3!? (19 ♗f4 ♗xe2! 20 ♖f2 ♗d1! 21 ♖f1! =; 21 ♗d2/e3? ♗xf3! ∓) and we are again at a cross-roads:

a11) 19...♘d5!? 20 ♗d4 (20 ♘xd5? ♖xd5 21 ♕f4 ♗xe2 22 ♖f2 g5! −+) 20...f6 21 ♕d2!? (21 ♕c1 ♘xc3 22 ♕xc3 ♗xe2 23 ♖f2 ♕d7! 24 ♗xa7 ♕a4 with counterplay) 21...♘e3 22 ♕xe3 (22 ♗xe3? ♖xd2 23 ♗xd2 ♗xe2 24 ♖fe1 ♕d7! ∓) 22...♖xe3 23 ♗xe3 ♗xe2! 24 ♖f2! is very double-edged.

a12) 19...♗xe2!? 20 ♘xe2 (20 ♖f2? ♗xf3 21 ♖xf3 ♘g4) 20...♖d5 21 ♕f4 (21 ♘f4? ♕xf1+) 21...♖de5 22 ♗xa7 (22 ♗f2 ♖xe2 23 ♕xc7?! ♘d5 24 ♕c6 ♘b4! ∓) 22...♖xe2 23 ♗f2 ♖xb2 24 a4 (24 ♕xc7 h6!? planning ...♘h7-g5) 24...h5!? 25 a5 ♘d5 26 ♕h4 ♕f5 with counterplay.

a2) 18 ♕f2 ♘d5 19 ♖e1 ♘b4 20 ♖b1 (20 b3 ♗a6 21 ♖b1 ♘c2 22 ♖f1 can be met by 22...♕a5 23 ♗b2 ♖e3!?; however, 22...♘d4 23 ♗e3

c5 intending ...♕e5 is the safe way to equality) 20...♘c2 21 ♖f1 ♘d4 22 ♗e3 c5 and Black has sufficient compensation for the material.

b) 13 ♘c3! ♘e4!? (13...♗e6 is also possible, but on principle Black should exchange knights if given the chance) 14 ♕xc4 ♘xc3 15 ♕xc3! (15 bxc3 ♗e6 16 ♕d3 ♖ad8 17 ♕e3 ♕b5 is not worse for Black despite the pawn minus) 15...♕xe2 16 ♖e1 ♕b5 17 ♖e5 ♕d7 18 ♗f4 ♗b7 19 ♖c5 ♖fd8! 20 f3 ♕d3! 21 ♗xc7 ♖d7 22 ♖f1 ♖e8 23 ♗f4 ♕e2 24 ♖e5 ♖xe5 25 ♕xe5 ♕xe5 26 ♗xe5 ♖d3 27 f4 ♖d2 28 ♖c1! f6 29 ♖c7 fxe5 30 ♖xb7 exf4 31 gxf4 a5 32 a3 a4 and Black drew easily in Korchnoi-Kotronias, Haifa Echt 1989.

12 ♕xc4

White has nothing better. After 12 ♘c3 ♕b4 13 ♕c6 ♗b7! 14 ♕xc7 ♘d5 15 ♘xd5 ♗xd5 Black gets excellent positional compensation for the pawn.

12...♗a6 13 ♕c2 *(D)*

13...♖fd8!

This looks more natural than 13...e5, which was played in the game C.Hansen-Vaganian, Esbjerg 1988. Although Vaganian obtained the advantage in that game after 14 dxe5 ♕xe5 15 ♘c3 ♖fe8 16 ♖e1 ♗b7 17 ♗f4 ♕c5! 18 ♖ad1 ♘e4 19 ♖f1 g5! 20 ♗c1 ♖a6 21 ♕b3 ♘xc3 22 ♕xc3 ♕xc3 23 bxc3 ♖xe2 I'm not entirely convinced that everything was forced. White could have considered 16 ♗f4!? when Black's compensation is not so clear, e.g. 16. ♕h5?! 17 ♖fe1 ♘g4 (17...g5? 18 ♕f5) 18 h4 ♕c5 19 e3! (19 e4? ♗d3! =) and the attack has faded away. Better is 16...♕c5!? 17 ♖ac1! h6!? with a complicated position which certainly requires a lot of analysis.

14 ♖d1

Also possible is 14 ♗e3 when Polak's suggestion of 14...c5!? 15 dxe5 ♘d5 (15...♘g4!?) 16 ♗f4 (16 ♗d4 ♘b4!; 16 ♗d2 ♕xe5 =) 16...♘xf4 17 gxf4 ♕h4! gives fine compensation for the pawns. The text move allows Black the opportunity to swap his weak c-pawn, and approach with his pieces to the vicinity of the white monarch.

14...c5! 15 dxc5 ♖xd1+ 16 ♕xd1 ♕xc5 17 ♘c3 ♘g4 18 ♕f1 *(D)*

After 18 ♘e4?! Black has the choice between 18...♕d5 19 ♕xd5 cxd5 20 ♘c3 d4 – and the more aggressive 18...♕h5. 18 ♕e1 can be met by 18...♗b7 19 h3 ♘e5 20 ♕f1 (20 ♗e3? ♕c6 21 f3 ♘xf3+ with a clear plus for Black; 20 ♔h2?! ♕c6 21 f3? {21 ♕g1!} 21...♕xf3! ∓) 20...h6 (Polak), keeping the pressure on White's position.

18...h6?!

It is quite understandable that Black was in a hurry to make this useful move, which rules out backrank mates, but here it was more important to concentrate on restraining White's movements. After 18...♖c8! 19 ♗d2 (19 h3?! ♘e5 only helps Black; 19 ♗f4 ♕b6! 20 ♖b1 c5 21 ♗d2 ♖d8 22 ♗e1 h5!? is unclear) 19...♕h5 20 h3 ♘e5 21 ♕g2!? ♘c4 22 ♗c1 ♕f5! 23 e4 ♕f6! Black has a strong initiative for the pawn.

19 h3 ♘e5 20 ♗f4! ♘g6?

Allowing White to consolidate. With 20...♘f3+! 21 ♔h1 ♘d4 (to be followed by ...e5) Polak could have hindered his opponent's plan of untangling his pieces. Now Stohl manages to reach a more or less harmonious configuration.

21 ♗e3! ♕b4 22 ♕c1 ♖c8 23 ♕c2 ♕c4 24 ♖c1!

The d-file is of no particular importance. After 24 ♖d1 ♗b7 25 ♔h2 ♕c6 (to be followed by ...♘e5) Black's pressure compensates for the pawn, while now White is planning to harass the black queen once she lands on c6.

24...♕c6 25 f3 ♘e5 26 b3 ♗b7

After his mistakes on moves 18 and 20 Black has to fight for a draw, and this task would have been extremely difficult if White had now continued with 27 ♕d1!. The only reasonable continuation 27...♕a6 28 ♘a4 ♖xc1 29 ♗xc1 ♕a7+ 30 ♔g2 leaves White well on top, but it is much better than Polak's recommendation of 27...♗a8 (a misprint?), which loses immediately to 28 ♘d5.

27 ♕e4?

A time-pressure blunder, allowing tactical possibilities to spring out of nowhere.

27...♕c7! 28 ♕f4

The queen has to keep an eye on g3. 28 ♕d4? would have lost forcibly to 28...♘xf3+! 29 exf3 ♕xg3+ 30 ♔f1 ♗a6+ 31 ♘e2 ♖xc1+ 32 ♗xc1 ♕xf3+.

28...g5! 29 ♕f6 ♘xf3+! 30 ♔f2! ♕e5 31 ♕xe5 ♘xe5

The situation has clarified. Black has recovered his pawn and has the sounder structure on the kingside, but his weakness on a5 should still give White a slight edge after, e.g., 32 ♗b6. The fact that White loses in less than ten moves can be attributed to fierce time trouble.

32 ♘b5?! ♖xc1 33 ♗xc1 ♗c6 34 ♘a3 ♘d7 35 ♗d2 a4 36 b4?

Blundering away a pawn. After the simple 36 bxa4 the players could have shaken hands.

36...♗d5 37 b5 ♗xa2 38 ♘c2?! ♗d5?!

Preferable was 38...♗c4! as White could have now played 39 ♘e3!

keeping his disadvantage to a minimum.

39 ♘b4?! a3?

39...♗c4! ∓.

40 ♗c1??

The final mistake. As Polak shows in *Informator 50* White could have drawn with 40 ♘xd5! a2 41 ♗c3 exd5 42 ♔e3 f5 43 ♔d4 ♔f7 44 ♔xd5 h5 45 ♗a1! ♔e7 46 e3! and Black can make no headway.

The text loses a vital tempo and the game.

40...a2 0-1

After 41 ♗b2 ♔f8 42 ♘xd5 exd5 43 ♔e3 ♔e7 44 ♔d4 ♔d6 White's position would be hopeless.

Despite its imperfections, this is an important game from Black's point of view. The improvement 18...♖c8! offers him good chances to play for a win in a variation that is generally considered to be drawish.

5) Geller's system: 8 ♘xc6 bxc6 9 ♘a3!? (and other 9th moves)

Game 19
Vladimirov – Vaganian
Moscow 1990

1 d4 ♘f6 2 ♘f3 d5 3 c4 e6 4 g3 ♗e7 5 ♗g2 0-0 6 0-0 dxc4 7 ♘e5 ♘c6 8 ♘xc6 bxc6 9 ♘a3!? *(D)*

White pursues a strategy analogous to that of Game 17. By developing his knight at the edge of the board he allows his pawn structure to be weakened, but gets in return a powerful pair of bishops. This factor is not in itself sufficient to grant White the advantage, but it may prove so if Black fails to create strong-points for his pieces, especially the knight. The resulting positions are rich in positional finesse and a lot depends on how well can Black utilize his front c-pawn, a valuable asset for winning purposes.

Besides the double-edged move 9 ♘a3!?, White has been sporadically employing several less recognized continuations, most of them without any particular success. Since they can be used from time to time as a surprise weapon it is worth consulting the information presented below:

a) 9 ♗xc6 (the most natural) 9...♖b8 10 ♘c3 ♗b7! (it is important to exchange light-squared bishops; the alternative 10...♘d5 has been less successful) 11 ♗xb7 (11 ♗b5 ♕d6!? is unclear; Gheorghiu's 11 ♕a4?! can be met by 11...♕xd4 12 ♗e3 ♗xc6! 13 ♕xc6 ♕d6 14 ♕xc4 ♖b4! 15 ♕d3 ♕xd3 16 exd3 ♖xb2 with the better position for Black) 11...♖xb7 and now:

a1) 12 ♖b1 ♕d7! (Gulko's suggestion) 13 e4 ♖fb8, to be followed by ...♗b4, leads to a good game for Black.

a2) 12 e4?! c5 13 d5 ♖d7 14 ♕a4 exd5 15 exd5 ♘xd5 16 ♕xc4 ♘b6 ∓ Mikenas-Shevelev, Vilnius 1979.

a3) 12 e3 c5 13 ♕f3!? (13 dxc5 ♗xc5 14 ♕f3 {14 ♕e2 ♕d3!? 15 ♕f3 ♖bb8} can be met by 14...♕a8 15 ♖d1 = Wojtkiewicz-Rozentalis, Manila 1992, but 14...♕c7! planning

...♖fb8 is ∓) 13...♖d7 (13...♕c7?! 14 d5!) 14 dxc5 ♕c7 (14...♗xc5 15 ♕f4!) 15 c6 ♖d6 16 ♘b5?! (16 ♖d1 =) 16...♕xc6 17 ♕xc6 ♖xc6 18 ♖d1 ♖b8 ∓ Johansson-Mraz, corr. 1990.

b) 9 ♘c3 ♖b8 and now:

b1) 10 ♗xc6 ♗b7 transposes to line 'a'.

b2) 10 e4?! c5 11 d5 exd5 12 exd5 ♗f5 13 ♕a4 ♗d3 14 ♖e1 ♗d6 15 ♕xa7 ♖e8! 16 ♗g5 ♖xb2 17 ♗xf6 gxf6 18 ♘e4 ♗c5 ∓ Podgaets-Ivanov, USSR 1975.

b3) 10 ♘a4!? ♗a6! gives Black excellent counterplay.

b4) 10 ♕c2 ♘d5! (10...♕xd4?! 11 ♗e3 is unfavourable compared to Larsen-Speelman below as the a-pawn is now hanging) 11 ♕a4 (11 ♖d1?! ♘b4 12 ♕a4 ♖b6!) 11...c5 (11...♖b6!? looks to me even better) 12 dxc5 ♘xc3 13 bxc3 ♗xc5 14 ♕xc4 ♕d6 15 ♗f1 (Webb-Tisdall, Hastings 1977/8) 15...♕b6!? ∓.

c) 9 ♕a4?! ♕xd4! and now:

c1) 10 ♘d2 ♖b8 11 a3?! ♗d7 12 ♗xc6?! ♗xc6 13 ♕xc6 ♗c5 14 ♘f3 ♕d5 15 ♕xc7 ♘e4 16 ♕e5 ♖fd8 was manifestly superior for Black in Calvo-Robatsch, Mallorca 1972, but White's play was dreadful.

c2) 11 ♕xc6, as played in Sygulski-L.Spasov, Warsaw 1983, although even here Black should be able to claim some advantage with 11...♘d5! instead of the game continuation 11...♗c5 12 e3 ♕d6 13 ♘xc4 ♕xc6 14 ♗xc6 ♗a6 =.

c3) 10 ♖d1 ♕b6 11 ♗e3!? was played in the game Hennings-Brameyer, E.Germany 1977/8. It seems that Black should continue grabbing pawns by 11...♕xb2, White's opening being merely a bluff as the following analysis by Neishtadt shows: 12 ♗d4 ♕xe2 13 ♘c3 ♕h5 14 ♕xc6 (14 ♗xc6 e5!) 14...♖b8! 15 ♕xc7 ♗d7! and Black holds on to the extra pawn.

d) 9 ♕c2 ♕xd4 10 ♗e3 ♕d6 11 ♘d2 ♘d5 12 ♘xc4 ♘xe3 13 ♘xe3 ♗a6 14 ♖ac1 ♖ad8 15 ♗xc6 ♗g5 16 ♗f3 ♕b6 was slightly better for Black in Larsen-Speelman, London 1980.

e) 9 e3!? is the most commendable of White's 9th move alternatives:

e1) 9...♘d5 10 ♕a4 ♘b6 and now:

e11) 11 ♕xc6 ♖b8 gives Black good counterplay.

e12) 11 ♕c2 ♖b8 12 ♖d1 (12 ♗xc6 ♗b7 =) 12...♕e8! 13 ♘d2 ♗a6 14 b3 c5 15 ♗b2 cxd4 16 ♗xd4 (Arsović-Cvetković, Yugoslavia 1994), and now the improvement 16...f6! (instead of 16...♗b5) seems to shake the theoretical evaluation ±, e.g. 17 ♘xc4 ♘xc4 18 bxc4 c5 19 ♗b2 ♖b4 20 ♗f1 ♗b7 or 17 ♗xb6 cxb6 18 ♘xc4 ♗c5. In the resulting positions only Black can be better.

a13) 11 ♕a5! and White stands well.

e2) 9...♗a6! (this is the best line for Black) 10 ♗xc6 ♖b8 11 ♘c3 ♕d6! (11...♘d5 12 ♘xd5! exd5 13 ♕f3 ♗b7 14 ♗xb7 ♖xb7 15 b3! cxb3! {15...c3?! 16 e4! ±} 16 axb3 was a trifle better for White in Seirawan-Ivanchuk, Tilburg 1992) 12

♕a4!? (12 ♗g2 c5 =) 12...♖b6 13 ♗g2 c5 14 dxc5 ♕xc5 15 e4 (15 ♕c2 ♕c8; 15 ♖d1 ♕c8) 15...♕c8! and the threatened knight invasion on d3 (via d7 or g4) ensures Black a good game.

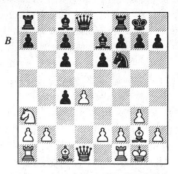

9...♗xa3 10 bxa3 ♗a6!

This is superior to the alternative 10...♘d5 11 ♕a4 ♘b6 12 ♕xc6 ♖b8 13 ♕c5! which has earned a reputation as a solid line for White. The knight manoeuvre ...♘f6-d5-b6 is time-consuming and as the reader might have noticed rarely leads to active play for Black.

11 ♗xc6

In Antunes-Karpov, Tilburg 1994, White played here the less ambitious 11 ♗g5 h6 12 ♗xf6 ♕xf6 13 ♗xc6 but despite the apparent simplicity of the position he was slowly squeezed to death in 73 moves. The game is worth quoting in full as it is a perfect illustration of Karpov's ability to utilise small advantages: 13...♖ab8 14 ♕a4 ♖b6 15 ♖fd1 ♖d8 16 ♗f3 c6 17 ♔g2 ♕e7 18 e3 ♖c8! 19 h4 ♗b5 20 ♕b4 c5! ∓ 21 dxc5 ♖xc5 22 ♖d8+ ♔h7 23 ♖ad1 ♗c6!

24 ♕c3 ♗xf3+ 25 ♔xf3 ♖f5+ 26
♔g2 ♕b7+ 27 ♔g1 ♕f3 28 ♖f1? (28
♖8d2 ∓) 28...♖c6? (28...♖b1!! 29
♖xb1 ♕xf2+ 30 ♔h1 ♕f3+ 31 ♔h2
♕e2+ 32 ♔h3 {32 ♔h1 ♖f2 –+}
32...♖f2 33 ♖h1 ♕f3 34 ♖h2 ♕f5+
would have resulted to a quick win;
now Karpov has to summon all his
energy to get back to the winning
track) 29 ♖d4 ♕e2 30 ♖d2 ♕f3 31
♖d4 ♕e2 32 ♖d2 ♕h5 33 ♖b1 ♖d5
34 ♕c2+ ♔g6 35 ♕xg6+ ♔xg6 36
♖c2 ♖d3 37 a4 ♖a3 38 ♖b4 c3 39
♔f1 ♖a6 40 ♖b3?! (40 ♖g4+! ♔f6
41 ♖f4+ ♔e7 42 ♖c4 ♖3xa4 43
♖4xc3 ♖xa2 44 ♖c7+ ♔f6 45 ♖2c4!
offered the best drawing chances)
40...♖3xa4 41 ♖cxc3?! (41 ♖bxc3 is
better; after the move played Black
is again in control of the situation)
41...♖xa2 42 ♖b7 ♖b6! 43 ♖xb6
axb6 44 ♖b3 ♖a6 45 c4 ♔f6 46 f4
♔e7 47 ♔e2 ♔d6 48 g4 ♖a2+ 49
♔e3 ♔c6 50 ♖c3+ ♔b7 51 ♖d3 ♖c2
(Black has regrouped successfully
and is ready to advance his passed
pawn) 52 h5 b5 53 c5 ♔c7 54 ♖a3
♔b6 55 ♖a8 ♖c3+ 56 ♔d4 ♖c4+ 57
♔e3 ♖c3+ 58 ♔d4 ♖c4+ 59 ♔e3
♖c7! 60 ♖g8 b4 61 ♔d3 b3 62 ♖b8+
♔b7 63 ♖c8 ♔a7 64 ♖c1 ♖b5 65
♖b1 ♔b6 66 ♔c3 ♔c5 67 ♔b2 ♖b4
68 ♖f1 ♔d5 69 ♖f3 ♔e4 70 ♖f1 ♖b7
71 ♖f2 ♔e3 72 ♖f1 ♔e2 73 ♖g1 ♔f2
0-1.

A fine technical achievement by
Karpov, but at the same time torture
for the Portuguese player, who might
have ended up regretting that his opponent missed the tactical shot on
move 28.

An obscure recommendation to
be found in several theoretical manu-
als (including *ECO*) is 11 ♕a4 ♗b5
12 ♕a5 c3 13 ♕xc3 ♗xe2 14 ♖e1 ±.
The final assessment is probably
correct, but the simple 12...♕xd4
(11...♕xd4 12 ♗e3 ♗b5! is also
good) 13 ♗e3 ♕d6! looks like a
refutation, e.g. 14 a4? ♕a3! or 14
♖fd1 ♘d5 and I can't see a decent
follow-up for White. It seems that
the whole idea was based on a miscalculation, its originator probably
overlooking the resource ...♕d6-a3
which prevents White from winning
the enemy bishop.

11...♖b8 12 ♕a4 *(D)*

12 ♗f3?! ♕d7! is fine for Black.

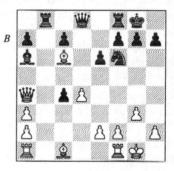

12...♖b6 13 ♗g2

An important alternative is 13
♗d2 ♕d6!? (13...c3 14 ♗xc3 ♗xe2
15 ♖fc1 ♘d5!? is not out of the question, e.g. 16 ♗a5 ♖b2 17 ♖ab1 ♘b6!
or 16 ♗xd5 ♗b5 17 ♕b3 exd5 18
♗b4 ♗c4 =) 14 ♗f3 ♘d5 15 ♖fb1
♖fb8 16 ♖xb6 ♕xb6 17 ♖c1. Then:

a) 17...♗b5 18 ♕a5 ♕xd4 19
♖b1 h6 20 ♖xb5 led to an immediate
draw in Ribli-Balashov, Dortmund

1987 in view of 20...♖xb5 21 ♕xb5 ♕xd2 22 ♕e8+ ♔h7 23 ♕xf7 ♘f6! = (Balashov).

b) It seems to me that Black could have played for more with 17...h6!?. For example, 18 e4 c3! 19 ♗e1 (19 ♗xh6 gxh6 20 exd5 ♕b2 21 ♕d1 ♗d3!) 19...♕b2 20 ♕d1 ♗b5!! 21 exd5 ♗a4 22 ♘xc3 ♗xd1 23 ♗xb2 ♗xf3 ∓ or 18 ♗b4 ♗b5 19 ♕d1 ♘xb4 20 axb4 ♕a6 21 ♕d2 ♕a3! and Black has all the pressure. With a pair of rooks gone the passed c-pawn gains in strength and Black should be alert in exploiting the tactical opportunities which are likely to occur.

On the other hand, 13 ♗f3 is similar to the text. In Beliavsky-Geller, Moscow IZ 1981, the players fought to a draw with 13...♘d5 14 ♕a5 c3 15 ♖e1 ♕f6 16 ♗xd5 exd5 17 ♕xc3 ♖c6 18 ♕b3 ♕xd4 19 ♗e3 ♕e4 20 ♖ad1 ♖c4 21 ♗xa7 c6 22 ♕e3, but this signifies little as they were probably too cautious in view of the tournament situation. In any case, there is little difference between 13 ♗g2 and 13 ♗f3 and Black may follow the same line of play that Vaganian adopts in our main game.

13...♘d5 14 ♕c2?! *(D)*

This is an imprecision. The immediate 14 e4? fails on account of 14...♘c3 15 ♕c2 ♕xd4! (Vaganian gives only 15...♘b5 16 d5 ♘d4 ∓) 16 ♗e3 ♕d3 17 ♕xd3 cxd3 18 ♗xb6 cxd6 and Black will regain the exchange with interest. Thus White prepares an advance of his e-pawn, but if Black prevents this plan it is

not clear what he can do next. Vaganian's suggestion of 14 ♕a5!? would have preserved some pressure on Black's queenside, thus maintaining dynamic equilibrium.

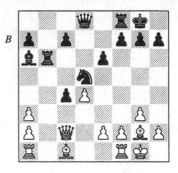

14...f5!

Of course! The knight radiates energy in all directions and it would be a pity to allow its eviction from d5. After the move played it can already be asserted that Black enjoys a slight advantage as in this semi-blocked position his minor pieces co-operate more harmoniously than the white bishops.

15 e4 fxe4 16 ♗xe4 h6!

An improvement over Palatnik-Kruppa, Kherson 1989, in which the weaker 16...♘f6?! was played. It turns out that Black can afford to make this concession as White has too many problems with his co-ordination to have real prospects of attack on the b1-h7 diagonal.

17 ♗g2?

A pointless move, but also after the better 17 ♗e3!? ♕f6 18 ♖fb1 ♖fb8 (Vaganian) White would have been reduced to a purely defensive role. Now, however, his situation becomes critical, as the fearsome c-pawn is allowed to advance, creating the unpleasant threat of a rook invasion on b2.

17...♕f6 18 ♗e3 c3 19 ♖fb1 ♗c4!

Preparing to double rooks on the b-file. To prevent this White is practically forced to take on b6 but that amounts to an admission of defeat as it redeems Black in one go from his wrecked pawn structure. Strategically the game has been decided but the execution still requires a lot of accuracy.

20 ♖xb6 cxb6 21 ♖e1 b5! 22 f4 ♘xe3!

White intended ♗f2 followed by ♗h3, but Vaganian's simple move nips the idea in the bud. Black will now lose his valuable passed pawn but the resulting endgame is lost for White as all the black pieces enjoy tremendous activity.

23 ♖xe3 ♕xd4 24 ♕xc3 ♖d8 25 ♗f3 a5!

Black is not in a hurry. The rash 25...♕xc3?! 26 ♖xc3 ♖d2 allows White some drawing chances after 27 a4 ♖xa2 28 axb5 ♗xb5 and then 29 ♖c7 or 29 ♗h5!?.

26 ♕xd4

Exchanges bring Black closer to victory, but Vladimirov had nothing better. The following variations by Vaganian illustrate the helplessness of White's situation: 26 ♔f2? ♕d2+ and Black wins; 26 ♕e1 ♕d2 (26...♗xa2 ∓) 27 ♗g4 ♕xe1+ 28 ♖xe1 ♔f7 ∓.

26...♖xd4 27 ♗e2 ♔f7 28 ♗xc4 bxc4

Black is practically a pawn to the good in the rook ending. The rest witnesses White's desperate attempt to save the game but the Armenian's exemplary technique leaves him no chances.

29 ♖c3 e5! 30 fxe5 ♔e6 31 ♔f2 ♔xe5 32 ♔e2 ♔f5!

Avoiding the last trap: 32...♖e4+ 33 ♔d2 ♔d4?! 34 ♖f3 c3+? 35 ♖xc3! ♖e2+ 36 ♔xe2 ♔xc3 37 a4! and White draws. By threatening a king invasion on g4 Black forces his opponent to create some more weaknesses along the third rank.

33 h3 g5! 34 ♖f3+ ♔e5 35 a4 ♖d6! 36 g4 ♖f6 37 ♖e3+ ♔d5 38 ♔d2 ♖f2+

After some careful manoeuvring the rook has finally broken into the heart of the enemy position. The rest requires no comments as Black serenely collects the fruits of his hard work.

39 ♔c3 ♖xa2 40 ♖e8 ♖xa4 41 h4 gxh4 42 ♖d8+ ♔e5 43 ♖f8 h3 44 ♖f5+ ♔e4 0-1

6) Geller's system: 6 0-0 dxc4 7 ♕c2 a6 8 ♕xc4 b5 9 ♕c2 ♗b7

Game 20
Illescas – Epishin
Madrid 1995

1 d4 ♘f6 2 c4 e6 3 g3 d5 4 ♗g2 ♗e7 5 ♘f3 0-0 6 0-0 dxc4 7 ♕c2

This has undoubtedly been the most efficient continuation over the past decade. Its increasing popularity lies in the fact that White is assured of recovering his pawn without jeopardizing his pawn structure, while at the same time no big concessions are made in terms of development. In fact the queen move helps to add more firepower in the centre by vacating d1 for her fellow heavy pieces. The only disadvantage is that the queen's position may become slightly exposed once Black manages to execute ...c5 and this factor is the one that gives most substance to Black's efforts to create something out of the symmetrical positions tend to arise.

7...a6 *(D)*

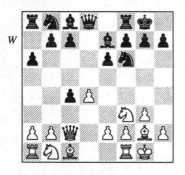

8 ♕xc4

The main alternative to this natural recapture, 8 a4, is dealt with in Games 22 and 23. Other moves are less logical and offer Black good possibilities of obtaining an advantage. Some examples:

a) 8 e4?! b5 9 a4 (*ECO* suggests 9 ♘g5!? but this looks very suspect

after 9...♘c6!) 9...♗b7 10 ♘c3 ♘c6! 11 axb5 axb5 12 ♖xa8 ♕xa8 13 ♘xb5? ♘b4 14 ♕xc4 ♗a6 with a clear advantage for Black, Enklaar-Zuidema, Holland 1965.

b) 8 ♖d1?! b5 9 ♘g5 c6 10 e4 h6 11 ♘h3 c5 was played in Chiburdanidze-Hjartarson, Linares 1988. The continuation 12 dxc5 ♕c7 13 e5 ♘d5 14 ♘f4 ♘xf4! 15 ♗xf4 (15 ♗xa8 ♘d3 ∓) 15...♗b7 left Black with clearly the better game but Hjartarson's suggestion 12 d5!? is no real improvement either: 12...exd5! (Hjartarson considers only 12...e5 in his notes) 13 e5 ♗xh3! 14 exf6 (14 ♗xh3 ♘e8 ∓) 14...♗xg2 15 fxe7 ♕xe7 16 ♔xg2 ♘c6 (or 16...d4) and Black's tremendous pawn mass on the queenside more than compensates for the missing piece.

c) 8 ♗g5 b5 9 ♗xf6 ♗xf6 10 ♘g5 ♗xg5 11 ♗xa8 ♕xd4 (11...c6!?) 12 ♗g2 ♘d7 13 ♘c3 f5! 14 b3! cxb3 15 axb3 ♕c5 16 ♖a2 ♗e7 17 e3 ♗d6 was slightly better for Black in Korchnoi-Vaganian, Montpellier Ct 1985.

d) 8 ♘bd2 b5 9 ♘g5 c6 10 b3 h6 (10...cxb3 11 ♘xb3 a5 12 ♖d1 ♗d7 13 ♘c5 h6 14 ♘f3 ♗e8 15 ♗b2 ♘a6 16 ♖ac1 ♕c8 17 ♕b1 ♘xc5 18 dxc5 ♘d7 19 ♘e5 ♘xe5 20 ♗xe5 ♖a7 ∓ Shabalov-Aseev, Barnaul 1988) 11 ♘gf3 ♗b7!? 12 bxc4 c5! 13 dxc5 (13 cxb5 cxd4 ∓) 13...b4! 14 a3 (14 ♘b3 ♘bd7 ∓) 14...bxa3 15 ♖b1 ♗c6 16 ♘e5 ♗xg2 17 ♔xg2 ♕c7 gave Black the better prospects in view of his outside passed pawn in Mikhalevski-Gofshtein, Beersheba 1991.

8...b5 9 ♕c2

This logical retreat is linked with the idea of impeding the advance ...c5 which is Black's traditional way of freeing his game in the Catalan. The unnatural 9 ♕b3 was treated cruelly in Larsen-Portisch, Havana OL 1966: 9...♗b7 10 ♖d1 (10 ♘c3 c5 11 dxc5 ♘bd7 12 ♖d1 ♗xc5 13 ♗g5 ♕b6 ∓) 10...♘bd7 11 ♗g5 c5 12 dxc5 ♕c7 13 ♘bd2 ♗xc5 14 ♘e1? ♗xf2+! 15 ♔xf2 ♕c5+ 16 e3 ♘g4+ 17 ♔g1 ♗xg2 18 ♘xg2 ♕xg5 19 ♘f3 ♕e7 20 a4 ♘de5 21 ♘d4? bxa4 22 ♖xa4 ♖ab8 23 ♕a2 ♕f6 and White resigned. 14 ♘e1? was, of course, a dreadful howler but the threat ...♕b6 had already created an unpleasant situation for the Dane, e.g. 14 ♖ac1 ♕b6 15 e3 ♘d5 and the stray bishop on g5 is in serious danger. 14 ♗xf6 may be better in a practical sense but does not automatically relieve White from his troubles in view of 14...♗d5! followed by 15...♘xf6; in this case the two bishops and the exposed position of the white queen offer Black a strong initiative.

9...♗b7 (D)

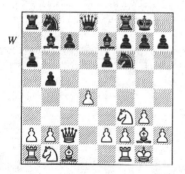

This is a standard position in the Catalan. The theoretical dispute over this position has centred so far on the problem of equalizing with Black but I think that the material presented here will even manage to pass the ball in White's court. The fact that White has been scoring rather well (60%) from the diagram can be attributed to the tendencies of most players on the black side, who usually regard their system of defence as a safe drawing device.

10 ♗g5

I have chosen this line as a starter because it is considered (not without reason) to be one of the most drawish in the whole range of opening chess literature. White plans to suffocate Black by means of ♘bd2-b3, followed by a timely exchange of the light-squared bishops that would accentuate the weakness of c6, a traditionally sensitive spot in Black's set-up. Of course, that can easily happen only in fairy tales and in practice Black has been able to attain comfortable equality though perhaps in too conservative a way.

Apart from the topical alternatives 10 ♗f4 and 10 ♗d2, which are both dealt under the next illustrative game, White can also develop his queen's knight at d2 or c3 but he usually refrains from that. The justification lies in the fact that the knight's early development interferes with White's play along the c-file, allowing Black to play ...c5 under more favourable circumstances. Some examples are:

a) 10 ♘bd2 ♘bd7 11 ♘b3 (11 ♖d1 c5! ∓; 11 e4 c5 12 e5 ♘d5 13 ♕e4 ♕b6 14 dxc5 ♘xc5 15 ♕g4 ♖ac8 ∓ Reshevsky-Rogoff, Lone Pine 1978) 11...♗e4! 12 ♕d1 c5 13 dxc5 ♘xc5 14 ♕xd8 ♖fxd8 15 ♘xc5 ♗xc5 ∓ Dely-Kluger, Hungarian Ch 1965.

b) 10 ♘c3 and then:

b1) 10...c5!? is interesting, e.g. 11 dxc5 ♗xc5 12 ♘xb5 (12 ♗g5 ♘bd7 to be followed by ...♕b6 is fine for Black; 12 ♘g5 ♗xg2 13 ♔xg2 ♘bd7 14 ♖d1 h6 is unclear) 12...♗xf2+ 13 ♖xf2 ♗e4! (and not 13...axb5? 14 ♘g5! ±) with excellent chances for a pawn.

b2) 10...♘bd7 11 ♖d1 ♕c8 12 ♗e3 c5 13 dxc5 ♗xc5 14 ♗xc5 ♕xc5 15 ♘d2 ♘b6 with a free game for Black although he eventually lost in Mi.Tseitlin-Plachetka, Trnava 1979.

c) An independent try is Uhlmann's 10 a4 which should come to nought, as it actually did, in Uhlmann-Drimer, Leipzig OL 1960: 10...♘c6 11 ♗f4 ♘b4 12 ♕c1 c5 13 dxc5 ♖c8 14 ♖d1 ♖xc5 15 ♘c3 ♘bd5 with an equal position. However, I believe that White's plan is extravagant and if any improvements exist they have to be on Black's side. This opinion is supported by the fact that 10 a4 has never appeared in tournament practice since the above-mentioned game.

10...♘bd7 11 ♘bd2

The actual move was 11 ♗xf6, but I have taken some liberties with the move order to show that White cannot profit by essaying the relatively more complicated 11 ♘bd2.

11...♖c8 12 ♗xf6

The alternative is 12 ♘b3!? ♗e4 13 ♕c1 (13 ♕d2 c5 =) 13...c5 *(D)* and here:

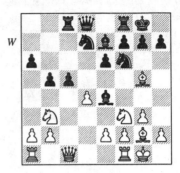

a) 14 ♗xf6 ♘xf6 15 dxc5 a5 transposes to a line discussed under 12 ♗xf6.

b) 14 dxc5 allows Black an extra possibility in 14...a5!? 15 a4?! (15 ♖d1!? ♗d5! is unclear) 15...♗d5 16 ♗xf6 ♗xf6 (16...♘xf6 is also good) 17 ♘fd2 ♘xc5! 18 ♘xc5 ♗d4!, recovering the piece with an initiative.

c) 14 ♘xc5! ♘xc5 15 dxc5 ♖xc5 16 ♕e3 ♕a8 17 ♗xf6 gxf6 with a double-edged position in Larsen-Ribli, Amsterdam 1980. The game continuation 18 ♖fd1 ♖d5! 19 ♘e1 ♗xg2 (19...♖xd1 20 ♖xd1 f5!? is worth analysing) 20 ♘xg2 ♖fd8 21 ♕b3 a5! 22 ♖xd5 ♕xd5 23 ♘f4 would have left Black slightly better had he now played 23...♕e5!, so I expect attention to focus on 18 ♖ad1!?, which offers White better chances to exploit Black's weakened kingside.

12...♘xf6 13 ♘b3 ♗e4!

I believe that this is the best move in the position. 13...c5 was successful in Andersson-Petursson, Reggio Emilia 1989/90, after 14 dxc5 a5 15 a4 ♗e4 16 ♕c3 b4 17 ♕e3 ♗d5! 18 ♖fd1 ♕c7 19 ♘fd4 ♗xg2 20 ♔xg2 ♗xc5 21 ♖ac1 ♗xd4 22 ♕xd4 ♕b7+ 23 ♔g1 ♕a6 24 ♕e5 ♘d5 25 ♘c5 ♕c6 26 ♖d2 ♘b6 27 ♖dc2 ♖cd8 28 ♘b3 ♖d1+! ∓ (0-1, 50) but I have the impression that White was a bit careless to allow this. 24 ♖xc8 or 25 e4 would have yielded an easy draw.

14 ♕c3

This is apparently stronger than 14 ♕c1, which disrupts the co-ordination of the white rooks. After 14...c5 15 dxc5 a5! Black has sharpened the struggle to good effect, e.g. 16 a4 ♕d5! 17 ♘xa5?! (17 ♕e3! is unclear) 17...♖xc5! (17...♗xc5 18 ♕d1! {18 ♕f4 e5 19 ♕h4 b4 ∓} gives White counterchances) or 16 ♖d1 ♗d5 17 a4?! bxa4 18 ♖xa4 ♕c8! 19 ♖a3 a4 when the position must be assessesd as at least slightly better for Black.

14...♘d5 15 ♕d2

15 ♕c6!? has not been tried, but looks OK for Black after 15...♕d6 16 ♘e5 (not 16 ♖ac1? ♕xc6 17 ♖xc6 ♘b4 −+, nor 16 ♖fc1?! ♕xc6 17 ♖xc6 ♘b6!) 16...♗xg2 17 ♔xg2 f6! 18 ♕xd6 cxd6, with a balanced endgame.

After 15 ♕c1 Black can easily equalize by means of 15...c5 16 ♘xc5 (16 dxc5 ♗xc5 {16...♕c7 =} 17 ♘xc5 ♗xf3 18 ♗xf3 ♕c7 also

leads to an equal position) 16...♗xc5 (16...♕b6, as in Andersson-Karpov, Moscow 1981, 17 ♘xe4!? ♖xc1 18 ♖fxc1 might be just a trifle better for White) 17 dxc5 ♕e7, but I like the look of 15...♘b6!?, planning ...♘a4 followed by ...c5. This idea paid off handsomely in Hulak-Gligorić, Zlatibor 1989, after 16 ♖d1 (16 ♕f4 ♕d5 17 ♘bd2 f5!?) 16...♘a4 17 ♘c5 (17 ♘bd2 ♗d5! is unclear as 18 b3 ♘b6 takes away b3 from the white knight while 18 e4?! ♗b7 dangerously weakens the dark squares) 17...♗xc5 18 dxc5 ♕f6! ∓ 19 b4? (19 ♘d4!? offers better chances of salvation) 19...♘c3 20 ♖e1 ♘xe2+ with Black emerging a clear pawn up, but Gligorić misplayed the rest of the game, allowing the Croatian a laborious draw on move 76.

That rounds up the rational moves, but in the game Shipov-Masternak, Katowice 1992, White opted for the insane-looking continuation 15 ♕a5. After 15...♗b4 16 ♕xa6 c6 17 ♘e5 ♗xg2 18 ♔xg2 ♘e7 the white queen was locked in but Black could not find a way to trap it and the game ended in a draw by repetition: 19 ♖fc1 f6 20 ♘f3 ♖a8 21 ♕b7 and then 21...♖b8 22 ♕a7, etc. Perhaps 21...♕d6 22 a3 ♖fb8 is a way to play on but White could have prevented this by retreating his knight to d3 on move 20. At this moment I cannot see a clear-cut refutation of 15 ♕a5 but the whole line is certainly debatable and I don't expect it to reappear in tournament practice.

15...c5

This is a healthy move, but Black may also consider the more refined 15...♘b6 or 15...♗b4!?. The former is most appropriate in win-or-die situations while the latter is designed to enforce the advance ...c5 by driving the white queen to the first rank. For example:

a) 16 ♕d1 (16 ♕g5 ♕e8!?) 16...c5 17 a3 (17 dxc5 ♗xc5 is a significant improvement over the main game as after 18 ♘xc5 ♖xc5 19 ♖c1 and then 19...♕c7 or 19...♖xc1 20 ♕xc1 ♕a8 Black gets to the c-file first but this represents White's best chance to avoid complications) 17...c4 18 axb4 cxb3 19 ♕xb3 (19 ♖xa6?! ♖c2) 19...♕d6 (19...♖c4!?) 20 ♘e5 ♗xg2 21 ♔xg2 was Spiridonov-Kotronias, Corfu 1989, and now instead of 21...♘xb4 as played in the game, I should have preferred 21...♕xb4, with a slight pull in the ensuing ending.

b) 16 ♕c1 c5 17 dxc5 ♗xc5 18 ♘xc5 ♗xf3 19 ♗xf3 ♕e7 = is a transposition to the note accompanying White's 15th, but Black can also play the more fighting 16...♘b6!? in the spirit of the above-mentioned game Hulak-Gligorić.

16 ♘xc5 ♗xc5 17 dxc5 ♖xc5 18 ♖fc1 ♖xc1 19 ♖xc1 ♕a8! 20 ♕d4 ♘f6 *(D)*

The reduced material means that neither side is risking too much: White's possession of the c-file is counterbalanced by Black's grip on the long diagonal, while the slight weakness of c6 remains unimportant as long as plenty of pieces are still on

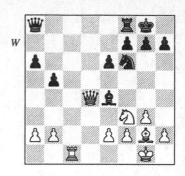

the board. Black should in principle try to keep the queens on, avoiding rook and knight endgames which could be extremely dangerous, provided that White still controls the critical file.

21 ♕c5

In Spiridonov-Geller, Moscow GMA 1989, the continuation 21 h3 h6 22 ♖c7 ♖c8 23 ♖xc8+ ♕xc8 produced a level position which has, surprisingly, been awarded a ± by some distinguished commentators. After 24 ♘e5 ♗xg2 25 ♔xg2 ♕c7 it is hard to detect any advantage for White and in fact it is Black who should have won, were it not for a tragic blunder on move 40: 26 ♘d3 ♕c2 27 ♘f4 ♕c7 28 ♘d3 ♕c2 29 e3?! ♕c6+ 30 ♔g1 ♘e4! ∓ 31 h4?! ♘d2! 32 ♕d8+? (32 ♘e5! ♕c1+ 33 ♔h2 ♕e1 34 ♕d8+ ♔h7 35 ♕d3+ f5 36 ♔g2 may hold) 32...♔h7 33 ♘e5 ♕c1+ 34 ♔h2 ♘f1+ 35 ♔h3 ♘xe3! 36 ♕d3+ f5 37 ♔h2 ♘d5 38 ♕e2 ♘f6 39 b3 ♕c5 ∓ 40 ♘d3 ♘g4+?? 41 ♕xg4 and Black resigned shortly afterwards. It is difficult to believe that an experienced player like Spiridonov was outplayed from the position of the diagram but for the non-believers here is a second example: 21 ♕b6 h6 22 h3 ♖d8 23 ♔h2 ♘d5 24 ♕a5 ♖b8 25 ♖c5 ♕a7 26 b4 ♕b7 27 ♕a3 ♘b6 28 ♕c1 ♖c8 29 ♖xc8+ ♘xc8 30 ♕c5 ♘b6 31 ♕d4 ♗d5 32 ♘e1 ♗xg2 33 ♘xg2 ♘d5 34 ♕c5 ♕b6 35 ♕xb6 ♘xb6 36 ♘e1 ♘a4 and Black went on to win in 61 moves in Mirallès-Vaganian, Haifa Echt 1989.

21...h6 22 a3 ♖d8 23 h3 ♗b7

Both players are shifting wood, waiting for the other side to make a threatening gesture. This is the kind of position in which one should play just logical moves, accepting the fact that half a point is better than nothing, or as a Greek saying would put it 'take care of your clothes to make sure you'll have half of them'.

24 ♕b6 ♖b8 25 b4 ♗d5 26 ♕c7 ♘e8 27 ♕f4 ♕b7

Black has been pushed back for the moment, but now he is planning to bring the c4-square under control by means of ...♖d8 followed by ...♘d6. The Spanish grandmaster, on the other hand, has prepared in reply an unusual interpretation of a flank attack which forms part of a restriction process.

28 h4 ♖d8 29 ♖c5 ♘d6 30 g4! ♕e7 (D)

30...f6?! would have been inferior to the solid game continuation in view of 31 g5! ♘e4 32 ♖c7 (32 ♖c1!?) 32...e5 33 ♕c1 ♕b6 34 e3 and White has managed to maintain some pressure.

31 g5

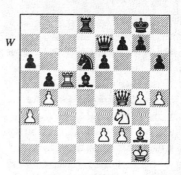

Stabilizing the situation on the kingside and taking away f6 from the enemy queen. Conceding control of f5 is not so important as Black may use this square only for defensive purposes.

31...hxg5 32 hxg5 ♗xf3

After 33...♘c4?! 34 ♖c7 ♖d7 35 ♖xd7 ♕xd7 36 ♕b8+ ♔h7 White has 37 g6+!, causing Black serious distress. The text eliminates all possibilities based on ♘e5, and should have been sufficient to maintain the status quo.

33 ♗xf3 ♘f5?!

But not like this. Black should be aiming for ...e5, which would highlight the pawn on g5 as a potential weakness. 33 ♘c4 was therefore best and could have led to a draw by repetition after 34 ♖c7 ♖d7 35 ♖c8+ ♖d8 36 ♖c7, etc.

34 e4! ♘d4 35 ♗g4 ♕d6 36 ♕xd6 ♖xd6 37 f4 f5 38 gxf6 gxf6 39 ♔f2 ♔g7 40 ♔e3

White has an edge due to the superior position of his pieces. It is not clear, however, whether he could have made progress had Black now chosen to remain passive.

40...e5?

After this White's initiative grows to alarming proportions. 40...♔g6 was preferable by far.

41 fxe5 fxe5 42 ♖xe5 *(D)*

Despite the diminished material Black is in serious danger as the white king becomes tremendously active in the next few moves.

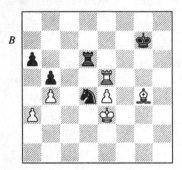

42...♘c2+ 43 ♔f4 ♘xa3 44 ♖e7+ ♔f8 45 ♖a7 ♘c2 46 ♔e5?

After 46 e5! ♖d4+ 47 ♔g5 ♘xb4 48 ♗f3! (48 e6? ♘c6 =) it is hard to see how Black would have saved himself. The attempt to attack the black monarch is bound to end in failure without the assistance of the dangerous e-pawn.

46...♖h6 47 ♗e6 ♘xb4 48 ♖f7+ ♔g8! 49 ♔f5 ♘d3 50 ♖a7+

The draw is now inevitable as 50 ♖d7+ can be met by 50...♖xe6!.

50...♔f8 51 ♖a8+ ♔e7 52 ♖a7+ ♔f8 and the players decided to split the point.

The way events evolved in this game may seem a bit discouraging, but one shouldn't forget that the improvements available to Black should offer him better chances than he actually obtained.

7) Geller's system: 6 0-0 dxc4 7 ♕c2 with 10 ♗f4 or 10 ♗d2

Game 21
Kirov – Vera
Timisoara 1987

1 ♘f3 ♘f6 2 g3 d5 3 ♗g2 e6 4 0-0 ♗e7 5 d4 0-0 6 c4 dxc4 7 ♕c2 a6 8 ♕xc4 b5 9 ♕c2 ♗b7 *(D)*

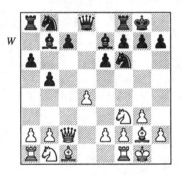

10 ♗f4

The alternative 10 ♗d2 has been played a lot but seems to place fewer obstacles in Black's path towards a complicated middlegame. White's idea, to arrange pressure on the c-file by posting his bishop on a5, does not look very aesthetic and in practice Black has been able to attain double-edged positions, offering him excellent chances to play for a win. Some examples:

a) 10...♘c6 (a bold way to prevent White's manoeuvre, but it has the disadvantage of blocking the c-pawn) 11 e3 ♖a7!? 12 ♖c1! (12 e4?! ♕a8 13 ♖e1 ♘b4 14 ♕b3 a5 15 e5 ♘e4 16 ♗xb4 axb4 was fine for Black in the game Hjartarson-Short, Belgrade 1989) 12...♕a8 13 ♘e1! (after 13 ♕d1, 13...♖d8?! 14 ♕e2 ♗d6?! 15 e4 e5? 16 ♖xc6! +− was Suba-Amura, Andorra 1994, but Black could have done better with the immediate 13...♗d6, planning ...e5, when the position is unclear) 13...♘b8 14 ♗a5 (14 ♗xb7 ♕xb7 15 ♗a5 c5! 16 dxc5 ♖c8 17 ♘d3 ♘c6 18 ♗b6 ♖aa8 19 a4 bxa4 20 ♖xa4 ♘d7 21 ♘c3 ♘xb6 22 cxb6 ♕xb6 23 ♖c4 ♘a7 24 ♘a4 ♕b5 25 ♘ac5 h6 26 h4 ♖ab8 27 ♘e4 ♖xc4 28 ♕xc4 ♖c8 was equal in Salov-Rotshtein, France 1993) and now:

a1) 14...♗xg2!? 15 ♘xg2 ♘fd7 16 b4 e5 17 ♘d2 exd4 18 exd4 ♗f6 19 ♘b3 ♖d8 20 ♖d1 ♘b6! 21 ♗xb6 cxb6 22 ♖ac1 ♖ad7 23 ♘e3 ♗e7 24 a3 a5! gave Black good counterplay in Marin-Veingold, Seville 1994 and may in fact be Black's best line.

a2) 14...♖c8 and then:

a21) Timman's suggestion of 15 ♗b6 ♗xg2 16 ♘xg2 ♖b7 17 ♗c5 does not offer White anything special: 17...♗xc5 18 ♕xc5 (18 dxc5 ♘c6 =) 18...♘fd7! and Black is ready for ...c5.

a22) 15 ♗xb7 ♕xb7 16 b4!? is worth trying, since the enterprising 16...e5 17 dxe5 ♘g4 runs into difficulties after 18 ♘d3 ♘bd7 19 e6! fxe6 20 ♕b3.

a23) 15 ♘d2 ♗xg2 16 ♘xg2 c5! 17 ♗b6 ♖d7 18 ♗xc5 a5 19 a4 (19

a3!? e5! 20 b4 exd4 21 exd4 ♘c6! 22 ♕b2! ♗xc5! 23 dxc5 axb4 24 axb4 ♕b7 is approximately balanced as White has no satisfactory way to meet the annoying ...♖d4, restoring material equality) 19...b4 20 ♘f4 ♖dc7 21 ♘d3 ♘bd7 22 ♕c4 (Timman-Short, Hilversum (1) 1989) and now 22...e5! 23 ♘b3 ♘e4 (planning ...♘g5) would have given Black sufficient compensation according to Timman.

b) 10...♗e4 11 ♕c1 ♘bd7 (this configuration is strongly recommended) 12 ♗a5 ♖c8 *(D)* and from this position White has been unable to prove any advantage:

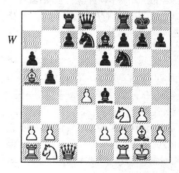

b1) 13 a4 (rather a feeble reply) 13...bxa4! 14 ♘c3 ♗xf3 15 ♗xf3 ♘b6 16 ♖d1 (or 16 ♘xa4 ♕xd4 ∓) 16...♘c4 17 ♖xa4 ♘xa5 18 ♖xa5 c5 19 ♖a6 (19 ♖a4 cxd4 20 ♖axd4 ♕b6 21 e3 ♗b4 is slightly better for Black) 19...cxd4 20 ♕f4 ♖c4 and a draw was agreed in the game Espig-Cvetković, Harkany 1987. In my opinion Black should have played on as both 21 ♘b5?! (Cvetković; 21 ♖a4?? dxc3! −+) 21...e5! and 21

♘e4 ♘d5!? (21...♖b4 22 ♘xf6+!
{22 ♘d6?! ♗xd6 23 ♖xd6 ♕a5!, intending ...e5, is ∓ in view of Black's
superior pawn structure} 22...♗xf6
is a shade better for Black) 22 ♕e5
♕c8! lead to positions where Black
enjoys some initiative without being
in the slightest danger of losing.

b2) 13 ♘bd2 ♗a8 with the alternatives:

b21) 14 ♘b3 ♕e8 15 ♘e5 (15
♘c5 ♘xc5 16 dxc5 ♘e4 17 c6 ♕xc6
18 ♕xc6 ♗xc6 19 ♖ac1 ♗d5 ∓)
15...c5 = Vaganian.

b22) 14 ♖e1?! ♕e8 15 b4 ♘e4!
16 ♘xe4 ♗xe4 17 ♕f4 f5 18 ♖ac1
♗d6 19 ♘e5 ♗xg2 20 ♔xg2 ♘f6 21
♕f3 ♘d5 22 a3 was agreed drawn in
Polugaevsky-Geller, Moscow 1985,
although Black enjoys clearly the
better position after 22...♗xe5 23
dxe5 f4!, e.g. 24 g4 h5 (24...♕g6!?)
25 ♔h1 (25 h3 hxg4 26 hxg4 ♕g6
planning ...♖f5 is also unpleasant)
25...hxg4 26 ♕xg4 ♖f5 27 ♖g1 ♕f7
28 ♖c6 (28 ♖g2? f3!) 28...♖xe5 29
♖xa6 ♘c3 ∓ (in this line the helplessness of the a5-bishop is particularly glaring).

b23) 14 ♕b1!? ♕e8 15 b4 ♘b8
16 a3 ♘c6 17 ♘b3 was slightly better for White in the game Marin-
Wells, Odorheiu Secuiesc 1993, but
the immediate 14...♘b8 looks like
an adequate reply.

b24) 14 ♖d1 ♕e8 15 b4 should
be met by 15...♘d5 and 16...f5 rather
than 15...♗d6 16 ♕c2 e5?! 17 ♘xe5
♗xg2 18 ♔xg2 ♘xe5 19 dxe5 ♕xe5
20 ♘f3 ♕e7 21 ♘d4 c5 22 ♘f5
♕b7+ 23 ♔g1 and Black was in

slight difficulties in Suba-Morović,
Dubai 1986.

b25) 14 ♕c2 ♕e8 15 b4 ♘d5 16
a3 f5! 17 e3 ♕h5 18 ♖ac1 ♗d6 19
♕d1 ♕h6 20 ♕e2 ♘7f6 21 ♖fd1
♘e7!? (21...♘g4 22 ♘f1 f4!! 23 e4
{23 exf4? ♘xf4! 24 gxf4 ♖xf4 ∓}
23...♘de3!? 24 fxe3 fxg3 25 hxg3
{25 h3 ♘f2 is unclear} 25...♗xe4
with unclear play, is analysis by Vaganian) 22 ♘e1 ♗d5! led to a finely
centralized position for Black in
Galdunts-Vaganian, Moscow 1991.
The continuation is instructive as
Black made excellent use of his advantages: 25 ♘d3 ♘e4 24 ♘xe4
fxe4 25 ♘c5 ♗xc5 (Black gladly
agrees to this exchange as it signifies
the end of White's counterplay) 26
♖xc5 c6 27 ♕g4 ♘f5! 28 ♕f4?! (28
♗xe4? loses at once to 28...♘xe3!
but 28 ♖c3!? ♘d6 29 ♗b6 offered
better survival chances) 28...♕xf4!
29 exf4 e3 30 ♗f1 *(D)* (loses rapidly
but 30 ♗xd5 exd5 31 fxe3 ♘xe3 32
♖e1 ♘c4 33 ♖e6 ♖f6 is also bad for
White according to Vaganian).

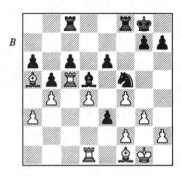

30...g5! 31 fxe3 (31 fxg5 ♘xd4!)
31...♘xe3 32 ♖c1 gxf4 33 gxf4 ♘f5

34 ♗h3 ♘xd4 35 ♖e3 ♖xf4 36 ♗b6
♔f7 and 0-1. The way White's position collapsed is not surprising if we take into account that he played the whole game practically a piece down!

b3) 13 ♘c3 (probably the best move) 13...♗b7 (13...♗a8!? 14 a4 ♖b8 15 axb5 axb5 16 b4 ♗d6 17 ♕c2 ♕e7 18 ♖ab1 e5 19 e4 g6! was unclear in Beliavsky-Vaganian, Brussels 1988) 14 a4 h4! 15 ♘a2 ♕e8 16 ♗xb4 and now the logical 16...c5 17 dxc5 ♘xc5 18 ♕d1 ♖d8 19 ♕c2 ♗e4 20 ♕c4 ♗d5 21 ♕f4 ♗d6 22 ♕e3 ♘b3 23 ♗xd6 ♖xd6 24 ♕f4 ♗xf3 25 ♕xd6 ♗xg2 26 ♔xg2 ♘xa1 27 ♖xa1 ♕xa4 28 ♕b4 ♕c6+ led to a dead-level position which was agreed drawn in Beliavsky-Speelman, Amsterdam 1989. Instead, the alternative 16...♗xh4!? 17 ♘xb4 c5 is worthy of attention, luring the white knight to the slightly unnatural square b4. I believe that this factor grants Black good compensation for the pawn in a more complicated form, but, of course, practical tests are required to substantiate this evaluation.

10...♘c6! *(D)*

The best answer, offering Black fluid piece play. 10...♘d5 11 ♘c3 ♘xf4 12 gxf4 is inferior since this merely strengthens White's central control.

11 ♘c3

I have chosen this as main line because it is the only move currently thought to give White some advantage.

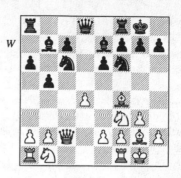

a) The frequently used 11 ♖d1 is more annoying, and has earned a reputation as being one of the most solid options against Black's set-up. After 11...♘b4 12 ♕c1 ♖c8 (Black should also equalize after 12...♕c8) 13 ♘c3, 13...♘bd5 14 ♘xd5 and then 14...♗xd5 or 14...♘xd5 has been the introduction to many short draws so I suggest that supporters of the black side should take up the untried 13...♕e8! (intending ...c5) which looks like an interesting attempt to complicate the issue. The normal objection to such moves is that they allow White to cramp his opponent on the queenside with a3 and b4, but in our case this particular formation does not seem to fulfil expectations: 14 a3 ♘bd5 14 b4 a5! 15 bxa5 c5 16 ♘xd5 ♘xd5 17 dxc5 ♖xc5! 18 ♕d2 ♘xf4 and Black's pair of bishops gives him reasonable chances to exploit the situation on the queenside after either 19 gxf4 ♕a8! or 19 ♕xf4 ♖c4!.

b) Another possibility for White is 11 ♘bd2, intending to hinder ...c5 by means of a subsequent ♘b3. In Mochalov-Itkis, USSR 1983 play continued 11...♖c8 (11...♘xd4 12 ♘xd4 ♗xg2 13 ♘xe6 fxe6 14 ♔xg2 is slightly better for White) 12 ♘b3 ♘b4 13 ♕c1 ♗d5 and then 14 ♕d1 ♗e4 (14...c5!? =) 15 ♘e1 c5 16 ♘xc5 ♗xc5 17 dxc5 ♖xc5 with balanced chances, but in his notes to the game Mochalov claims that 14 ♘fd2 ♗xg2 15 ♔xg2 ♕d5+ 16 f3 ♕a8 17 ♗e3 (planning ♗g1 followed by e4) would have given White the advantage. His assessment of the final position is probably correct but Black can certainly play better on move fifteen: 15...c5! 16 dxc5 a5! (it is useful to have the moves ...a5 and a4 thrown in for the upcoming complications) 17 a4 (17 ♖d1 ♘bd5 18 a4 ♘xf4+ 19 gxf4 ♕d5+ 20 f3 ♘g4! is good for Black) 17...♕d5+ 18 f3 ♗xc5! 19 e4 ♕h5 20 g4 ♘xg4 21 fxg4 ♕xg4+ 22 ♗g3 (22 ♔h1 ♗e3 23 ♕d1 ♕xd1 24 ♖axd1 ♗xf4 25 ♖xf4 gives Black more than enough for the piece after either 25...♘d3 or 25...bxa4) 22...♗b6 23 ♕d1 ♕xd1! (23...♕g6?! 24 axb5! {24 ♖c1 bxa4 ∓} 24...♘c2 25 ♕e2! {25 ♔h1?! ♘xa1 26 ♕xa1 ♖fd8 ∓} 25...♘xa1 { or 25...♖fd8 26 ♖a4!} 26 ♘xa1! ± {not 26 ♖xa1? ♖c2 ∓}) 24 ♖axd1 (24 ♖fxd1 ♘c2 25 axb5 ♘e3+ 26 ♔f3 ♘xd1 27 ♖xd1 a4 28 ♘a1 ♖fd8 ∓) 24...bxa4 and in this complicated endgame it is White who must fight for a draw.

11...♘b4 *(D)*

The alternative 11...♘xd4 is not highly respected, but nevertheless led to victory for Black in Ninov-Lechtynsky, Stara Zagora Z 1990: 12 ♘xd4 ♗xg2 13 ♖fd1 (13 ♘xe6 fxe6 14 ♔xg2 c5 is also unclear because the white knight stands less well on c3 than on d2) 13...♗b7 14 ♘xe6 ♕e8 15 ♘xf8 ♕c6! 16 f3 b4 17 ♖ac1 bxc3 18 ♕xc3 ♕xc3 19 ♖xc3 ♔xf8 20 ♖xc7 ♗d5 21 b3 a5 22 e4 ♗e6 23 ♖b7 a4 24 ♗d6 ♗xd6 25 ♖xd6 axb3 26 axb3 g5 27 ♖d2 ♖a3 28 ♖b2 g4 29 ♔f2 ♖a5 30 ♖b4 ♖h5 31 ♔e3 gxf3 32 ♔xf3 ♘g4 33 h4 ♖c5 34 ♖b6 ♘e5+ 35 ♔g2 ♖c3 and Black transformed his advantage into a win in eight more moves. It may seem that White was wrong in allowing ...g4, which let his pawn structure on the kingside be torn apart, but the natural 27 g4 is also not devoid of problems: 27...♖a1+ 28 ♔f2 ♖a2+ 29 ♔g1 ♔e8!? and it suddenly transpires that Black is threatening the dangerous manoeuvre ...♘d7-e5, questioning the safety of the enemy monarch. White may have some improvement at an earlier stage, but I have not been able to discover one, so for the moment this line holds good promise to become a viable alternative to the main continuation.

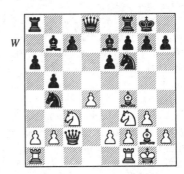

12 ♕b1!?

This move is the chief point behind 11 ♘c3 (12 ♕c1 ♖c8 13 ♖d1 is a direct transposition to 11 ♖d1). White avoids placing his queen on the c-file (where she might be exposed to harassment after a subsequent ...c5) and at the same time keeps an eye on e4 and h7. The only other move of independent significance, namely 12 ♕d2, gives Black a fine game after 12...c5 13 a3 ♘bd5 14 ♘xd5 ♗xd5 15 dxc5 ♗xc5.

12...c5! 13 dxc5 ♗xc5 14 ♗e5?!

Threatening ♘g5, but the whole idea looks artificial. In J.Horvath-Sulskis, Budapest 1994, White revealed a good sense of danger by opting for wholesale exchanges by 14 ♘g5 ♗xg2 15 ♔xg2, and after 15...h6 16 ♘ge4 ♘bd5 17 ♗e5 the draw was soon inevitable. I believe that the immediate 15...♘bd5!? gives Black chances for a tiny edge, for example 16 ♘ce4 h6! 17 ♘xf6+ (17 ♘xc5?! ♘xf4+ 18 gxf4 hxg5 ∓) 17...♘xf6 18 ♘f3 ♕b6 or 16 ♖d1 ♘xf4+ (16...♘xc3!? 17 ♖xd8 {17 bxc3 ♕b6 18 ♗c5 h6 19 ♗xf6 hxg5 ∓} 17...♘xb1 18 ♖xa8 ♖xa8 19 ♖xb1 h6 20 ♘f3 ♘e4) 17 gxf4 ♕e7, but in any case Horvath's decision looks much wiser than the ambitious text move.

14...♘g4 15 ♘c4 ♗xe4! 16 ♕xe4 f5! 17 ♕b1

In his notes to the game Vera considers the alternative 17 ♕f4 to be no improvement, giving the following analysis: 17...♕b6 (17...♘c2 is dismissed as inferior in view of 18 ♖ac1

♘ge3 19 ♖xc2! ♘xc2 20 ♘g5 ±) 18 ♗d4 e5 19 ♗xc5 ♕xc5 20 ♕d2 e4 and Black is slightly better. Nevertheless, the whole line was repeated in Inkiov-Speelman, Novi Sad OL 1990, with the Bulgarian GM employing 17 ♕f4 to good effect: 17...♘d5 (a possible explanation of Speelman's rejection of 17...♕b6 18 ♗d4 e5 could lie in 19 ♗xc5 {19 ♘xe5!?} 19...♕xc5 20 ♘xe5! ♘xe5 21 ♖fc1! ♕d6 22 ♗xa8 ♖xa8 23 ♕xf5 ±, pointed out by Inkiov in *Informator*) 18 ♕d2 ♕b6 19 ♗d4 ♖ad8 20 ♖ac1 ♗xd4 21 ♕xd4 ♕xd4? (21...♕b8) 22 ♘xd4 ♘f4 23 gxf4 ♖xd4 24 ♖c6 and White gradually assumed control in this endgame.

Were it not for a last, formal check-up, I would have believed in White's cause, but, to my great astonishment, I found a gaping hole in Vera's analysis. After 17...♘c2! 18 ♖ac1?? Black has 18...♘xf2!! 19 ♖xf2 ♗e3, winning immediately, while 18 ♖ab1 ♕b6! (18...♘ce3 19 h3!? is not so clear) is hardly what White had been dreaming of either. Thus, it seems that Black obtains the better chances after all, although it would require a monstrous chess machine to figure out all the ramifications in this extremely complicated position.

17...♕h6 18 e3 (D)

18...♗xe3! 19 fxe3 ♘xe5!

This excellent exchange sacrifice forces White on the defensive for the rest of the game. Black gets sufficient compensation from the purely material point of view, as well as

long-term pressure against the white king.

20 ♘xe5 ♕xe3+ 21 ♖f2 ♕xe5 22 ♗xa8 ♖xa8 23 a3?!

This merely drives the knight to a better square. Kirov could have renounced any intentions he might have had about winning by choosing 23 ♕e1!? ♕xe1+ 24 ♖xe1 ♘d3 25 ♖xe6 ♘xf2 26 ♔xf2, when the resulting rook endgame offers White considerable drawing chances.

23...♘c6!

Revealing another dark side of his opponent's last move. Had White played 23 ♕d1 he would have at least prevented the text (23...♘c6? 24 ♕f3) but now it's an entirely different story as Black threatens to set up the formation knight on d4, queen on d5, and pawn on e5, which, according to Vera, should be enough for a winning advantage.

24 ♕e1 ♕f6 25 a4!?

White is searching for counterplay by opening more lines for his rooks. 25 ♖d1! e5 25 ♖d5! (Vera) looks more accurate, but it is doubtful whether it would have saved White in the long run.

25...♖d8 26 axb5 axb5 27 ♖a6 ♘d4 28 ♕a5!? h6 29 ♕c7! ♔h7 30 ♖d6? *(D)*

In this type of position White should be trying to exchange queens as his main source of trouble is the poor pawn cover around his king. To this end 30 ♖a7 was best, intending ♕e7, while now Black gets the chance to penetrate, bringing the game to a drastic end.

30...♖a8 31 ♕c3 ♖a4!

31...♖a1+? 32 ♔g2 ♖d1 is a bad mistake in view of 33 ♖d2! while 31...♖d8 is met by 32 ♕c7. After the text Black is ready to undertake decisive action as all of his pieces have attained maximum activity.

32 ♖d2 ♖c4 33 ♕e3

33 ♕d3 ♘c6 is unpleasant for White but still that was preferable to the game continuation.

33...f4! 34 gxf4

Allowing a mating attack, but 34 ♕e4+ (34 ♕d3+ ♘f5 35 g4 ♕g6 −+) 34...♘f5 35 ♕xe6 ♘xd6 36 ♕xf6 gxf6 37 ♖xd6 fxg3 38 hxg3 ♖c1+ 39 ♔g2 ♖c2+ 40 ♔h3 ♔g6 (Vera) is also hopeless.

34...♕g6+ 35 ♔f2 ♘f5 36 ♖xe6 ♕g4 0-1

8) Geller's system: 6 0-0 dxc4 7 ♕c2 a6 8 a4 ♗d7 9 ♖d1 (and 9 ♘e5)

Game 22
Kochiev – Aseev
Leningrad 1989

1 d4 ♘f6 2 ♘f3 e6 3 g3 d5 4 ♗g2 ♗e7 5 0-0 0-0 6 c4 dxc4 7 ♕c2 a6 8 a4 *(D)*

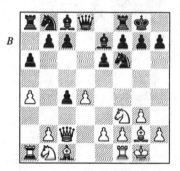

The most interesting continuation, presenting Black with some problems regarding the development of his queenside. White judges that the newly created weaknesses at b4 and b3 are relatively unimportant and trusts that his central superiority will finally emerge as the dominant factor in the position.

8...♗d7!

The bishop evidently belongs on the long diagonal, but playing 8...b6 would give Black fewer chances of obtaining active play. In the game

Hübner-Spassky, Bad Kissingen 1980, the ex-world champion managed to equalize after 9 ♘e5 ♖a7 10 ♖d1 ♗b7 11 e4 ♘c6 12 ♘xc6 ♗xc6 13 ♘c3 ♗a8 14 ♕e2 c6 15 ♕xc4 b5 16 ♕e2 b4 17 e5 bxc3 18 exf6 c2! 19 ♕xc2 ♗xf6 20 ♗c3 ♖d7 21 ♖ac1 ♖d6, but I would rather bet on White's chances of finding improvements over this.

9 ♖d1!?

This is the main alternative to the straightforward 9 ♕xc4 which is the subject of our next illustrative game. A third option, namely 9 ♘e5, has led to many uninteresting draws after 9...♗c6 10 ♘xc6 ♘xc6 11 e3 ♘a5 12 ♘d2 c5 13 dxc5 ♖c8 14 b4 cxb3 15 ♘xb3, so I suggest the little-known 9...♘c6!? when White has the following choice:

a) 10 ♘xc6 ♗xc6 11 ♗xc6 bxc6 12 ♖d1 (12 ♕xc4 ♕d5! 13 ♘d2 ♖fd8 =; 12 ♘a3 ♕d5!? {12...♕xd4} 13 ♘xc4 ♕h5! 14 ♘e5 c5 15 ♘f3 ♖ab8 16 ♗d2 cxd4 17 ♘xd4 ♘g4 18 h4 ♗c5 19 ♘f3 ♖fd8 was fine for Black in Liebert-Barczay, Szolnok 1975) 12...♕d5 13 ♘a3 (Klemens-Schüssler, Hamburg 1980) 13...♕h5! with unclear play.

b) 10 ♕xc4 ♘d5! (this keeps the position as complicated as possible without any structural or spatial concessions; in Jukić-Anand, Frunze 1987, Black played the premature 10...♘xc5 and after 11 dxe5 ♘d5 12 ♖d1 ♕c8 13 ♘c3 he couldn't avoid wholesale exchanges: 13...♘xc3 14 ♕xc3 c5 15 ♗e3 ♗c6 16 ♗xc5 ♗xc5 17 ♕xc5 ♗xg2 18 ♕xc8 ♖axc8 19

♔xg2 ♖c2 20 ♔f3 ♖xb2 21 ♖db1 and a draw was soon agreed) 11 ♖d1 (11 ♗xd5 ♘xe5 12 dxe5 exd5 13 ♕xd5 ♗c6 {13...♕c8!?} 14 ♕xd8 ♖axd8 gives Black good compensation for the material; 11 ♘xd7 ♘a5! 12 ♕c2 ♘b4 13 ♕c3 ♕xd7 is unclear) 11...♘a5 12 ♕c2 ♘b4 13 ♕c3 and now both 13...♖c8 and 13...♗e8 look quite promising for Black.

c) 10 ♖d1!? ♘d5!? 11 ♘xc4 is worth further analysis even though Black should have no problems after 11...b5!.

Among White's 9th move alternatives 9 ♘bd2 is undoubtedly the least popular. This move is linked with the idea of intensifying control over e5 after recapturing on c4 with the knight, but it appears harmless as Black can in the meantime increase his own central influence over the light-square complex. For example: 9...♗c6 10 a5 (10 ♘xc4 ♗e4 11 ♕c3 {11 ♕d1 ♘c6 12 ♘cd2 ♗g6 13 ♘b3 ♘b4 14 ♘e1 c6 was unclear in the game Smyslov-Kluger, Polanica Zdroj 1966} 11...♘c6 12 ♘ce5 ♘d5 13 ♕b3 ♘a5 {13...♘xe5!?; 13...♘cb4!?} 14 ♕d1 c5 15 ♗d2 ♘b4 16 ♖c1 cxd4 17 ♗xb4 ♗xb4 18 ♕xd4 ♕xd4 19 ♘xd4 ♗xg2 20 ♔xg2 ♖fd8 was equal in G.Kuzmin-Vaganian, USSR Ch 1980/1) 10...b5 11 axb6 cxb6 12 ♘xc4 ♗e4 13 ♕d1 ♘c6 14 ♗g5 ♘b4 15 ♕d2 a5 16 ♖fc1 ♖c8 was excellent for Black in Kaidanov-Wells, London 1990.

9...♗c6 10 ♘c3 ♗xf3

The only other way to stop White's intended e4 is by playing

10...♗b4 but the text move is better as it allows Black to develop his queen's knight with gain of tempo.

11 ♗xf3 ♘c6 12 ♗xc6 bxc6 13 ♗g5

13 a5!? is more thematic as White gets the possibility of attacking the weak c-pawns by making use of a4. Black has two plausible ways of meeting his opponent's intentions:

a) 13...♕b8!? 14 ♖a4! (after 14 ♕a4 c5! 15 ♕xc4 cxd4 16 ♖xd4, 16...c5 17 ♖d1 ♕b4 18 ♖a4 was equal in Razuvaev-Geller, Moscow 1982; the more ambitious 16...♕b7 comes strongly into consideration) 14...♕b3! 15 ♕xb3 cxb3 16 ♖c4 c5! 17 dxc5 ♖fd8 18 ♖xd8+ ♖xd8 19 ♗e3 ♘d5. There was not much left to do for either side in the games Kaidanov-Tukmakov, Irkutsk 1986 and Krasenkov-Khalifman, Vilnius 1988.

b) 13...♖b8 (more aggressive) 14 ♕a4 (14 ♖a4 ♖b4) 14...♖b4! 15 ♕xc6 ♕d6 16 ♕f3 and now in the game Romanishin-Brunner, Altensteig 1992, Black chose the unfortunate 16...♖fb8?! which led to his quick demise: 17 e4 ♕c6 18 d5 exd5?? 19 e5 ♘e8 20 ♘xd5 ♔f8 21 ♕h5 ♖4b5 22 ♕xh7 f6 23 ♕g8+! 1-0. Much better was 16...♖d8! (16...♘d5 17 e4 ♘xc3 18 bxc3 ♖b3 19 ♗f4 ♕d7 20 d5!? = is also playable) 17 e4 (17 ♗f4 ♕d7 18 ♖a2 ♘d5 is unclear; after 17 ♖a2, there is 17...♘d5 = and 17...h6!?) 17...♕c6 18 ♕e2 ♕b7 19 ♖a2 (19 ♖b1 ♖b3!?) 19...c5!? as 20 d5 exd5 21 exd5 h6! (preparing ...♗d6) looks good for

Black, e.g. 22 ♗f4?! ♘xd5! 23 ♘xd5 ♖xd5 24 ♖xd5 ♕xd5 25 ♕xe7 c3!. This is hardly forced but serves to emphasize the importance of posting the rook on the d-file, where it helps to soften the consequences of a potential d5 advance.

13...♖b8 14 a5

Kochiev decides that this pawn push is necessary after all. Black could have prevented it by playing 13...a5 himself, but, as the previous note indicates, it is not clear that a5 grants White any significant advantages. In fact, the pawn may turn out to be a liability, and Black should work towards this direction by pursuing favourable simplification.

14...♖b4 15 ♖a4?!

Falling in with Black's plans. Better was 15 e3 although it is hard to say whether White has sufficient compensation for the pawn minus.

15...♕b8 16 ♖xb4 ♕xb4 17 ♗xf6 gxf6 18 ♘a2 ♕b5 19 ♖c1 ♖d8 20 e3 c5! 21 dxc5 ♕xc5 22 ♕e2 ♕xa5 23 ♘c3 f5 24 ♕xc4 *(D)*

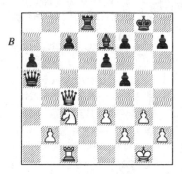

The situation has clarified: Black has maintained the extra pawn and should be looking forward to exploiting it, aided by his bishop vs knight advantage. Things are not so easy, however, because of his ruptured pawn structure on the kingside which presents White with possibilities of counterplay.

24...♗f6 25 ♖c2 ♕b6 26 ♘a4 ♕b5 27 ♔g2 ♔g7

The king is heading for g6 where it will be less exposed to a perpetual check. 27...♖d3!? was also interesting.

28 b3 ♔g6?!

28...♕b7+!? would have been more difficult to meet. For example: 29 ♔h3 h5! 30 ♘c5 ♕f3 (threatening ...h4) or 29 ♕c6 ♕xb3 30 ♘o5 ♕b6 31 ♘xa6 ♖d6 32 ♕xb6 cxb6 when the resulting endgame promises White few chances of salvation. 29 f3 is hardly an improvement as the weakness along White's second rank will sooner or later prove decisive.

29 ♘c5 ♕c6+ 30 ♔h3! a5 31 ♕e2!

The defects of Black's 28th move slowly come to the fore. White is now threatening ♘d3-f4+, highlighting the unfortunate placement of the black king.

31...♕d5 32 e4! fxe4 33 ♘xe4 ♕f5+ 34 ♔g2 ♖d4

This poses White no problems. 34...♗e5 appears better even though Black has no realistic chances of winning in view of his insecure king position.

35 ♘xf6 ♔xf6 36 ♖xc7 ♕d5+ 37 ♔h3 ♕f5+

37...♕xb3?? 38 ♕h5 is suicidal, so Black settles for perpetual check. **38 ♔g2 ♕d5+ 39 ♔h3 ½-½**

9) Geller's system: 6 0-0 dxc4 7 ♕c2 a6 8 a4 ♗d7 9 ♕xc4

Game 23
Korchnoi – Hjartarson
Saint John Ct (8) 1988

1 c4 ♘f6 2 d4 e6 3 g3 d5 4 ♗g2 ♗e7 5 ♘f3 0-0 6 0-0 dxc4 7 ♕c2 a6 8 a4 ♗d7 9 ♕xc4 (D)

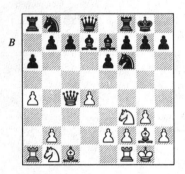

Restoring material equality at the cost of allowing Black a freer hand in the fight for the central square e4. Nevertheless, this is the most annoying continuation for Black as the possibility of carrying out ...c5 looks more remote than ever.

9...♗c6 10 ♗f4!

Tying Black to the defence of his c-pawn. White has interesting alternatives in 10 ♘c3 and 10 ♗g5 but they both allow Black some counterplay in the centre:

a) 10 ♘c3 b5! and now:

a1) 11 ♕a2? b4 12 ♘d1 ♗d5 13 b3 c5 14 dxc5 ♘e4 (14...♘bd7!?) 15 ♘e3 ♘c3 16 ♕d2 ♗e4! left Black superbly placed in the game Polugaevsky-Braga, Mar del Plata 1982. After the forced reply 17 ♖e1 Black should have chosen 17...♘d7! 18 ♗b2 ♘xc5 19 ♗xc3 bxc3 20 ♕xc3 ♖c8! with the superior game, rather than 17...♗xc5 18 ♗b2, which let White slip away from his difficulties and eventually win.

a2) 11 ♕d3 b4 12 ♘b1!? (12 ♘d1? ♗e4 13 ♕d2? ♘c6 14 e3 ♘a5 –+) 12...♗e4 13 ♕d1 (13 ♕e3?! ♘bd7 14 ♘bd2 ♗d5 15 ♕d3 c5 16 e4 ♗b7 17 e5 ♘d5 18 ♘e4 h6 19 b3 a5! 20 ♘fd2 ♗a6 21 ♘c4 ♖c8 22 ♖d1 ♘5b6 was clearly better for Black in L.Spassov-Ionescu, Spain 1991) 13...c5 14 ♘bd2 ♗d5 15 dxc5 ♘bd7 16 c6! (16 ♘b3?! ♘xc5 ∓) 16...♗xc6 17 ♘c4 (17 ♘b3?! ♖c8 18 ♗f4 ♗e4 19 ♖c1 ♘d5 20 ♗d2 ♘7b6 21 ♘bd4 ♘c4 gave White severe difficulties in Peng Zhaoqin-Bojković, Novi Sad OL 1990) 17...♘c5 18 ♗d2 ♖b8 19 a5!? with a double-edged position in Dizdarević-Brunner, Suhr 1990. Black can try to improve his play by 17...♖c8!? when the temporarily unstable position of the knight on c4 may cause White some inconvenience.

b) 10 ♗g5 and now:

b1) 10...♘bd7 (a very reliable, albeit drawish continuation) 11 ♘c3 h6 and now:

b11) 12 ♗f4 ♘b6 13 ♕d3 (13 ♕b3 a5 14 ♖fd1 ♖a6!? intending

...Nbd5, is unclear; the immediate 14...Nbd5 is less good in view of 15 Ne5) 13...Nbd5 14 Be5 a5 15 Bxf6 Bxf6 16 e4 Nb4 17 Qd2 e5 18 d5 Bd7 19 h3?! c6 was slightly better for Black in Kaidanov-Karpov, Tilburg (20') 1993.

b12) 12 Bxf6 Nxf6 with the further branch:

b121) 13 Rfe1 Bd5 14 Qd3 Bxf3 15 Bxf3 c6 16 Red1 ½-½ Tukmakov-Cvetković, Yugoslavia 1991.

b122) 13 Rfd1 a5 14 e3 Bb4 15 Qd3 Qe7 = Vukić-Cvetković, Yugoslavia 1991.

b123) 13 Rac1!? a5 14 Ne5 Bxg2 15 Kxg2 c6 16 e3 Qb6 17 Rfd1 Rfd8 18 Qe2 Rac8 19 Nc4 Qa6 was equal in Nogueiras-Pigusov, Santa Clara 1991.

b2) 10...Bd5!? is given as best in *ECO*. This move is linked with the idea of carrying out the thematic thrust ...c5; surprisingly, it has scored badly in practice so I will try to redress the balance here:

b21) 11 Qc2 Be4 and then:

b211) 12 Qc1!? shouldn't worry Black: 12...Nc6!? (12...c5?! 13 dxc5! Nhd7 14 Nc3! ±) 13 e3 Bb4!? 14 Nc3 Bxc3 15 bxc3 Qd5 16 c4 Qf5 17 Bf4 h6 with counterplay on the light squares.

b212) On 12 Qd1 Black has a choice between the safe 12...c5 13 dxc5 Bxc5 14 Nc3 Bc6 = (Polugaevsky-Geller, Leningrad 1977) and 12...Nbd7 13 Nc3 Bc6 14 Qc2 h6 15 Bf4 Bb4 16 a5 Rc8 17 Rfe1 Bd6 18 Bd2 Bxf3 19 Bxf3 c6 20 Bg2 Re8 with more complicated play, as

in the game Yusupov-Almasi, Groningen 1994.

b22) 11 Qd3 Be4 (11...c5 is also perfectly playable) 12 Qe3!? Bc6 13 Nc3 Nbd7 14 Qd3 Bb4 15 Rfe1 h6 16 Bf4 Rc8 17 Qc2 (17 e4? Nc5) 17...b6! 18 e4 Bb7 19 Rad1 Re8 20 Ne5 Nxe5 21 Bxe5 Nd7 22 Bf4 Qe7 23 Re2! c5! reaching a critical position:

b221) 24 Red2?! was played in Yusupov-Portisch, Linares 1989. After 24...cxd4 25 Rxd4 Nf6 26 Bd6 Bxd6 27 Rxd6 b5 28 axb5 axb5 29 Qb3 Bc6 30 Qb4 Qb7 31 h3 Rb8 32 Kh2 the players agreed to a draw but it seems to me that 24...Nf6! would have yielded interesting play, e.g. 25 dxc5 e5! 26 Be3 bxc5!? or 25 d5 cxd5 26 cxd5 Qd7 27 d6?! Bxg2 28 Kxg2 Bxc3 29 bxc3 g5! 30 Be3 Rc6 and White's passed pawn is in trouble. These lines serve to illustrate that the doubled rooks are not necessarily a tower of strength as their activity is hampered by the presence of many pieces on the board.

b222) 24 d5! is Khalifman's improvement from his game against Lautier at the 1993 Interzonal in Biel. After 24...e5 25 Be3! (25 d6? Qe6 26 Be3: 26...Nb8! ∓; 26...c4!?) 25...Qd6 26 Bh3 Rc7 27 Nb1! White obtained the better game in view of his agile knight but it seems to me that 24...Bxc3!? would have rendered the situation unclear: 25 d6 Qf6 26 bxc3 e5 27 Bh3! (27 Be3 Qe6!, planning ...Bc6, ...Rf8 and ...f5 offers interesting possibilities for counterplay) 27...♖cd8 28 ♗c1!? (now 28 ♗e3 ♕f3 29 ♗g2 ♕g4 {29...♕h5!?} 30 f3 ♕e6 31 h4 ♗c6! 32 c4 {32 ♔h2 ♕c4} 32...♕g6 intending ...♘f8-e6 is double-edged) 28...♗c6 and although the position requires careful manoeuvring I believe that Black's chances are not inferior. This assessment needs practical verification but the static nature of White's pawn structure minimizes the effectiveness of the bishop pair.

10...a5! 11 ♘c3 ♘a6 12 ♖ae1!?

An imaginative way of preparing e4. The alternative 12 ♖fe1 looks more natural but Black can obtain excellent chances by exploiting the temporary weakness of the square c2: 12...♘b4! (12...♗d5!? 13 ♘xd5 exd5 14 ♕b5 ♕c8 15 ♕b3 c6 16 ♘e5 ♗b4 17 ♖ed1 ♕e6 is also good, as played in Donchenko-Geller, USSR 1979, but 13 ♕b5!? seems to force a draw as Black has nothing better than 13...♗c6) 13 ♖ac1 ♗d6! 14 ♗g5 (14 ♗xd6 cxd6 =; 14 e4?! ♗xf4 15 gxf4 ♘h5 ∓) 14...♗d5! 15 ♘xd5 exd5 16 ♕b3 (16 ♕b5?? c6! 17 ♕xb7 ♖b8 18 ♕a7 ♖e8 −+) 16...♖e8 and Black's firm control over b4 and e4 easily outweighs White's bishops.

In Kramnik-Lautier, Dortmund 1995, the young Russian attempted to improve on White's play by 12 ♖ac1!?, ruling out the above-mentioned possibility, but the loss of tempo entailed allowed Black to equalize by different means: 12...h6 13 ♖fe1 ♗b4! 14 ♗e5 ♗xf3 15 ♗xf3 c6 16 ♖ed1 ♕e7 17 ♗f4 ♘d5

18 ♗d2 ♖fd8 19 ♕b3 ♘f6 20 ♗e3 ♘d5 =.

12 ♕d3 is, on the other hand, the least critical way of preparing e4 as the simple 12...♘b4 13 ♕b1 ♗xf3 14 ♗xf3 c6 15 ♖d1 ♗d6! guarantees Black a good game.

12...♘b4

Allowing e4, but in the present instance this is acceptable as the odd configuration of White's rooks offers Black tempi for counterplay. More circumspect is 12...♗d5!? 13 ♘xd5 exd5 14 ♕b5 ♕c8 = (Hjartarson), but one should take notice that after 13 ♕b5!? the objectively strongest line is 13...♗c6! 14 ♕c4! (14 ♕xa5?! ♘d5! 15 ♘xd5 exd5 leads to the loss of an exchange; 14 ♕b3 ♘b4 15 e4? ♘d3 ∓) 14...♗d5 with a draw by repetition.

13 e4 ♘d7

The knight is heading for b6, reminding White that his 12th move has weakened the defence of a4. In doing so it unblocks the f-pawn, which, according to circumstances, may jump to f5, contesting the centre.

14 ♖a1?!

A strange move, withdrawing the rook from the theatre of action for no serious reason. Better is 14 ♕e2 (14 ♖d1 ♗d6 15 ♗g5 ♕e8; 14 ♖e2 ♘b6 15 ♕b3 ♗d6! 16 ♗g5 {16 ♘e5 ♗xe5! 17 ♗xe5 ♘d3 ∓} 16...♕d7) 14...♘b6 15 b3 ♗d6 16 ♗g5 (Birnboim-Verat, Lugano 1989) although it is debatable whether the time gained (in comparison to our main game) grants White the advantage.

14...♗d6 15 ♗e3 ♘c2! 16 ♗g5

Hjartarson gives 16 d5 ♘xe3 17 fxe3 ♘b6 18 ♕d4 exd5 19 exd5 ♗d7 as unclear, a weird evaluation. In fact Black enjoys a clear advantage here in view of his bishop pair and superior pawn structure.

16...♘b6 17 ♕d3 ♘b4 18 ♕e2 ♕e8 19 b3 *(D)*

19...f5!

A powerful move in both a theoretical and psychological sense: Black creates a valuable outpost on d5 for his minor pieces and at the same time warns his illustrious opponent that he is not the only one playing for a win. Given the importance of the encounter (the winner of this game would advance further in the world championship cycle) one can easily draw the conclusion that tension was about to reach considerable heights.

20 ♖ac1 h6 21 ♗e3 ♕h5 22 d5?

An unsuccessful attempt to shake Black's control on the light squares. Korchnoi should have been content with the equal endgame resulting from 22 ♘d2 ♕xe2 23 ♘xe2 fxe4 24 ♘xe4 ♘6d5 while now his centre is going to collapse like a house of cards.

22...fxe4 23 dxc6?

Sealing his fate, but the alternative 23 ♘xe4 ♘6xd5 24 ♗c5 ♗xc5 25 ♘xc5 ♖ae8 was also unattractive.

23...exf3 24 ♕d1 bxc6

Less convincing is 24...♖ad8?! 25 cxb7! ♗xg3 26 fxg3 ♖xd1 27 ♘xd1! when, according to Hjartarson, White obtains strong counterplay due to his dangerous b-pawn. White's swindling chances are now reduced to a minimum but the particular conditions under which this game was played (1 hour for each contestant) encouraged Korchnoi to put up a determined resistance.

25 ♗xb6 cxb6 26 ♕xd6 fxg2 27 ♖fd1

27 ♕xe6+ ♔h8 would have left White with a sad choice between 28 ♔xg2 ♖ae8 29 ♕c4 ♕f3+ 30 ♔g1 ♘d3 31 ♖c2 ♘e1! and 28 ♖fd1 ♖xf2! 29 ♔xf2 ♕xh2 30 ♔e3 ♕xg3+ 31 ♔e2 ♖f8 32 ♕e3 ♕g4+ 33 ♔d2 ♖d8+ (Hjartarson). By keeping the e-file closed Korchnoi averts the intrusion of the enemy forces, yet his two pawn deficit means that he has no real chances of saving the game.

27...♕f5 28 ♕d2 ♘d3 29 ♖c2 ♘e5?!

29...♖ad8! would have been more conclusive. The text allows White to regain one of the pawns but in view of his vulnerable queenside the result is never in doubt.

30 ♕e2 ♖ad8 31 ♔xg2 ♘f3 32 ♖xd8 ♖xd8 33 ♖c1 ♘d4 34 ♕e3 c5

35 ♖d1 ♛c2 36 h4?

36 ♛d3 would have been more tenacious. The game continuation gives Black the opportunity to finish off efficiently.

36...♖f8 37 ♖c1 ♖xf2+! 38 ♛xf2 ♛xc1 and in this hopeless position White exceeded the time limit.

10) Korchnoi's Line: 1 d4 ♘f6 2 c4 e6 3 g3 d5 4 ♗g2 dxc4 5 ♘f3 ♗d7

Game 24
Sosonko – Korchnoi
Wijk aan Zee 1984

1 d4 ♘f6 2 c4 e6 3 g3 d5 4 ♗g2 dxc4 5 ♘f3

The alternative 5 ♛a4+!? has the advantage of keeping the position simple: 5...♗d7 (5...♘bd7 is more complicated, but White can employ the move-order 5 ♘f3 ♗d7 6 ♛c2 to avoid it) 6 ♛xc4 ♗c6 7 ♘f3 (7 f3 ♛d5! 8 ♛c3 e5 9 dxe5 ♘g4 10 e4 ♛b5 11 a3 ♘xe5 12 ♗f1 ♛c5 13 ♗e3 ♛xc3 14 ♘xc3 ♘bd7 ∓; Black's minor pieces are very active and White has some weaknesses on the light squares that may be exploited at a later stage) 7...♗d5!:

a) 8 ♛c2 ♘c6! 9 ♛d1?! (9 ♛a4) 9...e5 10 dxe5 ♘xe5 was slightly better for Black in Mastrokoukos-Ninov, Sofia 1994.

b) 8 ♛a4+ ♛d7 9 ♛xd7+ (9 ♛d1 c5 10 dxc5 ♗xc5 11 0-0 ♗c6 12 ♛c2 ♛e7 13 ♗g5 ♘bd7 =) 9...♘bxd7 10 0-0 c5 11 ♘c3 ♗c6 12 ♖d1 ♗e7 led

to a drawish ending in Bronstein-Smyslov, USSR Ch 1952.

c) 8 ♛d3 ♗e4:

c1) 9 ♛e3 c5 (9...♘c6!? is a more aggressive move) 10 dxc5 ♘bd7 11 b4 a5 12 ♗d2 axb4 13 ♗xb4 ♗xb1 (13...♘xc5!?) 14 ♖xb1 ♘d5 15 ♛d2 ♘xb4 = Neishtadt.

c2) 9 ♛d2 ♘c6 10 0-0 ♗b4 11 ♘c3?! 0-0 12 a3 ♗xc3 13 bxc3 ♘a5 14 ♛b2 ♛d5 15 ♗f4 ♘c4 16 ♛a2 ♖ac8 ∓ Smyslov-Konstantinopolsky, USSR 1950.

c3) 9 ♛b3!? ♛d5!? 10 ♘bd2 (10 ♛xd5 exd5 11 0-0 ♘c6 12 ♘bd2 ♗d6 is unclear) 10...♛xb3 11 ♘xb3 ♗b4+ 12 ♗d2 ♗d6 =.

c4) 9 ♛d1 c5 10 ♘c3 ♗c6 11 0-0 ♘bd7 12 ♗f4 cxd4 13 ♛xd4 ♗c5 14 ♛d3 0-0 15 e4 (Hübner-Lutz, Germany 1992) 15...h6!? =. It is obvious that these lines are not likely to produce another 'Evergreen', yet one shouldn't forget that the potential for beauty in a game of chess is mostly determined by White's opening choice rather than the quality of Black's response.

5...♗d7!?

An interesting idea, introduced into modern tournament practice by Viktor Korchnoi. Black intends to oppose bishops on the long diagonal without weakening c6, thus avoiding all the risks that such a way of developing would entail. The manoeuvre ...♗d7-c6 is well-founded in terms of development and centralization and has formed part of the repertoire of several of the world's best players.

6 ♘bd2

The safest way of recovering the pawn lies in 6 ♕c2, when 6...♗c6 leads to the note to White's 5th. The main continuation 6 ♘e5 will be discussed under the next game while 6 0-0 leads to the type of game Black is hoping for: 6...♗c6 7 ♘bd2 b5 8 a4 a6 9 ♕c2 ♗e7 and although it cannot be denied that White has some pressure in positions of this kind, an extra pawn is certainly worth the suffering.

6...♗b4

Black clings on to the pawn. The alternative 6...c5 is not promising in view of 7 0-0 ♗c6 8 ♘xc4 ♘bd7 9 ♗f4! cxd4 (9...♘b6 10 ♘ce5 ±) 10 ♕xd4! ♗c5 11 ♘d6+ ♚e7 12 ♕d2 ♘b6 13 ♖ad1 ♗d5 14 ♘b5 and White has good chances of exploiting the insecure position of the enemy king.

7 ♕c2

a) After 7 0-0!?:

a1) In the game Kožul-Abramović, Pljevlja 1989, White got the advantage after 7...♗xd2 8 ♗xd2 ♗c6 9 ♕c2 b5 10 ♗g5 ♘bd7 11 b3 ♘b6 12 ♗xf6 ♕xf6 13 a4 0-0 14 bxc4 bxa4 15 c5 ♘d5 16 ♘e5.

a2) It seems to me that the critical test of Kozul's idea is 7...c3!?:

a21) 8 ♘c4 cxb2 9 ♗xb2 ♗c6 10 ♘ce5 0-0 11 ♕b3 a5 looks OK for Black.

a22) White does best to continue 8 bxc3 ♗xc3 9 ♖b1 ♗c6 10 ♗a3 a5 11 ♕c2 ♗b4 12 ♗xb4 axb4 13 ♖xb4 0-0 14 e4 ♘bd7, reaching a position in which his central preponderance

compensates for the weak pawn on a2.

b) Another possibility is 7 ♘e5!? ♘c6 8 0-0 (Sosonko-Korchnoi, Zurich 1984) and now instead of the game continuation 8...♘xe5?! 9 dxe5 ♘d5 10 ♘xc4 ±, Sosonko recommends 8...♗xd2 9 ♕xd2 ♘xe5 10 dxe5 ♘d5 as unclear. Even stronger looks 7...♗c6!? 8 ♘xc6 ♘xc6 9 ♗xc6+ bxc6 10 ♕a4 ♕d5 11 0-0 a5!? with more than sufficient counterplay for Black.

7...♗b5! 8 0-0 ♘c6 9 ♖d1 *(D)*

9...♘xd4

9...♘a5 10 e4 0-0 11 ♘e5!? ♗xd2 12 ♗xd2 ♕xd4 13 ♗e3 ♕b6 14 ♕d2 ♘c6 15 ♕g5 h6 16 ♕h4 was unclear in the game Kožul-Liang Jinrong, Novi Sad OL 1990.

Interesting is 9...♕d5!? 10 e3! ♕f5! 11 ♕xf5 exf5 12 ♗f1 ♘a5 13 b3 (13 ♘e5 ♗a4 14 b3 cxb3 15 axb3 ♗d7 is unclear) 13...♗c6 14 bxc4 ♗a4 15 ♖e1 c5! (intending ...0-0-0 and ...♖he8) with chances for both sides. The text leads to a complex position where White has compensation for his sacrificed pawns.

10 ♘xd4 ♛xd4 11 ♘e4

Sosonko is playing for higher stakes than merely regaining pawns. He could have done that by 11 ♗xb7 ♖d8 12 a4! ♛b6 (12...c3? 13 bxc3 ♛xc3 14 ♛xc3 ♗xc3 15 axb5! ♗a1 16 ♗a3 ±) 13 axb5 ♛xb7 14 ♘xc4 = (Matanović) but the game continuation is very hard to resist if one is not familiar with the defensive resources of Black's position.

11...♛b6 12 ♗e3 ♛a6 13 ♗d4 ♗e7 14 ♗xf6 gxf6

Matanović thinks that 14...♗xf6 is also possible, giving the following analysis: 15 ♘xf6+ (15 ♘c5? ♛b6 ∓) 15...gxf6 16 ♛c3 e5 17 ♛f3 (17 ♗h3!?) 17...♔e7 18 ♛xb7 ♛xb7 ∓.

The text is typical of Korchnoi's style but it involves a lot more risk as White's next forces a serious weakening of Black's protective cover on the kingside.

15 ♛c3 e5 16 ♛f3?

Sosonko is in a hurry to re-deploy his knight, the most appropriate piece for exploiting the newly created weaknesses, yet, as the continuation suggests, Black is able to cover all the holes, and steer the game to a victorious conclusion. Imperative was 16 ♗h3! when White would have obtained definite positional compensation in the form of excellent control over e4 and f5.

16...♗d7! 17 ♛h5 ♛e6 18 ♘c3 c6 19 ♘b5!

The only chance, preventing the Black king from castling into safety. 19...cxb5?? would now be a ghastly error in view of the reply 20 ♗d5.

19...♖c8! 20 ♖xd7!

But not 20 ♘xa7? ♖c7! and the knight cannot get out: 21 ♘b5 cxb5 22 ♗d5 ♛g4 23 ♛xf7+ ♔d8 −+. The text keeps White alive by maintaining some pressure on the light squares.

20...♛xd7 21 ♗h3 ♛d2?

Now it is Korchnoi's turn to go wrong. Better was 21...♛d8 22 ♘c3 ♛c7 23 ♗e6 ♖f8 with a clear advantage to Black (Matanović), but from the practical point of view the move played is strong as it conceals a devilish trap.

22 ♗xc8 cxb5 23 e3?? (D)

Walking head-first into Black's trap, whereas he could have refreshed his chances with the simple 23 ♗xb7. This is the type of blunder that often occurs in a period of relaxation after a complicated sequence of moves.

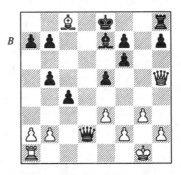

23...c3! 24 ♛h3

White is stone dead. 24 ♖d1 c2! 25 ♖xd2 c1♛+ 26 ♖d1 ♛xc8 loses a piece, while now the passed c-pawn marches to triumph.

24...♛xb2 25 ♛f1 c2 0-1

11) Korchnoi's Line with 5...♗d7 6 ♘e5

Game 25
Birnboim – Csom
Tel Aviv 1988

1 d4 ♘f6 2 c4 e6 3 g3 d5 4 ♗g2 dxc4 5 ♘f3 ♗d7 6 ♘e5

The most critical continuation, leading to dynamic positions with chances for both sides.

6...♗c6 7 ♘xc6 ♘xc6 8 e3

Given as best in *ECO*, this move safeguards the d-pawn in preparation for ♕e2. White has various alternatives at this point but for the moment Black seems able to come up with a good reply against each of them:

a) 8 ♗xc6+ (a direct attempt at refutation) 8...bxc6 9 ♕a4 ♕d5 10 0-0 ♘e4 11 ♖d1 (11 f3 ♘d6 12 ♘c3 ♕xd4+ 13 ♔g2 ♕b6 14 ♗e3 ♕b7 15 b3! cxb3 16 ♖ab1 a5! 17 ♖xb3 ♕a6 18 ♗b6 ♔d7! is unclear according to Cserna) 11...♕b5 12 ♕c2 (Kottke-Cserna, Dortmund 1986) and now Cserna gives 12...♘d6 13 ♘a3 ♕a6 14 ♗f4 ♖b8 15 ♖ac1 ♖b4 16 ♗xd6 cxd6 17 ♘xc4 ♗e7 with an equal game. Also possible is 9...♕d7 (intending ...c5), as 10 ♕xc4 ♕d5! leads nowhere for White.

b) 8 ♕a4 ♕d7 and now:

b1) 9 e3? is problematic: Hulak-Korchnoi, Sarajevo 1984 continued 9...♘b4! 10 ♕xd7+ ♔xd7 11 ♘a3 ♘d3+ 12 ♔e2 ♗xa3 13 bxa3 ♖ab8 14 ♗d2 b5 with a clear advantage for Black.

b2) 9 ♕xc4 ♘xd4 10 ♗xb7 ♗b4+! is unclear according to Lukacs. In Sosonko-Lukacs, Volmac-Spartacus 1987, White sacrificed a pawn by 10 0-0?! but after 10...c5! 11 ♘c3 (11 e3? b5 −+) 11...♖d8! 12 ♗g5 (12 ♖d1? b5 13 ♕d3 b4 14 e3 ♘f3+ −+; 12 a4 ♗e7 13 ♖d1 ♘d5! Lukacs) 12...b5! he had no real compensation (13 ♕d3 ♗e7! 14 ♗xf6 gxf6! ∓ Lukacs).

b3) 9 ♗xc6 ♕xc6 10 ♕xc6+ bxc6 11 0-0 0-0-0 12 ♗e3 c5 13 dxc5 ♘g4 14 c6 ♘xe3 15 fxc3 ♗c5 was slightly better for Black in Hübner-Greenfeld, Biel 1986.

c) 8 0-0 ♗e7!? (8...♘xd4?! 9 ♗xb7 ♖b8 10 ♗g2 ♗c5 11 ♘d2 was better for White in Gulko-Korchnoi, Amsterdam 1989; 8...♕d7 is the main line but White has been scoring quite well against it lately) and here:

c1) 9 ♕a4 0-0:

c11) 10 ♖d1? b5!! 11 ♕xb5 ♘xd4 12 ♕a4 ♘xe2+ 13 ♔f1 ♘d4 14 ♗e3 c5 15 ♘c3 ♖b8! 16 ♕xa7 ♖xb2 17 ♗xd4 cxd4 18 ♖xd4 ♗d6! 19 a4 ♘d5 20 ♗xd5 ♗e5! 21 ♖dd1 ♗xc3 22 ♗xc4 ♕f6 23 ♖a2? (23 ♖ac1 ♗a5! ∓) 23...♕f3! 0-1 Sulava-Farago, Vinkovci 1993.

c12) Better is 10 e3 ♘b4 11 a3 ♘bd5 12 ♕xc4 c6 13 b4 ♕d7 14 ♘d2 a5! with a level game, C.Horvath-Lukacs, Budapest 1994.

c2) 9 e3 e5!? 10 ♗xc6+ (10 dxe5 ♕xd1 11 ♖xd1 ♘xe5 12 ♗xb7 ♖b8 13 ♗g2 0-0 14 ♘d2 ♖fd8 15 ♖f1 ♗b4 16 ♘e4 ♘d3 was fine for Black in Gyorkos-Farago, Zalakaros 1994) 10...bxc6:

a21) 11 ♕a4!? is worth a try although after 11...♕d5!? 12 ♘c3 ♕e6 13 dxe5 ♘d7 14 f4 0-0 15 e4 ♗c5+ 16 ♔g2 ♗d4 intending ...♖ad8 and ...♘c5-d3, possibly combined with a well-timed ...g5, Black certainly has good counterplay.

a22) 11 dxe5 ♕xd1 12 ♖xd1 ♘d7 13 f4 0-0-0 14 ♗d2 f6!? 15 e6 ♘b6 16 ♘c3 f5 17 e4 ♗c5+ 18 ♔g2 g6 19 a4 a5 was very double-edged in Tratar-Wells, Bled 1995. Plans involving ...e5 are very interesting as Black's pawn structure gets ruined but in return he conquers space and increases the activity of his pieces.

8...e5!? 9 0-0?!

White should play 9 ♗xc6+! bxc6 10 ♕a4, when 10...♕d5 11 0-0 ♗e7 transposes to the note accompanying Tratar-Wells above, while 10...♕d7 11 dxe5 ♘g4 12 0-0 (12 ♕xc4 ♘xe5 13 ♕e4 ♕d5 =) 12...♘xe5 with complicated play is worth considering.

9...exd4 10 exd4 ♗e7 11 ♘a3?!

White probably disliked the position resulting after 11 ♗xc6+ bxc6 12 ♕a4 0-0 13 ♕xc4 ♕d7, but the text is very risky as it allows Black to obtain a dangerous passed pawn.

11...♗xa3 12 bxa3 0-0

This position compares favourably with those arising in the 7 ♘a3 variation of the Geller system as the absence of the e-pawns means that d4 will soon fall. White's hopes for counterplay are pinned on the bishop pair which, however, lacks sufficient targets to show its real strength.

13 ♖b1 ♘xd4 14 ♖xb7 c5 (D)

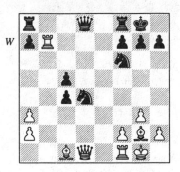

15 ♕a4 c3 16 ♕c4 a5!

Csom calmly safeguards his a-pawn as White can hardly play 17 ♕xc5: 17...♘e2+ 18 ♔h1 ♖c8 and the passed pawn is close to promotion.

17 ♖e1?

After this White's situation becomes critical. He should have tried at all costs to get rid of the monstrous pawn and to this end best was 17 ♔h1 c2 18 ♗e3 ♖c8 19 ♗h3 with chances to hold.

17...c2 18 ♖ee7 ♔h8!

Underlining White's inability to undertake anything positive. The Israeli's pieces are all impressively placed but, alas, the little pawn on c2 is worth more than a whole army.

19 h3

A last mistake, which only serves to accelerate the end in a position which held no prospects of salvation.

19...♘f5 20 ♖e5 ♕d1+ 21 ♕f1 ♖ae8 22 ♖xc5 ♖e1 23 ♗b2 ♘d4 24 ♗xd4 c1♕ 25 ♖xc1 ♕xc1 0-1

Index of Variations